From Page to Proclamation

"In this book, Clare Schwantes brilliantly moves beyond traditional biblical scholarship to explore how the scripture text is actually received in the context of worship. Everyone will benefit from seeing where and how God's word is revealed to us on a particular occasion, in different texts set side by side to work together and heard within the communal liturgy."

—TOM ELICH,
former director, Liturgy Brisbane

"Clare Schwantes provokes us to interpret the Scriptures as proclaimed in the worshiping community. She is not putting forward low energy biblicism or high passion enthusiasm. Calling upon Gadamer's sense of festival, with its dynamism and recall of corporate memory, we are invited to fuse multiple horizons ever respectful of contemporary biblical scholarship. Here is a practical theology of proclamation to challenge liturgists and exegetes alike, while nourishing the faithful with a contemporary diet."

—GERARD MOORE,
principal, BBI–The Australian Institute of Theological Education

"This is what we have been waiting for. Finally, a liturgical theologian has emerged with the boldness and creativity to produce a major hermeneutic work on the Lectionary. *From Page to Proclamation* offers a brilliant adaptation of Gadamerian concepts that is thoroughly theological and eminently practical."

—NEIL PEMBROKE,
associate professor in pastoral theology, Trinity College Queensland

"*From Page to Proclamation* embodies the need and desire of Pope Francis to have liturgical research based on actual experience. This book is a valuable addition to the academic array of material in liturgy, because it embraces in depth four different methodologies and each of them is comprehensively researched and presented with clarity and conviction. The Word of God comes to us through proclamation and how that is received is what we believe."

—ANGELA MCCARTHY,
adjunct senior lecturer theology, University of Notre Dame Australia

From Page to Proclamation

Interpreting Scripture in the Context of Liturgy

CLARE SCHWANTES

foreword by Jason McFarland

PICKWICK *Publications* · Eugene, Oregon

FROM PAGE TO PROCLAMATION
Interpreting Scripture in the Context of Liturgy

Copyright © 2024 Clare Schwantes. All rights reserved. Except for brief quotations in critical publications or reviews, no part of this book may be reproduced in any manner without prior written permission from the publisher. Write: Permissions, Wipf and Stock Publishers, 199 W. 8th Ave., Suite 3, Eugene, OR 97401.

Pickwick Publications
An Imprint of Wipf and Stock Publishers
199 W. 8th Ave., Suite 3
Eugene, OR 97401

www.wipfandstock.com

PAPERBACK ISBN: 979-8-3852-2026-7
HARDCOVER ISBN: 979-8-3852-2027-4
EBOOK ISBN: 979-8-3852-2028-1

Cataloguing-in-Publication data:

Names: Schwantes, Clare, author. | McFarland, Jason J., foreword.

Title: From page to proclamation : interpreting scripture in the context of liturgy / Clare Schwantes ; foreword by Jason McFarland.

Description: Eugene, OR : Pickwick Publications, 2024 | Includes bibliographical references.

Identifiers: ISBN 979-8-3852-2026-7 (paperback) | ISBN 979-8-3852-2027-4 (hardcover) | ISBN 979-8-3852-2028-1 (ebook)

Subjects: LCSH: Bible—Hermeneutics | Liturgical movement—Catholic Church. | Bible—Liturgical use. | Catholic Church—Liturgy.

Classification: BV176.3 .S38 2024 (paperback) | BV176.3 .S38 (ebook)

VERSION NUMBER 11/15/24
First paperback edition December 2024.

Scripture quotes are from the New Revised Standard Version, Updated Edition. Copyright © 2021 National Council of Churches of Christ in the United States of America. Used by permission. All rights reserved worldwide.

Image Permissions

© Archbishop's Diocesan and Cathedral Library (Digital), *Gospels,* Cod. 56 (Dom Hs. 56), Cologne, Germany, f.13r, https://nbn-resolving.org/urn:nbn:de:hbz:kn28-3-1791-p0029-4. © The British Library Board *Odalricus Peccator Gospel Lectionary*, Digital Collections, Harley MS 2970, f.22, http://www.bl.uk/manuscripts/Viewer.aspx?ref=harley_ms_2970_fs001ar © The British Library Board *Cistercian Missal*, Digital Collections, Harley MS 1229 Page: f.3v – 4r, http://www.bl.uk/manuscripts/Viewer.aspx?ref=harley_ms_1229_fs001r

Contents

Foreword by Jason McFarland | vii

Chapter 1	Introduction	1
Chapter 2	Dimensions of Practical Theology	18

PART I — DESCRIPTIVE THEOLOGY

Chapter 3	The Structure of the Lectionary and Its Impact on the Meaning of Texts	35
Chapter 4	The Catholic Liturgical Paradigm	58

PART II — HISTORICAL THEOLOGY

Chapter 5	The History of Scripture Proclamation in the Mass	95

PART III — SYSTEMATIC THEOLOGY

Chapter 6	The Event of Meaning: Understanding the Proclamation of Scripture	121
Chapter 7	Corporate Memory and Tradition	145
Chapter 8	Liturgical Proclamation as Social Event and Personal Encounter	171

PART IV — STRATEGIC PRACTICAL THEOLOGY

Chapter 9	Identifying Issues in a Liturgical Hermeneutic of Scripture	193
Chapter 10	Conclusion	218

Bibliography | 227

Foreword

JASON J. MCFARLAND
AUSTRALIAN CATHOLIC UNIVERSITY

God's word is living and active, keenly sharp, able to enter even into the darkest and farthest recesses of our being (cf. Heb 4:12). From the perspective of Christian experience, this view of Scripture as active and transformative is self-evident. The believer reads or hears the word and is somehow not the same as before. Still, the question lingers: How does the word transform?

Up to now, Scripture scholars of recent centuries have taken up quintessentially post-Enlightenment and post-modern modes of answering this question. We can know how the word transforms by unearthing what it truly means or by viewing it through a lens of concern that activates new meanings. In our post-critical world, to be sure, there are literally limitless ways of reading anything, and the Bible is read a lot more than most things.

If we ask how the word transforms, we are in a sense really asking one of the most post-critical questions of all: How does it mean? Clare Schwantes in *From Page to Proclamation* takes us on a painstakingly researched and cleverly written journey toward answering this question. In short, Schwantes answers: the word means liturgically.

If the word means liturgically, then it "means" outside the typical vision of engagement with the Bible, wherein one is sitting with the book, probably at a desk or as part of a Bible study group, reading with careful attention to critical annotations, perhaps with a commentary and concordance at hand, with the aim of deepening understanding for the purpose of spiritual development, scholarly interpretation, or sermon preparation. But this is not how the word "means" and is not at all what Schwantes is getting at in this book. She offers not another method of interpreting the Bible—and this point is crucial as well as a welcome liberation from armchair biblical interpretation—but rather an exploration of the influence of liturgical context(s) upon how the word means and makes meaning, namely through the event of official corporate worship or liturgy.

Her approach resonates soundly with the disciplines of liturgical studies and liturgical theology, which assert the profound and even primary place of corporate worship in shaping and expressing what Christians believe. In a sixth-century axiom often attributed to Prosper of Aquitaine, for example, we have an ancient expression of this reality: *ut legem credendi lex statuat supplicandi* (the law of prayer establishes the law of belief, or, more simply, worship shapes doctrine). In the Constitution on the Liturgy of the Second Vatican Council, *Sacrosanctum Concilium* (hereafter SC), we hear that "the liturgy is the summit toward which the Church's activity is aimed and at the same time the source of its power" (SC 10). For Catholic liturgical scholars and liturgical theologians, both the axiom and the Constitution are held as authoritative expressions of how liturgy functions in the Christian life and in a sense comprise the foundations of both disciplines as they exist today.

In asserting her liturgical hermeneutic of Scripture, Schwantes is affirming liturgical context as a (or even *the*) primary mode in which the word "means." This affirmation is well-justified, indeed, given (1) liturgy is where most Christians have most often encountered and continue to encounter Scripture and (2) liturgy is an ancient and originating context for Scripture's appropriation within and among Christian communities. Somehow it is still largely unknown that what appears in the canonical Bible today was profoundly influenced by the liturgical and catechetical usage of particular gospels and letters among early Christian communities. Indeed, the Lectionary in many ways comes before the Bible. From this perspective, Schwantes's work becomes even more important and pressing in that it provides a remedy to the prevalent and harmful *liturgievergessenheit*[1] within the biblical and theological academies.

The liturgical word is revealed in context: in community, in the organization and juxtaposition of texts in the Lectionary, by preaching, in human ritualizing, etc., and is inseparable from the tradition of liturgical worship by multitudes of communities over the course of two millennia. While this way of understanding how worship works is well known to liturgical scholars, *From Page to Proclamation* makes an immense contribution to the academy in that it not only asserts this truth but also provides a theoretical model by which to prove it, drawing on Gadamer's concept of the "fusion of horizons" and Browning's "dimensions of fundamental practical theology."

---

1. See Geldhof, *Liturgical Studies as a Research Program*, 8. I have tried to make a similar effort at remembering liturgy in theology with McFarland, "Why and How of Liturgical Theology," 265–90.

Schwantes achieves with this book something very hard to do: a hermeneutic that opens the liturgical proclamation of Scripture to nearly limitless further study—the results of which have the potential to be actually useful, not only to scholars, but also to the originating contexts that I gather were the inspiration for this book in the first place: local worshiping communities.

So, the word is revealed. Then it can 'mean.' Then communal and individual appropriation of the word can lead to understanding, wherein lies the possibility of conversion of the believer's (or seeker's) heart. God's word is living and active, indeed, one might say after reading this book, God's word lives and is activated in the liturgy.

CHAPTER 1

Introduction

I. IN SEARCH OF A LITURGICAL HERMENEUTIC OF SCRIPTURE

Theologians across several centuries have employed a variety of methods in an attempt to interpret the Scriptures, yet these hermeneutics do not adequately explain the process of interpretation that takes place when readings are proclaimed from their Lectionary arrangement and heard within a corporate, ecclesial context such as the Catholic Mass. Existing interpretive approaches presume a solitary reader employing analytical skills from a range of possible methodologies including historical-critical, socio-rhetorical, literary-narrative, canonical-critical, reader-response, cultural-critical, ecological, and social-scientific criticism. Some hermeneutical approaches analyze the biblical text through the lens of contemporary issues such as feminism or liberation theology.[1]

Yet despite this wealth of scholarly approaches, the key context in which most modern-day Catholics encounter the Scriptures is during Sunday Mass. In this context, they hear scriptural extracts (pericopes) proclaimed aloud, they hear extracts juxtaposed with other biblical readings according to the Lectionary's unique structure, all while being immersed in the multisensory context of the eucharistic liturgy and surrounded by the ecclesial community.

The liturgical hermeneutic suggested here does not contradict existing approaches to biblical interpretation but adds another tier to the interpretive enterprise. It aims to demonstrate that the liturgical event and the arrangement of the Roman Catholic Lectionary exert a unique influence on the interpretation of Scripture texts, and that an additional hermeneutical

---

1. Stovell and Porter, "Trajectories," 12–20.

lens is therefore required. It will be argued that the Scripture passages contained in the Lectionary acquire a different meaning to their native biblical context, due to the juxtaposition of scriptural passages with previously unrelated texts, the decision about where pericopes begin and end, the omission of verses or entire chapters of Scripture, and the liturgical day to which readings are assigned.

The fact that Lectionary texts are heard within the experiential context of the liturgical event suggests that more than a literary analysis is required. The assembly gathers, not for private prayer and meditation, but to participate in corporate worship. The Lectionary texts are proclaimed within this ecclesial body, accompanied by gestures, singing, symbols, and ritual which highlight the sacramental encounter taking place. The texts are not heard in isolation; rather they are illuminated by the homily and surrounded by other biblical fragments which abound in the prayers of the liturgy.

It is proposed that the philosophical notion of "play" and the concept of a "fusion of horizons" espoused by German philosopher, Hans-Georg Gadamer, have direct implications for the dynamic interpretation of meaning which takes place in the communal liturgical event. The aim, therefore, is to develop a hermeneutical model for interpreting Scripture texts proclaimed from the Lectionary within the liturgical event by placing liturgical and biblical theology into a critical dialogue with philosophical hermeneutics. Extrapolating from Gadamer's model, which proposed a two-way fusion of horizons between an author and a reader or between a speaker and a listener, it will be argued that a liturgical hermeneutic of Scripture must incorporate four horizons—the Bible text, the Lectionary text, the homilist, and the worshiper—and that new meaning emerges when these four horizons collide in the context of the liturgical event and the ecclesial community.

II. THE UNIQUE INTERPRETIVE INFLUENCE OF LECTIONARY AND LITURGY

The term "liturgical hermeneutic" has been used in the literature with varying emphases. English Benedictine monk, priest, and liturgy professor, James Leachman, used the term "liturgical hermeneutic" to refer to his methodology for interpreting liturgical texts and rites, excluding the Scripture readings. His work involves firstly an analysis of Latin grammar and secondly an in-depth textual analysis of the liturgical prayers.[2]

Anglican liturgist and theologian, Bridget Nichols, presents an approach to interpreting liturgical rites which seeks to overcome any sense of

---

2. Leachman, "New Liturgical Hermeneutic," 223.

competitive dichotomy between the liturgical text and its performance. She claims that these two elements are not only inseparable but mutually sustaining. Nichols proposes principles for interpreting liturgy in the Anglican tradition based on the premise that liturgical rites are simultaneously text and performance, and refers to these principles as "liturgical hermeneutics."[3]

American theologian, Scott Hahn, argues that Scripture was written for liturgy and about liturgy, and therefore proposes a liturgical reading of the entire canonical text. He explores the liturgical content and context of Scripture and highlights the liturgical trajectory and teleology of the Bible. He calls this liturgical reading of Scripture a "liturgical hermeneutic."[4]

The current enterprise, however, is not directed towards an interpretation of liturgical texts and rites, nor reading the entire biblical canon through a liturgical lens. Instead, it examines how the liturgical event, and the Lectionary from which the Scriptures are proclaimed, uniquely influence the interpretation of Scripture. There has not been a great deal of research to date on the subject of interpreting Scripture in the liturgy, but existing scholarship in a number of closely related fields will help to situate the current project.

The Lectionary as a Distinct Entity from the Bible

Australian liturgist and Catholic priest, Tom Elich, has proposed that the meaning of readings in the liturgy is influenced by their position in the Lectionary, the liturgical day to which they are assigned, and the liturgical act of reading.[5] He claims that hearing a text in its liturgical setting on a particular feast, interwoven with other Scripture texts that have also been extricated from their native biblical context, creates a new layer of meaning.[6] For example, the Exodus story of the parting of the Red Sea which is read at the Easter Vigil (and which is also heard in the blessing of water for baptism), evokes undertones of Christian initiation, despite the fact that the story has nothing at all to do with baptism in its biblical context.[7] Further, when a series of previously unrelated biblical pericopes are regularly heard together in a single liturgical event, connections are formed between them. Through their liturgical usage, pericopes in the Lectionary can be seen to possess

---

3. Nichols, "Liturgical Hermeneutics," 1–48.

4. Hahn, "Worship in the Word," 101–3.

5. Elich, "Word in Worship," 94; Power, *Word of the Lord*, 4, 20; Sloyan, "Lectionary as Context," 43.

6. Elich, "Word in Worship," 100; De Clerck, "In the Beginning," 13.

7. Irwin, *Context and Text*, 186.

a semantic autonomy, independent of their biblical context, which allows them to relate to other lections in new ways.

The Lectionary's Role in Balancing Written and Communal Memory

American liturgical scholar, Fritz West, purports that the selection and arrangement of Scripture texts in the Lectionary reflects an attempt to balance the written and communal memory of the Christian Church.[8] The written memory of the Christian Church, recorded in the Bible and encompassing the entire story of salvation history, is placed within the framework of the communal memory enshrined in the liturgical year.[9] West argues that Scripture is carried through "containers of communal memory" such as liturgical celebrations, and is interpreted through the memory of the community.[10]

Biblical passages such as the healing of the blind man, the Samaritan woman at the well, and the raising of Lazarus which have been used over many centuries at the end of Lent have become infused with connotations of penance, conversion, and preparation for Christian initiation even when they are heard or read outside of a liturgical context.[11] Through their repetition in specific liturgical contexts, these pericopes take on extra layers of meaning which become embedded in communal memory.

The Nature of Oral Proclamation

The oral proclamation of Scripture in the Catholic liturgy has ancient roots. The canonical texts chosen for inclusion in the Bible were selected because early church communities repeatedly used them in liturgical gatherings, and the texts thus became a treasured communal memory.[12] The biblical texts, in their original language, are rich with oral features such as rhyme, rhythm, balanced clauses, and repetition of root words.[13] The mnemonic devices and performative language which saturate the Scriptures also signify that the canonical texts were the written transcription of an oral tradition.[14]

8. West, *Scripture and Memory*, 8.
9. West, *Scripture and Memory*, 5–6.
10. West, *Scripture and Memory*, 51–65.
11. Elich, "Word in Worship," 100.
12. O'Loughlin, "Sharing the Living Word," 11.
13. Waterford, "Hearing and Reading," 336.
14. West, *Scripture and Memory*, 46.

Further, lections have the particular characteristics of being both written and oral because, from their printed form in the Lectionary, they are proclaimed publicly and received aurally. As written text, the pericopes convey a sense of authority and stability; as spoken words they embody the qualities of presence and participation.[15] Meaning is conveyed not only through the words of the Scripture text, but through the act of public proclamation; the ritual act of reading imbues the texts with a sense of constancy and wisdom, and affirms their normative status.[16] The ritual actions, gestures, and responses throughout the Liturgy of the Word enhance the shared event of reading, and form part of the multisensory, corporate context within which the various horizons collide to produce meaning in the liturgical event.

The Catholic Liturgical Paradigm

It is instructive to trace the hermeneutical trajectory of lections out of the Bible into the Lectionary cursus, where they are juxtaposed with other lections and become facets in a mnemonic composition, before eventually taking their place in the liturgical celebration. The lections proclaimed in the liturgy possess accumulated meanings from their biblical context, from their position in the Lectionary cursus, and from the liturgical complex consisting of the ceremonial surrounding the readings and the homily that follows.[17]

Fritz West examines the differences between the Catholic and Protestant liturgical paradigms, noting that each ecclesial tradition places a different interpretive framework on the Lectionary and has a significantly different experience of worship. A pivotal feature of the use of Scripture in the Catholic liturgical paradigm is its residual oral-aural character in which pericopes are organized according to the framework of the liturgical year and printed for the purpose of being proclaimed and heard publicly. Further, the sacramental presence of Christ, which resides not in the book but in the proclamation in the midst of the assembly, directly impacts the interpretation of Scripture in the liturgy;[18] the dialogical responses, veneration of the book, communal acclamations, and the proclamation of the Scripture readings constitute an ecclesial event which takes place *with* Christ rather than simply being *about* Christ.[19]

---

15. West, *Scripture and Memory*, 38; Graham, *Beyond the Written Word*, 157.
16. Irwin, *Context and Text*, 170; West, *Scripture and Memory*, 38.
17. West, *Scripture and Memory*, 25.
18. Catholic Church, *General Instruction of the Roman Missal*, 29 (hereafter GIRM).
19. McCarron, "Context for Preaching," 52.

Communal Dimension of the Liturgical Event

As distinct from traditional reader-response approaches to biblical interpretation, which envisage a reader sitting and reading alone, pericopes that are proclaimed from the Lectionary in the liturgy are heard in a corporate, ecclesial event where the entire assembly actively participates in the reception of the word and the appropriation of meaning. American Catholic priest and professor of liturgical and sacramental theology, Paul Janowiak, describes the scriptural proclamation as a communal, creative, and social transaction where the movement towards a genuine communal identity takes place amid the opposing quest for personal transcendence.[20] The interpretation of sacred texts can never be an individual enterprise according to Janowiak, since it is impossible for individuals to separate themselves from their historicity or their state of being implanted in a culture.[21] Similarly, the texts themselves are embedded in a culture and possess a historicity which enters into the interpretive event.

Functioning as communal texts which have a treasured meaning for a sociocultural group, the Lectionary texts are not static, univalent entities that are transmitted unchanged through the generations nor even from one "reading" to the next. Indeed, inaccessible and complex interactions occur between the author, the tradition, the readers and hearers, and the cultural background that has shaped the perspectives, beliefs, and assumptions of those present at the liturgical event. Janowiak argues therefore that the meaning of sacred texts is constantly negotiated by the community as an interpretive entity.[22] The communal nature of a liturgical hermeneutic helps to ease concerns regarding potentially limitless individual interpretations of the Scripture texts.

Research has also revealed that an individual's interpretation of a text in a communal setting is influenced by the centrality of interests within the group. While the beliefs, culture, and experience of the individual are pivotal in the interpretive process, each person's perception is stimulated by the group dynamics and by the responses of other individuals.[23] This has interesting implications for the current investigation which examines the process by which worshipers construct meaning from Lectionary texts proclaimed within an ecclesial assembly.

---

20. Janowiak, *Holy Preaching*, 165.
21. Janowiak, *Holy Preaching*, 167.
22. Janowiak, *Holy Preaching*, 167.
23. Colburn and Weinberg, *Orientation to Listening*, 17.

INTRODUCTION

Gadamer's Philosophical Hermeneutics

Fusion of Horizons

Gadamer refers to the mediation of meaning between a text and an interpreter, between past and present, as a "fusion of horizons."[24] A person's horizon can be conceptualized as their current range of vision or worldview, and comprises that which can be understood from their current vantage point. It includes assumptions, values, and beliefs acquired from past experiences. Each horizon is fluid and temporal, continually shaped and expanded as prejudices are tested in new situations.[25]

Gadamer's notion of horizon reveals the importance he accords to history within the hermeneutical process; one's horizon of understanding is the product of experience, and this horizon is in a constant state of reconstruction as one engages with tradition.[26] The awareness that a person's interpretation is influenced by history, referred to by Gadamer as "effective historical consciousness," allows the interpreter to engage authentically with the past while gaining insight into a disclosure of truth in the present.[27] A person's horizon, therefore, is the product of a historical tradition while also constituting an addition to it. Just as one's current horizon is imbued with horizons from the past, so also an understanding of the past is imbued with one's present horizon. A fusion of horizons occurs, according to Gadamer, when the interpreter's present horizon fuses with the past horizon of a traditionary text to produce a new, shared meaning.[28] Gadamer's theory is pivotal in a liturgical hermeneutic of Scripture because it preserves the historicity of both the Lectionary text and the interpreter, providing for the applicability of a scriptural pericope in a contemporary worship context while also preserving its unique historical origin.

The Interpretive Event as Play

In order to explicate the dynamic event of understanding that takes place in the Catholic liturgy, the fusion of horizons is best situated within the philosophical notion of "play". The play event, according to Gadamer, is a

---

24. Gadamer, *Truth and Method*, 313–17 (hereafter TM).

25. TM 315–17; Warnke, "Hermeneutics," 82.

26. TM 307, 313–15, 317; Bernstein, "Reviews," 421; Grondin, "Hans-Georg Gadamer," 399.

27. TM 369; Weinsheimer, *Gadamer's Hermeneutics*, 183.

28. TM 314–15; Grondin, "Hans-Georg Gadamer," 400.

dynamic process involving a dialogical and reciprocal movement between the players within a defined time and space. A player must willingly enter into the play of the game, with a deep commitment to the "rules of the game" and an openness to any shared articulation of truth which may emerge.[29]

Each player is engrossed by and becomes immersed in the game, engaging in dynamic conversation.[30] The spirit of play extends beyond the consciousness of the individual players such that the players are not so much in control of the game as they are played by it.[31] The players are not passive, indeed they choose to participate actively, but it is the play itself which results in the emergence of meaning. Each person tests their understanding, remaining open to potential meanings of the text and being prepared for their own understanding to be transformed.[32] The hermeneutical construct of play offers key insights for the interpretation of Scripture in the liturgy as it affirms the importance of active participation, emphasizes the corporate nature of the interpretive event above individual consciousness, and incorporates a presumption of faith in which worshipers come with an openness to being addressed and transformed by the sacred text.

III. THEORETICAL MODEL

Gadamer aimed to describe what happens when people are engaged in the activity of understanding, yet he did not prescribe methods or define techniques. Indeed, he argued that understanding transcends the limits of methodological reasoning. When investigating the process by which a person comes to understand a text, Gadamer imagined a two-way fusion of horizons between the author of a text and a reader, or the horizon of a speaker and a listener, which led to the emergence of meaning.[33] It is proposed here that meaning emerges in the play of the liturgy due to the collision of four horizons, thus extrapolating Gadamer's idea. More specifically, it claims that new meaning emerges when the horizons of the Bible text, the Lectionary text, the homilist, and the worshiper collide, and that these horizons are situated in and influenced by two contextual factors: the liturgical event and the ecclesial community.

---

29. TM 107–12.
30. Gadamer, "Text and Interpretation," 188; Grondin, "Hans-Georg Gadamer," 44.
31. TM 109; Vilhauer, "Beyond," 360; Weinsheimer, *Gadamer's Hermeneutics*, 104, 106.
32. TM 117; Gadamer, "Relevance of the Beautiful," 26.
33. TM xvi, 281, 317.

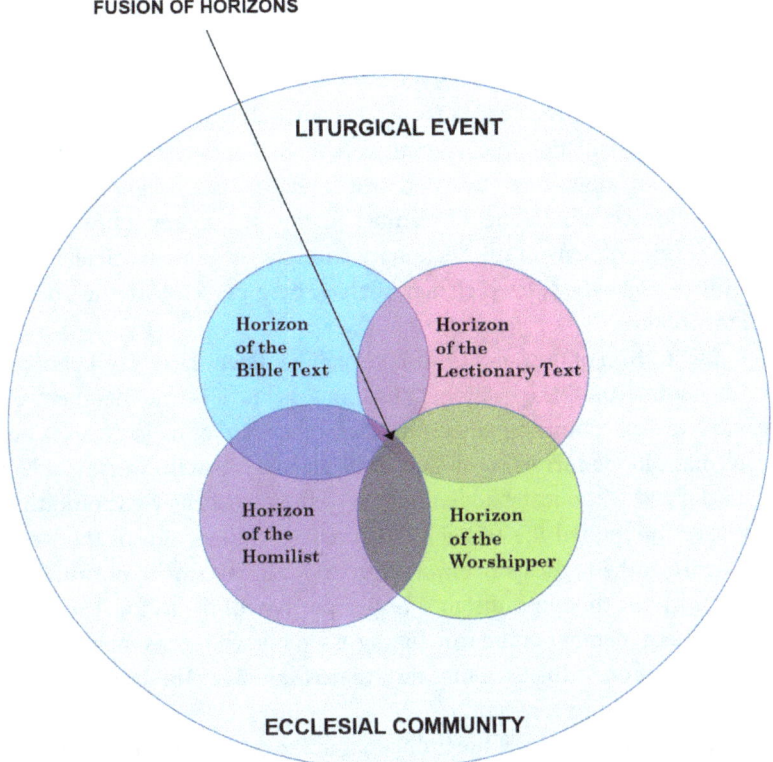

The Four Horizons

The vantage point of the *Bible text* is inescapably present in the liturgical proclamation, although a complete picture of the biblical horizon may be obscured due to the brevity of a pericope proclaimed. It cannot be presumed that the assembly will recognize the broader scriptural context from which a proclaimed pericope has been extracted; for this reason, the biblical horizon enters the hermeneutical event most directly when the homilist expounds the native historical and biblical context of a pericope.

While the presence of the Bible in the liturgy is most clearly manifest in the scriptural proclamation, it must be noted that the entire liturgical event is saturated with the texts of Scripture; antiphons, prayers, responses, and blessings in the Roman Missal and other ritual books frequently draw on biblical texts.[34] Hymn lyrics may also contain biblical texts which are

---

34. Lathrop, *Holy Things*, 15–32.

sung by the whole assembly. In order to contain the scope of this project, however, the focus will be limited to the Scripture texts that are proclaimed from the Lectionary in the Liturgy of the Word.[35]

The horizon of the *Lectionary text* is constituted by Scripture passages chosen for proclamation in corporate worship; it is influenced by decisions about where readings begin and end, which readings are assigned to which feasts, and the combinations of readings juxtaposed on any liturgical day. Some pairings of texts in the Lectionary strongly suggest a particular relationship between the two which may not have been perceived in their native biblical context.

The horizon of the *homilist* will inevitably influence the way a particular listener interprets the Lectionary readings. While it is true that there are as many vantage points on any given text as there are homilists, this is not problematic in the current model. The crucial issue is that if a worshiper had heard the text without the added impact of the preacher's viewpoint, they may have interpreted the text quite differently. The horizon of the lector is not part of the model, since worshipers do not have the opportunity to engage with the thoughts, insights, or perspectives of the lector. The lector is viewed as a member of the worshiping assembly who lends their voice to the proclamation of the Scripture text, thereby allowing the sacred texts to resound in the liturgical event.

Finally, the horizon of the individual *worshiper*, comprising their presumptions, values, and previous experiences, colors their interpretation of the Scripture readings in the liturgy. People come with unique life circumstances and perspectives to hear the same Scripture texts proclaimed; in the assembly there may be a grieving widow, a young graduate, a newly married couple, a person facing unemployment, a woman expecting a baby. These various life circumstances may cause the Lectionary texts to be received with varying emphases, which ultimately influences a worshiper's interpretation.

The Two Contextual Factors

In addition to these four horizons, it is claimed that interpretation of the scriptural proclamation is influenced by two contextual factors—the liturgical event and the ecclesial community. In the liturgy, reception of the texts is

---

35. The presence of the Bible in the liturgy also encompasses the biblical warrant for the Eucharist at the Last Supper (Matt 26:26–28; Mark 14:22–24; Luke 22:17–20; 1 Cor 11:23–25). Some scholars have further observed that the very structure of the liturgy reflects the biblical account of the Way to Emmaus in Luke's Gospel (24:13–35). See Chauvet, *Symbol and Sacrament*, 161–66.

influenced by features of the liturgical space (the ambo, baptismal font, altar, candles), by music, singing, and processions. Also of particular hermeneutical significance are liturgical symbols and symbolic actions such as sprinkling with holy water, breaking bread, drinking wine, proclaiming the word, burning incense, offering a sign of peace. The second contextual factor is the ecclesial community. The physical gathering for communal worship is a powerful corporeal symbol of the People of God, united not just within a particular parish church but indeed with Christians around the world, and with those who have gone before them. The ecclesial context serves as an interpretive framework within which members of the assembly attribute meaning to Lectionary texts. Beyond an interest in textual analysis common to many of the existing hermeneutical methods, the dialogue established in this investigation between theology and philosophy is ultimately practical and is directed towards understanding how the meaning of Scripture texts is influenced when heard within the ecclesial community as part of the multisensory liturgical event.

Delimiting the Scope

There are many specific elements of the liturgical event that are not named individually in the diagrammatic model. The General Intercessions are one such element of the liturgy that ideally build upon what has been proclaimed and give voice to the contemporary needs of the assembly, the church, and the world. Well-chosen liturgical music has a similar hermeneutical impact. For the purposes of this investigation, liturgical elements beyond the immediate proclamation event of lections and preaching will be considered as part of the context of the liturgical event rather than constituting separate horizons.

The role of the Holy Spirit has also been carefully considered. The interpretive impact of the Holy Spirit, which is ultimately a faith perspective, is not depicted diagrammatically in a theoretical model which has its basis in philosophical hermeneutics. However, the impact of the Holy Spirit is seen to pervade the entire interpretive process, having influenced the original composition of Scripture and its interpretation through the ages, opening hearts and minds to encounter other horizons in the liturgical event, uniting members of the assembly, and inspiring the dynamic vibrant energy circulating among those gathered. It is not in dispute that, for a faith-filled worshiper who participates in the liturgical event, the Holy Spirit is present in each element of the model.

IV. THE SIGNIFICANCE OF A LITURGICAL HERMENEUTIC

The worship event has constituted the primary setting for engaging with sacred texts throughout history; encountering sacred texts within community shaped the faith of early Christians, and the texts eventually became authoritative and were canonized as Scripture. As E. Byron Anderson notes, "Scripture and sacrament are born out of the liturgical activity of the church, survive (or not) because of their liturgical use, and receive their public authority in and through their public celebration."[36] Indeed, it is through the gesture, action, word, and song of the worshiping assembly, that the biblical texts are actualized as Scripture and continue to constitute the living word of God in the life of the ecclesial community.[37]

Since the liturgy is the primary, if not the only, context in which most contemporary Catholics encounter the Scriptures, the task of expounding a liturgical hermeneutic of Scripture is of great significance. Such a task aims to shed light on how members of the liturgical assembly come to interpret the Scripture readings, and, by implication, how a meaningful interpretation of Scripture might be facilitated so that it takes root in the hearts of worshipers and informs their lives beyond the bounds of the liturgical event. This work also offers an important contribution to the field of biblical hermeneutics in proposing an additional hermeneutic—namely a liturgical hermeneutic of Scripture. While written from a Roman Catholic perspective, the findings have broader application due to the adoption by other Christian Churches of the Revised Common Lectionary (1983, 1992) which is based on and derived from the Catholic Lectionary.

V. THE INVESTIGATIVE FRAMEWORK

It is important to acknowledge at the outset, that the human process of understanding, in a liturgical context or otherwise, is an inconceivably complex network for which an algorithm cannot be devised, nor a model designed, that would cover all possibilities or intricacies operating within the human mind and spirit. The multitude of facets which constitute religious tradition, human cognition, and contemporary culture invite the contributions of several disciplines including theology, philosophy, sociology, and the psychological sciences. Each of these could possibly illuminate the process by which worshipers make meaning of the scriptural proclamation.

---

36. Anderson, "Scripture and Liturgy," 188.
37. Anderson, "Practicing Scripture," 104.

However, to contain the scope of this project, there will be a focus on two of these disciplines whereby theology will be brought into conversation with philosophy in a critical correlational approach. Within this overarching approach, the investigation is structured according to the four levels of practical theological inquiry developed by American theologian Don Browning: descriptive theology, historical theology, systematic theology, and strategic practical theology.

This introductory chapter has provided an overview of the investigation and the theoretical model which underpins it. It has situated this project within the existing philosophical and liturgical scholarship and has highlighted the significance of developing a liturgical hermeneutic of Scripture.

Chapter 2 introduces a Roman Catholic perspective on practical theology and presents a rationale for the use of a critical correlational approach in achieving the aims of this project. Under the overarching framework of mutually critical correlation, the four dimensions of fundamental practical theology proposed by Don Browning are then introduced as the framework upon which this investigation is structured.

Part I constitutes the descriptive theology phase; it comprises the third and fourth chapters. Chapter 3 explores the structure of the Lectionary and its impact on the meaning of the Scripture texts it contains. Scripture is shown to be conveyed in the Catholic liturgy through pre-selected pericopes arranged in a Lectionary designed for liturgical proclamation. The organization of these texts according to the framework of the liturgical year and the ritual shape of the Catholic eucharistic event is examined. The chapter investigates the criteria for assigning readings to particular liturgical days and seasons across a three-year cycle of readings. It canvasses the factors which influenced the selection, omission, and juxtaposition of various pericopes and addresses the impact of decisions about where to start and finish a pericope.

Chapter 4 explores the hermeneutical influence of hearing Lectionary pericopes proclaimed in the multisensory, corporate context of the Mass characterized by ritual gestures and symbols, hymns, silence, prayers, and responses which comprise the Catholic liturgical paradigm. There is an examination of the features of the liturgical event which have a particular influence on the interpretation of Scripture. The first is the Catholic Church teaching that Christ is sacramentally present in the assembly, in the priest, in the word, and in the Eucharist, and that Christ speaks directly and dialogically with the gathered assembly in the liturgical proclamation. Further, the active working of the Holy Spirit in the liturgy is seen to occupy an important role in illuminating the Scriptures for successive generations, changing the hearts of interpreters, and facilitating a transformative encounter with the sacred text. The presumption of full, conscious, and active participation constitutes another hermeneutical influence, with bodily gestures, postures, and processions in the liturgy drawing together the exterior and interior elements of participation and creating a unique context in which to interpret the scriptural pericopes. The trajectory of the word event is traced from Lectionary text to a contemporary living proclamation, that is, from potentiality to actuality. The place of the homily is explored, with the listener viewed not only as an active participant but indeed as a co-author of the homily. The preacher is seen to stimulate and disturb the internal polyphonic dialogue of the worshipers "like an interlocutor in an ongoing internal dialogue."[38] This chapter also explores the multisensory features of the liturgy. The liturgy is seen to offer a complex interplay of auditory, visual, tactile, olfactory, and gustatory elements. The result is a profound affective response, which leads to the uncovering of meaning in ways that supersede mere literary competence.

Part II, the fifth chapter, presents the historical theology stage of the investigation. Chapter 5 examines the evolution of the scriptural proclamation in the liturgical event and traces the emergence of liturgical books for proclaiming Scripture, as distinct from biblical manuscripts. Jewish reading practices and reading selections are explored, leading to the identification of continuities and discontinuities between Jewish and Christian practices. The history of Christian scriptural proclamation within a liturgical context is noted to have progressed alongside the development of the Christian liturgical calendar with its feasts and seasons. The evolution of written manuscripts, and technologies which enabled the arrangement of texts into particular sequences, are seen to have facilitated the creation of an intertextual network for interpretation. Specific examples of ancient manuscripts are included as evidence of the evolution of liturgical books for proclaiming Scripture, which occurred in response to the emergence of liturgical ministries.

The impact of changing liturgical practice in the Middle Ages is explored, in which the priest proclaimed all texts of the Mass in Latin, including the readings, and which led to the production of a "complete missal" incorporating the Mass prayers and readings into one volume for the priest's use. The changes resulting from the Second Vatican Council are then presented as establishing a new hermeneutical context for the interpretation of Scripture texts in the liturgy. This historical investigation is ultimately directed towards understanding the present, ongoing worship life of liturgical

---

38. Gaarden, "Living Voice," 5.

communities. The implication for modern times is that the Lectionary must continue to be viewed as a living text, subject to adaptation, in response to changing socio-cultural and liturgical practice.

Part III, the systematic theology stage, comprises chapters 6, 7, and 8. It places theological explanations of the proclamation event into a mutually critical dialogue with Gadamer's philosophical hermeneutics. Chapter 6 explores key concepts of Gadamer's theory of interpretation and demonstrates how the concepts of play, festival, and a fusion of horizons can inform a hermeneutic for interpreting scriptural pericopes in the liturgy.

Gadamer outlines the need to identify one's prejudices at the outset of an interpretive event, as these prejudices form the basis of one's questioning of a text in an active dialogical process. He insists that each interpreter is hermeneutically and historically located, a product of their tradition, culture, and experiences, and claims that interpreters must remain open to being challenged and transformed by historical texts. He refers to the mediation of meaning between a text and an interpreter as a "fusion of horizons" and situates this event within the richer concept of "play". The construct of play is characterized by a dynamic, interactive, dialogical movement between the players in which meaning emerges through the activity that unfolds between the players as they remain open to the shared enunciation of truth.

Gadamer's concept of "festival" is then examined as an example of play which has a particular celebratory quality, and which comes to fruition in a community that gathers for a common festive purpose. The final part of the chapter undertakes a critical analysis of the ways in which Gadamer's notions of play, festival, and the fusion of horizons can account for the emergence of meaning in the liturgical proclamation of Scripture.

Chapter 7 endeavors to provide a synthesis of the hermeneutical impact of tradition and memory from the perspectives of both liturgical theology and philosophical hermeneutics in relation to the understanding of Scripture proclaimed in the liturgy. Tradition is not conceived as a static collection of doctrines, rules, and ritual practices, but rather as a dynamic process of transmission which keeps communal memory alive, and which is continually renewed in negotiation with shifting horizons. The role of liturgy in preserving and creating a living corporate memory is examined, noting the impact of the sensory system in creating memories. The reception history of a Scripture text is viewed as a hermeneutical bridge between the historical text and the contemporary understanding of it. It is argued that classic interpretations have become part of the text's history of influence and form part of the horizon of expectations for future listeners, although limitations of engaging with a text's reception history during the liturgical proclamation are acknowledged. It is proposed that a worshiper can be close enough to the tradition that their predispositions are guided by that tradition, and simultaneously distant enough that the truth of a text can be experienced, and a new perspective attained through a fusion of horizons.

Chapter 8 examines the scriptural proclamation within the liturgy as both a complex social event and a personal encounter. There is an acknowledgment of the unavoidable tension between the public, communal, ritualized proclamation of the Scripture texts on one hand, and the inward movement towards interiorization and silence on the other. Although personal autonomy and relational autonomy can seem to be a "philosophical dichotomy,"[39] it is proposed in this chapter that both are essential when considering how Scripture texts are interpreted in the liturgical event. There is reciprocity between the individual worshiper and the community during the liturgy such that each person individually, as well as the assembly collectively, is an active subject in a dynamic social event.

Part IV, the ninth chapter, is the strategic practical theology phase; it identifies specific practical concerns that inform a liturgical hermeneutic of Scripture. In line with Gadamer's philosophical hermeneutics, chapter 9 does not propose a method nor propose a formulaic procedure for understanding Scripture in the liturgy. Rather, it illustrates the capacity of the theoretical model to account for ways in which the meaning of Scripture is uniquely influenced by its arrangement in the Lectionary and by the liturgical context in which it is received. To facilitate a fusion of horizons in the liturgy, practical suggestions are offered for promoting engagement of the senses, creating space for corporate silence, and for encouraging worshipers to enter the play of the liturgy. This chapter highlights the way that the tradition of scriptural proclamation is molded and modified from within, and also draws attention to the ways in which worshipers can be formed for the liturgy and by the liturgy. It is further claimed that the Lectionary's use of Scripture texts has directly influenced the meaning of these Scripture pericopes over time such that their liturgical use has become part of their inherent meaning. It is proposed that the use of Scripture texts in the Lectionary and the liturgical year be considered in the field of biblical hermeneutics alongside other hermeneutical approaches used by biblical scholars.

Finally, the conclusion presents the significance and implications of the findings and, on this basis, defends the need for a liturgical hermeneutic of Scripture. The variety of recognized hermeneutical approaches to biblical interpretation rules out any suggestion that it would be possible to offer one correct way to interpret Scripture. However, since the liturgy is the predominant context in which Catholics receive the Scriptures in contemporary

---

39. Konigsburg, "Worship as Compatible," 129.

times, it will be proposed that a liturgical hermeneutic of Scripture must take its place alongside other commonly accepted biblical hermeneutical methods.

CHAPTER 2

Dimensions of Practical Theology

In order to develop a liturgical hermeneutic of Scripture, the current project brings liturgical theology into conversation with philosophical hermeneutics and contemporary culture using a mutually critical correlational approach. In this chapter, a Roman Catholic perspective on practical theology is presented, and the evolution of the critical correlational method is traced, before providing a rationale for the suitability of this approach for the current liturgical investigation. This is followed by an explication of the four dimensions of practical theological inquiry which will serve as the framework for this investigation.

I. PRACTICAL THEOLOGY

Practical theology is conducted using a variety of methodologies, all designed to make connections between the realm of human action, the human sciences, and the Christian tradition, in an endeavor to renew or restructure contemporary practice. For the current project, which seeks to bring theology into dialogue with philosophy and with contemporary culture, the most appropriate method is the critical correlational approach proposed by David Tracy and introduced into the domain of practical theology by Don Browning. This approach aims to facilitate a critical conversation between various disciplines, both theological and non-theological, and is open to the possibility of both conflict and congruence arising from interdisciplinary dialogue.

Academic contributions to practical theology since the 1990s have adopted a framework which begins with practice and experience, proceeds to an examination of theory, and finally returns to practice. Browning expressed this as a movement "from present theory-laden practice to a retrieval of normative theory-laden practice to the creation of more critically held theory-laden practices."[1] Recent scholarship emphasizes that practical theological thinking is located in the modern, embodied world and is therefore always "concrete, local, and contextual."[2] In the current exploration, practical theological thinking takes place in the contemporary, embodied, multisensory liturgical event in which a concrete, local assembly gathers in the context of corporate worship.

This investigation operates from the premise that practical theology is a dynamic, hermeneutical, dialogical, and contextual enterprise, and considers interpretation to be both an ecclesial and an individual task. It acknowledges that the place to begin is with practice. However, it also recognizes that theory, tradition, and practice are inextricably interwoven in complex ways, a phenomenon which is particularly evident in the liturgical event.[3]

Practical Theology: A Roman Catholic Perspective

Practical theology is concerned with issues such as praxis, performance, experience, transformation, engagement, and formation, all of which have a profound resonance within the Catholic tradition.[4] Catholic practical theologians work with several commitments in mind. They view theological anthropology through a communal and social lens and affirm a sense of sacramentality in regards to the human person, creation, and the incarnation.[5] They acknowledge the liturgy as the summit and source of Christian life, as a place where Christ is encountered and members of the assembly are transformed.[6] They operate with an ecclesial outlook, acknowledging the role of the Spirit in the task of interpretation while also attributing authoritative weight to church norms, doctrines, and the teachings of the magisterium. They recognize the central role of tradition and its embodiment in concrete practices.[7]

1. Browning, *Fundamental Practical Theology*, 7.

2. Muller, "Postfoundational Practical Theology," 3. Despite the focus on the present context, theological tradition is also acknowledged as an important contributor to practical theological research. See Bennett et al., *Invitation to Research*, 12.

3. Cahalan, "Locating Practical Theology," 14.

4. Wolfteich, "Reframing Practical Theology," 284.

5. Cahalan and Froehle, "Developing Discipline," 28; Wolfteich, "Catholic Voices," 330.

6. Vatican Council II, "Constitution, *Sacrosanctum Concilium*," 10 (hereafter SC).

7. Wolfteich, "Reframing Practical Theology," 285; Cahalan, "Locating Practical Theology," 15.

The Second Vatican Council, opened in 1962 by Pope John XXIII, has been described as a "practical theological revolution"[8] in which possibilities were opened for the relationship between theory and praxis to be explored. After a century of church resistance to secular culture and modernism, the key documents of the Council revealed a pendulum swing towards welcoming the insights of cultural, intellectual, and human sciences for their potential to illuminate the life of the Catholic Church.[9] This represented a profound reorientation from a dogmatic to a conversational theological approach, from an inwardly-focused, hierarchical structure, centered around the ordained clergy, to an outward-looking engagement with the contemporary world.

The first document promulgated by the Council, *The Constitution on the Sacred Liturgy*, gave expression to the new emphasis on encounter and experience in the liturgy. It declared that the liturgy is "an action of Christ the priest and of His Body which is the Church,"[10] and established that "full, conscious, and active" participation by all the people is the fundamental concern in liturgical celebrations.[11] While tradition was a foundation stone of the Council's work, there was nonetheless an emergence of new methods of theological and praxis-based reflection, with human experience recognized as a legitimate source of theological inquiry.[12]

II. A CRITICAL CORRELATIONAL APPROACH

In attempting to create a synthesis between the Christian tradition and the modern world in the aftermath of World War I, Lutheran theologian and philosopher, Paul Tillich, developed a way of doing theology known as the "method of correlation." He aimed to correlate questions raised by contemporary human experience in the secular world with answers provided by Christian texts and traditions.[13] Tillich's formulation of theological method attracted critics who argued that a truly correlational model must also account for the potential of contemporary culture to influence theology with answers of its own.[14]

8. Cahalan and Froehle, "Developing Discipline," 35.
9. Graham et al., *Theological Reflection*, 164.
10. SC 7.
11. SC 14.
12. Cahalan and Froehle, "Developing Discipline," 36.
13. Tillich, *Systematic*, 62–67.
14. Tracy conceded that, while Tillich's statement of method was problematic, Tillich may in fact have practiced a mutually correlative approach: ". . . the method

Tillich's colleague, Seward Hiltner, advocated instead that the correlation be envisaged as a "two-way street" where the dynamic of question and response would be a mutual and dialectical process.[15] Hiltner claimed that non-theological disciplines, human sciences, and the arts could offer fresh insights not accessible from the theological standpoint.[16]

American Roman Catholic theologian, David Tracy, subsequently proposed a revised model requiring "the mutually critical correlation of the interpreted theory and praxis of the Christian faith with the interpreted theory and praxis of the contemporary situation."[17] He claimed that theology must position itself at the intersection of common human experience (culture) and Christian claims to truth (classic texts) such that each is mutually corrective and critical of the other and such that each is open to transformation and revision.[18] According to Tracy, "contemporary fundamental theology is best understood as philosophical reflection upon both the meanings disclosed in our common human experience and the meanings disclosed in the primary texts of the Christian tradition."[19]

The influence of Gadamer's philosophical hermeneutical theory upon Tracy's model is indisputable. Like Gadamer, Tracy asserts that human understanding is acquired through "dialogue" or "conversation" where the interpreter's fore-understandings are consciously acknowledged and used to prompt their questioning of a text. Further echoing Gadamer, Tracy notes that, in any encounter with an ancient text, the text puts a question to the interpreter and speaks into the contemporary age. Tradition is regarded as a genuine partner in conversation.[20]

This mutually critical dialogical process guards against the danger of a Christian symbol, text, or belief being subsumed into a secular idea, yet also rejects the notion that Christian truths are decisively and authoritatively sealed. Furthermore, the revised model of mutually critical correlation preserves the privileged place of tradition while remaining committed to the conversational, communicative process of theological reflection.

---

of correlation is better formulated . . . not as Tillich formulated it but as he actually employed it: namely as an interpretive correlation of the questions and answers of the message with the questions and answers of the situation." Tracy, *Filaments,* 214.

15. Hiltner, *Preface to Pastoral Theology,* 22. Hiltner argues that dialogical questioning and answering must be "constant and discriminating" in order that theology remain relevant to the contemporary culture.

16. Hiltner, *Preface to Pastoral Theology,* 223.

17. Tracy, "Foundations of Practical Theology," 76.

18. Tracy, *Blessed Rage,* 43–46.

19. Tracy, *Blessed Rage,* 237.

20. TM 366; Tracy, *Blessed Rage,* 42–44.

Tracy further develops the concept of active dialogue, emphasizing that partners in a conversation risk change as they remain open to new possibilities that might change their beliefs.[21] He presents three potential outcomes that could result from the dialogue between theology and culture:

1. A Christian assertion and a cultural claim may say the same thing, resulting in a case of complete *identity*;
2. There may be similarity without total resemblance, resulting in a correlation of *analogy*;
3. The Christian viewpoint and the cultural perspective may be in a state of *non-identity*. In this case, the dialogical process of theological reflection which takes place between society, the academy, and the Christian Church, is directed towards discovering where truth is located.[22]

Don Browning, while professor of religious ethics and social sciences at the University of Chicago, introduced Tracy's model of mutually critical correlation to the field of fundamental practical theology. Browning affirms the mutually correlative nature of the theological task in establishing "a critical dialogue between the implicit questions and the explicit answers of the Christian classics and the explicit questions and implicit answers of contemporary cultural experiences and practices."[23] He holds the firm conviction that theology must be practical from beginning to end, moving from traditional theory-laden practices, to theory, and then back to new theory-laden practices.[24]

Browning argues that the process of theological reflection begins when a crisis is encountered, and theory-laden questions subsequently emerge.[25] The process of theological reflection continues with a description of current practices in order to better comprehend the questions emerging from the crisis. The resulting questions are then considered in light of the normative Christian texts such that a critical dialogue takes place between tradition and practice.[26] Browning makes it clear that a hermeneutical conversation with normative texts involves more than one interpreter. Rather, it is imbued

---

21. Tracy, *Plurality*, 93, 103.
22. Graham et al., *Theological Reflection*, 172.
23. Browning, *Fundamental Practical Theology*, 46.
24. Browning, *Fundamental Practical Theology*, 40.
25. Browning, *Fundamental Practical Theology*, 281–82. One hears the echo of Thomas Kuhn's structure of scientific revolutions in which a revolutionary change occurs in response to a period of crisis and results in a deficient paradigm being replaced by a new, more appropriate one. Kuhn, *Structure*, 18–20, 23–25.
26. Browning, *Fundamental Practical Theology*, 6.

with a group dynamic where the members of a community, each with their own effective histories, engage in an ongoing and mutually correcting conversation with the classic texts. In this way, the process of interpretation becomes open-ended and oriented towards the future.[27] The final stage in the process of theological reflection according to Browning, is the implementation of new interpretations of the normative texts, directly impacting both tradition and practice. Revealing a distinctly Gadamerian influence, Browning insists that application does not merely enter the conversation at the end; rather, he claims that the whole conversation is shaped by practical concerns that emerge from the current situation.[28]

Flowing on from this inherently practical view of hermeneutics, Browning proposes four dimensions or disciplines within the larger framework of fundamental practical theology: descriptive theology, historical theology, systematic theology, and strategic or fully practical theology.[29] The current investigation will be structured around these four dimensions of theological inquiry within the methodological framework of mutually critical correlation.

As a researcher shaped within the Catholic tradition of faith and a frequent participant in liturgical celebrations, it is acknowledged that I would be unable to conduct an entirely objective study with critical distance. Indeed, it is now well accepted in the academic community that the notion of an objective, bias-free researcher is illusory.[30] For this particular project it could, in fact, be argued that an involvement and familiarity with the liturgical event might actually be advantageous for discerning new insights. The chosen methodology allows for new questions and perspectives to emerge, prompts critical reflections on liturgical praxis, and engages the researcher and the practice in such a way that both might evolve and be transformed.

Critics of the Correlational Method

Critics of the correlational method argue that bringing theology into conversation with contemporary culture compromises the unique identity of the Christian Church, promotes an accommodation to modern secularism, and rejects the counter-cultural elements of the Gospel. Swiss theologian, Karl Barth, staunchly criticizes correlational approaches on the grounds that God's revelation in Christ is the central and normative source for all

---

27. Colapietro, "Dissenting Voice," 186.
28. Browning, *Fundamental Practical Theology*, 39; TM 318–19.
29. Browning, *Fundamental Practical Theology*, 8.
30. Dillen and Mager, "Research," 308–10.

theology, and he espouses the utter primacy of the Scripture text as divine, revealed word.[31] He rejects the possibility of nominating alternative starting points, such as philosophy or the social sciences, based on their "alien" frameworks.[32] Barth recognizes the potential for a theologian's work to be consistent with and confirmed by cultural understandings, but regards this as unnecessary.[33] By way of contrast, those who support a critical correlational model claim that the questions and answers being generated in contemporary society must indeed be correlated with theological questions in order for theology to remain relevant.[34]

Hans Frei, an American post-liberal biblical scholar and theologian, also offers strong opposition to correlational methods. Best known for his work in the area of biblical hermeneutics, Frei laments the "eclipse" of the biblical narrative beginning in the late eighteenth century, in which the narrative of the Bible was subjected to various hermeneutical methods in order to render the stories applicable to the lives of modern readers. For Frei, this represents "the great reversal" whereby interpretation becomes a case of "fitting the biblical story into another world with another story rather than incorporating that world into the biblical story."[35]

More recently, in the context of preaching, Lutheran pastor, Mark Ellingsen, argues that Scripture "functions as its own interpreter" and claims that reading it through the lens of an extrinsic discipline prevents the sacred text from speaking.[36] Yet, a correlational homilist would strongly reject the idea that merely recounting the biblical narrative gives it contemporary relevance, and would suggest the need to engage with prominent questions and issues in modern society. Foreseeably, most people in a Sunday congregation would be familiar with contemporary philosophical and psychological categories such as self-actualization, meaninglessness, optimism, and despair, because they have "sucked in the air surrounding these disciplines."[37] Consequently, the correlational homilist would claim that

31. Barth, *Word of God*, 26–28; Harrison, "Correlation," 70–73.

32. Rumscheidt, *Way of Theology*, 5–6.

33. Barth, *Church Dogmatics*, 277. John Milbank, who founded the movement known as Radical Orthodoxy, has argued against the critical correlational method, in particular, the use of the social sciences as a dialogue partner, on the basis that the social sciences are an expression of modern secularism and operate within a paradigm that is irreconcilable with the comprehensive Christian vision of reality. Milbank, *Theology and Social Theory*, 390.

34. Pembroke, "Theocentric Therapeutic Preaching," 319.

35. Frei, *Eclipse*, 130.

36. Ellingsen, *Integrity*, 19.

37. Pembroke, "Theocentric Therapeutic Preaching," 319.

these categories must be addressed explicitly if the Scripture text is to speak to the experience of contemporary listeners.

George Lindbeck, an American Lutheran theologian considered to be one of the fathers of the post-liberal movement and remembered for his work in Lutheran-Roman Catholic dialogue, rejects the revisionist-liberal correlational approach of translating faith into more readily accessible terms so that it might be more intelligible to a modern culture.[38] He views religion as a *verbum externum*, an external word that shapes and forms people and the world in which they live.[39] In regard to biblical hermeneutics, Lindbeck claims that reality must be described "within the scriptural framework rather than translating Scripture into extra scriptural categories."[40] Lindbeck thus rejects the notion that interpretation is influenced by the variety of questions brought to the narrative texts where those questions have been influenced by contemporary culture and practices, claiming that the inner coherence of the Christian narrative renders it distinct from the surrounding culture.

Proponents of the correlational approach also recognize some inherent challenges with this methodology. The correlational theologian is well aware that the insights from contemporary culture may distort the meaning of Catholic texts and practices rather than illuminate them. Consequently, there is a need to preserve the integrity of the biblical text and ensure that it is not contorted to fit the needs and interests of modern interpreters.[41] The converse also poses a risk, and so the correlative theologian ensures that cultural elements are not manipulated in order to align with theological interpretations. Since it is impossible to give equal and just treatment to each source and discipline involved in the dialogical process of correlation, the correlative theologian must make decisions about narrowing the field of focus and deciding which sources are most pertinent.

Strengths of the Correlational Approach

There are several advantages intrinsic to the method of mutually critical correlation for practical theological research. Firstly, it facilitates an interdisciplinary dialogue between contemporary cultural experience and the Christian tradition, elucidating integral aspects of Christian texts

---

38. Michalson, "Response to Lindbeck," 114.
39. Michalson, "Response to Lindbeck," 114.
40. Lindbeck, *Nature of Doctrine*, 118.
41. Pembroke, "Theocentric Therapeutic Preaching," 317.

and practices which may otherwise remain obscured.[42] It invites sources from the human sciences and modern culture to contribute an innovative perspective to elements of Christian tradition and, similarly, provides an avenue for Christian practices and traditions to influence contemporary human experience. The inevitable tension between religion and secular culture is not avoided, but rather embraced, in a mutually critical correlative model, with both theology and culture posing questions and offering answers. This methodology takes seriously "the dramatic confrontation, the mutual illuminations and corrections, the possible basic reconciliation" between the values and understandings of Christian tradition and modern culture.[43]

The revised correlational model aligns with the Second Vatican Council's focus on "aggiornamento," a throwing open of the doors of the Catholic Church in a desire to enter into dialogue with the modern world.[44] Correlating questions and answers from the Catholic liturgical tradition with questions and answers being generated in modern culture indeed affirms the contemporary relevance of theological research and affirms interdisciplinary differences as a fruitful ground for further dialogue and insight.

Rationale for a Critical Correlational Approach in Developing a Liturgical Hermeneutic of Scripture

The post-liberal approaches of Barth, Frei, and Lindbeck make a valuable contribution in emphasizing the integral importance of biblical narrative and tradition in the process of Scripture interpretation. It is recognized that their common rejection of the correlational method stems from their concern that the biblical text might be unduly compromised and forced to conform to the realm of the human sciences.

Yet, the current investigation proceeds with the strong conviction that philosophy and the human sciences can contribute insights about the process of understanding that takes place when scriptural pericopes are proclaimed during the liturgical event, and claims that an additional lens may allow the biblical text to speak more clearly. It acknowledges the need to avoid a situation where philosophical or psychological concepts become dominant or threaten the integrity of the biblical text such that the Scriptures are manipulated to fall in line with modern sentiments. It recognizes the need to guard against the danger of shaping the biblical text, rather than allowing it to shape the listener.

42. Pembroke, "Theocentric Therapeutic Preaching," 334.
43. Tracy, *Blessed Rage*, 32.
44. Butler, "Aggiornamento."

The chosen research framework is designed to circumvent the potential hazards of the correlational method. It avoids the danger of focusing purely on contemporary liturgical practice by treating tradition as a serious dialogue partner and by engaging with modern cultural experience. It guards against an individualist approach to interpretation by situating the hermeneutical process within the ecclesial community gathered for corporate worship, and recognizes that both individuals and communities are influenced by pre-existing philosophical, social, and cultural influences.[45]

The correlational approach adopted in this investigation is more than an elementary correlation between the Christian tradition and current experience as if these were static, fixed entities. Instead, it presumes that both tradition and experience are complex, evolving elements and that the conversational interaction between them is dynamic and fluid.[46] Within the liturgy, according to Catholic Church teaching, God takes the divine initiative in reaching down to humanity (catabasis) and the gathered worshipers respond (anabasis) thereby establishing a dynamic communication between humankind and God.[47] The dialogical and critical method of correlation, therefore, has particular merit for the current project in which the Catholic liturgy is viewed as both a human social event and an encounter with the divine presence.

III. BROWNING'S DIMENSIONS OF FUNDAMENTAL PRACTICAL THEOLOGY

i. Descriptive Theology

The task of this dimension (Part One) is to describe contemporary theory-laden practices and their meanings in order to better understand the emerging practical questions that have prompted the theological reflection. This dimension also involves an analysis of the various aspects of religious and cultural meaning that encircle current practices. Browning insists, however, that the descriptive phase must be a theological endeavor and not simply a task for the social sciences.

The critical dialogue at the descriptive phase is characterized by questions such as: *What is actually happening within this field of praxis? What are the authoritative sources relied upon to legitimate current practices? What are the symbols or values used to interpret the current practice?* A description

---

45. Graham et al., *Theological Reflection*, 152.
46. Miller-McLemore, "Introduction," 17.
47. Kunzler, *Church's Liturgy*, 15.

of the current practices inevitably leads to questions about what should in fact be happening and what ideals should actually be guiding praxis.[48] It also raises practical questions about whether the authoritative sources are being used consistently and prompts a fresh examination of the classic Christian texts and traditions.[49]

The descriptive phase of this investigation will identify the features of the Roman Catholic Lectionary and the principles underlying its construction (chapter 3). It will examine the synthesis of written and oral features of language in the proclamation and provide a rich analysis of the liturgical event which shapes how the Scriptures are heard in the ecclesial community (chapter 4). Both theological and non-theological disciplines will be drawn upon in the descriptive task in order to articulate the practical questions to be addressed in subsequent sections of this book.

ii. Historical Theology

The second dimension of fundamental practical theology (Part Two) takes the questions that emerge from the description of the theory-laden practices in the first phase and puts them to the normative classic texts which are part of the community's effective history. It asks: *What do the normative texts actually imply for current practice?*[50] It draws on biblical studies, Catholic Church history, and liturgical theology, and prompts an honest confrontation with the historical texts in order to identify implications for liturgical praxis.

This normative work involves tracing the history of the scriptural proclamation in the Mass, identifying continuities and discontinuities between early Jewish and Christian reading practices, and then examining the evolution of liturgical books for proclaiming Scripture in the worship event.

While the normative task examines the richness of church tradition, it is not a study of liturgical books and manuscripts within their historical contexts dissociated from the contemporary situation. Indeed, the focus remains firmly fixed on current practice with the presumption that the present has been shaped by tradition. It is accepted that historical texts and ritual practices have been assimilated into contemporary practices and understandings, and have therefore exerted complex and varied influences on the interpretation of Scripture in the liturgy.

---

48. Browning, "Mapping the Terrain," 20.
49. Browning, *Fundamental Practical Theology*, 49.
50. Browning, *Fundamental Practical Theology*, 49; Klaasen, "Practical Theology," 5.

It must be noted that there is an inherent danger in looking exclusively at the use of texts in modern contexts without reference to the context in which they were originally composed. It is irrefutable that stripping biblical manuscripts or ancient Lectionaries of their historical context and meaning is to ignore the place of history in the dialogical process of interpretation. Indeed, the current quest for a liturgical hermeneutic of Scripture accepts the work of historical-critical analysis but proposes to build on this foundation by investigating the additional hermeneutical impact of both the Lectionary cursus and the liturgical event within which the scriptural proclamation takes place.

iii. Systematic Theology

Browning's systematic dimension (Part Three) articulates a new construction of meaning arising from the previous two phases, and it critically searches for reasons to justify this newly created meaning.[51] Practical reasoning at this stage asks: *What new meaning emerges following the fusion of horizons between the vision implied in current praxis and the frame of reference implicit in the normative Christian texts?*

The systematic theology phase will examine three key themes. The first is the potential of Gadamer's philosophical hermeneutics to account for the process of understanding that takes place when scriptural pericopes are proclaimed in the liturgy. The fusion of horizons which occurs during the proclamation will be examined, as the liturgical event is viewed through the lens of Gadamer's concept of play (chapter 6). The second theme concerns the hermeneutical role of memory and tradition, and will involve an exploration of personal and corporate memory with regards to the liturgical proclamation. The dynamic tradition of the Catholic Church as expressed in the normative documents will be placed into dialogue with Gadamer's account of tradition and experience in the process of understanding, thus providing a synthesis of the role of memory and tradition from the perspectives of both liturgical theology and philosophical hermeneutics (chapter 7). Thirdly, this phase of the investigation will illuminate the scriptural proclamation as both a complex social event and a moment of personal encounter, whereby the ecclesial context serves as an interpretative framework within which members of the assembly attribute meaning to scriptural pericopes (chapter 8).

It must be mentioned that Gadamer was explicit in his intention *not* to present a "method" of interpretation. Rather, he spoke of interpretative

---

51. Browning, *Fundamental Practical Theology*, 51–52.

"experience" which occurs through the dialectical process of the fusion of horizons and results in the event of understanding.[52] In this current investigation, which aims to elucidate a liturgical hermeneutic of Scripture, theological explanations of the liturgical event will be placed into a mutually critical dialogue with philosophical theories of understanding, incorporating contemporary cultural experiences and practices, to arrive at a hermeneutic for interpreting scriptural pericopes proclaimed in the liturgy.

iv. Strategic Practical Theology

The final stage of the investigation (Part Four) returns to the specific, concrete questions that initially prompted the process of theological reflection; it is concerned with the purposeful implementation of the practical concerns that have been driving the theological reflection. Building on the information gleaned in the descriptive, normative, and systematic theology phases, it asks four questions.

Firstly: *How can this specific situation be understood?* This includes comprehensive questioning about elements particular to the concrete situation of liturgical proclamation, the history of the ecclesial community, the current needs of the community, and an investigation of the religious and cultural narratives that contribute meaning to the event.[53] Secondly, strategic practical theology asks: *What should the contemporary praxis be in this particular situation?* The outcomes identified throughout the descriptive, historical, and systematic theology phases, which have had a practical focus from the outset, are placed into conversation with the concrete situation.[54] Thirdly: *How can the norms of contemporary praxis be defended in this specific context?* This moment of critical reflection results in the construction of rational explanations to defend the theory-laden practices in a highly pluralistic society.[55] The final question to be asked in this stage is: *What strategies and resources can be used in this specific situation?* No matter how useful the suggestions at this point, they are necessarily provisional in nature. The new practices that emerge soon provoke fresh questions that set the hermeneutic spiral in motion again.[56]

---

52. Warnke, *Gadamer*, 69.

53. Browning, *Fundamental Practical Theology*, 55.

54. Browning, *Fundamental Practical Theology*, 55.

55. Cooper, *Don Browning*, 25.

56. Browning, *Fundamental Practical Theology*, 56; Whitehead and Whitehead, *Method in Ministry*, 3.

Contemporary hermeneutical practical theology focuses on human actions and practices which are "both ecclesial and extra-ecclesial, intra-communal and public."[57] However, the public and extra-ecclesial impact is beyond the scope of this book. While it is acknowledged that worshipers will carry the transformative effect of the scriptural proclamation beyond the liturgy into their daily lives, the practical concerns to be addressed will focus on the ecclesial and intra-communal dimension of the Catholic liturgical event.

The strategic practical theology stage will identify issues in a liturgical hermeneutic of Scripture, elucidating the ways in which the scriptural proclamation functions as an event of meaning and proposing strategies for facilitating a fusion of horizons in the liturgical event (chapter 9). It will articulate ways to draw worshipers into the play of the liturgy so that they can experience the proclamation as both corporate event and personal encounter, and will address the need for worshipers to be formed for the liturgy and by the liturgy. Ultimately this chapter proposes that a liturgical hermeneutic of Scripture take its place alongside other hermeneutical approaches, since the proclamation of pericopes from the Lectionary within the context of the liturgical event has directly influenced the meaning of these Scripture texts over time.

---

57. Brown, "Hermeneutical Theory," 120.

PART I

DESCRIPTIVE THEOLOGY

CHAPTER 3

The Structure of the Lectionary and Its Impact on the Meaning of Texts

This chapter explores the processes and principles of Lectionary construction adopted during the Second Vatican Council and investigates the extent to which the resulting architecture of the Lectionary balances the written and communal memory of the Catholic Church. There is an examination of the effect of juxtapositions, inclusions, omissions, and decisions about where to start and end readings, such that the Lectionary emerges as a particular interpretive stance on Scripture.

I. PROCESS OF LECTIONARY CONSTRUCTION

The Second Vatican Council (1962–1965) was called by Pope John XXIII to renew the Catholic Church by bringing it into dialogue with modern culture. During the three years of the Council, more than 2000 bishops from around the world, in consultation with thousands of advisers, issued a series of landmark documents which expressed a renewed vision. The first key document of the Council, *Sacrosanctum Concilium* (The Constitution on the Sacred Liturgy) was promulgated in 1963. Practical implementation of the liturgical reforms proposed in the constitution began immediately, sparking an enthusiastic sense of anticipation. Annibale Bugnini, secretary of the commission charged with implementing *Sacrosanctum Concilium*, promptly established working groups to oversee the composition of new liturgical books. Study Group XI was tasked with one of the most complex elements of the reform, namely the construction of the new Lectionary for Mass which took place between 1964 and 1967. Bugnini documents the meticulous work of this study group in *The Reform of the Liturgy*,[1] and reveals the aims and objectives of the Lectionary compilers as they selected particular passages, omitted others, and juxtaposed readings for a pastoral purpose. Guiding this work were provisions in *Sacrosanctum Concilium* which provided that Scripture should be "of the greatest importance in the celebration of the liturgy," that a "warm and lively appreciation of Scripture" be promoted, and that the "treasures of the Bible . . . be opened up more lavishly, so that a richer fare may be provided for the faithful at the table of God's word."[2]

Notwithstanding the overall tendency towards "aggiornamento" which underpinned the workings of the Council, the construction of the new Lectionary was not a spontaneous or impulsive move designed to give the impression of modernity, but was rather a meticulously researched and thoroughly considered response to the recognized deficiencies in the existing arrangement of readings for Mass.[3] In 1966, after two years of study and consultation, a comprehensive plan had been developed for the new system of readings for Mass. Despite the suggestion of some members that one of the first two readings be optional, the study group decided to adopt three obligatory readings for Sundays to preserve the unity of the two Testaments, to fulfil the Council's request for a "more representative portion" of Scripture to be presented to the people, and to continue the tradition of the early church as revealed in the writings of Augustine and Ambrose. There was also significant discussion about whether the Lectionary should contain three or four annual cycles. Due to the necessity for very short readings to create enough passages for a four-year cycle, and the need to include pericopes of minimal catechetical importance, the triennial cycle was chosen for Sundays.[4] The Weekday Lectionary was established as a separate entity independent of the Sunday Lectionary according to a two-year cycle with semi-continuous reading of the biblical books and no repetition of Sunday passages.[5]

The structure and composition of the new Lectionary marked a dramatic shift in the liturgical hearing of Scripture. Where the previous organization of readings had gradually evolved over many centuries with

---

1. Bugnini, *Reform of Liturgy*, 406–25.
2. SC 24, 51.
3. O'Loughlin, "Sharing the Living Word," 12.
4. Bugnini, *Reform of Liturgy*, 414.
5. Lent, Easter, Advent, and Christmas have the same weekday readings each year. In Ordinary Time, the first reading is arranged according to a two-year cycle (alternating between Old and New Testament readings), with the Gospel on a one-year cycle.

continual modifications to the calendar, the Lectionary for Mass compiled after Vatican II was the result of a clear and overarching vision.

The readings used at Mass prior to Vatican II did not appear in their own liturgical book, but rather were contained in the Roman Missal along with every prayer and text of the Mass. Since the readings were read by the priest (in Latin) there was no need for a separate Lectionary. This existing arrangement of readings remained substantially unchanged between 1570 and 1969.[6] It comprised only a single annual cycle of readings with the same readings read on Sundays and feast days every year. Each Sunday Mass had only two readings which were generally referred to as "The Epistle" and "The Gospel" since passages from the Old Testament were rarely used. Old Testament readings were only included on a few feasts, ember days, vigils, and as part of some liturgical octaves. Furthermore, the Gospel pericopes did not constitute a representative selection; only four pericopes from Mark's Gospel were included, for example.[7] Weekdays in Lent and in the octaves of Christmas, Easter, and Pentecost, were the only weekday Masses to have their own assigned readings. Readings for all other weekday Masses were taken either from the previous Sunday, or from a special Mass for saints, or from a votive or ritual Mass. Only 22 percent of the Gospels were included in the liturgical readings prior to Vatican II, along with 11 percent of the Epistles and only 0.8 percent of the Old Testament (excluding the Psalms).[8]

Some members of the Council therefore argued that worshipers would not be adequately prepared to understand large quantities of Scripture, but the eventual decision to include greater variety in the readings was supported by the fact that readings would now be heard in the vernacular instead of in Latin.[9] The pastoral considerations of preventing boredom and promoting prayer weighed in favor of expanding the selections offered prior to Vatican II. The Council also drew upon a provision of the Constitution

---

6. The 1947 edition of the *Missale Romanum* was predominantly the same as the 1570 edition promulgated by Pope Pius V, apart from a few changes including the addition of feast days for recently canonized saints. Further modifications were introduced in 1951 with the removal of the six Old Testament readings assigned to the Pentecost Vigil and a reduction in the number of Old Testament readings for the Easter Vigil from twelve to four. Just, "Lectionary Statistics."

7. West, *Scripture and Memory*, 25.

8. Just, "Lectionary Statistics."

9. Bugnini, *Reform of Liturgy,* 406. It is also noteworthy that the Lectionary text from which the vernacular translations were derived was the Latin Vulgate (a fourth-century Latin translation of the Bible), now the Neo-Vulgate (the revised translation of the biblical text promulgated as "typical" by John Paul II in 1979). This itself is a translation of the original Hebrew and Greek texts and therefore not exactly the horizon of the original text.

that Christ "is present in his word, since it is he himself who speaks when the holy Scriptures are read in Church"[10] and thus trusted that the truth of the Scripture texts would be made known to worshipers.

An extensive process of research was undertaken to produce over fifty comparative tables documenting the biblical passages that had been used in eucharistic celebrations for over eighteen centuries in both Catholic and non-Catholic communities.[11] There was a desire to safeguard and build upon liturgical traditions while ensuring that new additions would stem organically from traditional choices. Readings historically assigned to major liturgical feasts for their thematic correlation were retained, as was the traditional use of Isaiah in Advent. The working group also reinstated the ancient tradition of reading the Gospel of John during Lent.[12]

Thirty-one biblical scholars were tasked with suggesting passages from the Old and New Testaments that would be the most likely to be understood and that would most accurately convey the message of salvation.[13] The biblical scholars also suggested divisions between passages, verses to be omitted, and the liturgical feast or season to which a passage was particularly suited. Recommended passages were sent to approximately 100 pastors and catechetical experts for comment, yielding approximately 2500 responses.[14]

Following a two-year process of experimentation, a new organization of readings for Mass was presented at the Seventh General Meeting of the Consilium in October 1966. This comprehensive plan was then subjected to extensive scrutiny by approximately eight hundred experts on liturgy, Scripture, pastoral care, and catechesis. A further four hundred and sixty contributions were received prompting a substantial revision in January 1968 which involved the incorporation of additional passages, the elimination of pericopes judged to be too difficult, a review of the division of passages into verses, and the selection of different readings for the Sundays of Lent and some feasts.[15] Biblical texts used for Sundays, vigils, and major feasts in the revised Lectionary now included about 58 percent of the Gospels and 25 percent of the Epistles, with eighty-three out of one hundred and fifty psalms represented in whole or in part. Excluding the Psalms, 3.7 percent

---

10. SC 7.

11. Bugnini, *Reform of Liturgy*, 412.

12. Catholic Church, "General Introduction to Lectionary," 74 (hereafter GIL).

13. Bugnini, *Reform of Liturgy*, 412–13. Notably, twenty-nine of these biblical scholars were Europeans, and two were Canadians with no representation from other cultures. Sloyan, "What Kind of Canon?," 30.

14. Bugnini, *Reform of Liturgy*, 413.

15. Bugnini, *Reform of Liturgy*, 419–20.

of the Old Testament was to be read at Sunday Masses across the three-year cycle.[16]

The proofs for the revised Lectionary were given to Pope Paul VI in May 1969 and were promptly approved, reflecting the Pope's confidence in the expertise of those who had compiled and refined the texts. The *Ordo Lectionum Missae* (Lectionary for Mass) was promulgated for the universal church on 25 May 1969 by decree of the Congregation of Divine Worship. The full text of the readings was not provided, but rather a list of Scripture references in Latin for each liturgical day. In the case where a pericope was plucked from the middle of a biblical passage with no contextual information, an incipit was provided by way of introduction such as "Jesus said to his disciples," or "At that time," or "In those days."[17] According to the instructions which accompanied the Order of Readings, episcopal conferences around the world then approved vernacular translations of the full text of each Lectionary reading. The approval of two thirds of each Bishops Conference was required, as well as confirmation by the Holy See in each case.[18]

The revision and publication of other liturgical books continued at a rapid rate in the years following the Second Vatican Council. Consequently, a second edition of the Lectionary for Mass was published in 1981 which included readings for new Masses from the second edition of the Roman Missal and for sacramental rites published after 1969. This second edition of the Lectionary also included a significantly enhanced introduction explicating its design and vision and expounding the theological purposes and principles that guided its construction.[19]

The Liturgical Year

A necessary prelude to work on the Lectionary was the revision of the liturgical year. The architecture of the Christocentric liturgical year, with its solemnities, feasts, and memorials, provided the framework for the new Lectionary facilitating the assignment of scriptural pericopes to liturgical

16. When including Masses for weekdays, ritual and votive Masses, the propers and commons of saints, and Masses for Special Needs and Occasions, the *Lectionary for Mass* includes approximately 90 percent of the Gospels and 55 percent of the remainder of the New Testament, particularly from Acts, Revelation, and the Epistles. However, the representation of the Old Testament is still very low at a little more than 13 percent). Just, "Lectionary Statistics."

17. GIL 124.

18. Catholic Church, *Code of Canon Law*, 455.2.

19. West, *Scripture and Memory*, 77.

days and offering an organized way to present worshipers with a richer fare of Scripture passages.[20]

The large number of liturgical days devoted to saints before Vatican II meant that the continuous cycle of readings was frequently interrupted with readings for the various saints' days; any sense of continuity was difficult to detect.[21] The reform of the liturgical calendar, in which ninety-three saints were removed, was pivotal in facilitating the assignment of continuous pericopes to consecutive liturgical days.[22] The concern of the Lectionary compilers that the biblical passages be proclaimed in continuous fashion was further reflected in the clearly stated priority for readings of the day to be used for obligatory and optional memorials, rather than the readings of the saint.[23] This new compilation of biblical readings was designed to meet the needs and interests of those gathered for worship, giving them "an ever-deepening perception of the faith they profess and of the history of salvation."[24]

The Three-Year Cycle

The Order of Readings for Sundays and for solemnities was arranged according to a three-year cycle, with one of the Synoptic Gospels assigned to each year to more fully reveal the unique features of each Gospel.[25] The Lectionary thus preserved the distinct voice of each of the evangelists.[26] Irish Catholic priest and professor of historical theology, Thomas O'Loughlin, notes the great achievement of the Lectionary compilers in explicitly addressing the challenge of incorporating the rich Gospel inheritance of the

---

20. Boisclair, *Word of the Lord*, 32, 34; West, *Scripture and Memory*, 25.

21. Jungmann, *Mass of Roman Rite*, 399.

22. Paul VI, *Mysterii Paschalis*.

23. Higher ranking solemnities and feasts were also reduced, with very few having priority over a Sunday. All octaves, apart from Christmas and Easter, were also removed, facilitating the hearing of continuous readings. Boisclair, *Word of the Lord*, 33–34; Federici, "Bibbia Diventa Lezionario," 198.

24. GIL 60.

25. Matthew's Gospel is heard in Year A, Mark's Gospel in Year B, and Luke's Gospel in Year C. Passages from John's Gospel are read each year during the seasons of Christmas, Lent, and Easter, and are also used to fill the Sundays in Year B since Mark is the shortest of the Synoptic Gospels.

26. Lathrop refers to this as the Lectionary's capacity to "take quite seriously the fourness of the Gospel witness and the juxtaposition of the differing voices in those four." Lathrop, *Saving Images*, 129.

Christian Church into the structure of the liturgical year.[27] It has been argued that reading one Gospel semi-continuously for much of the year could lead to the false assumption that the Lectionary is designed to present the story of Jesus' life in chronological order. However, it is not the sequence of Jesus' life and ministry which is being followed, but rather the order of texts as presented in the particular Gospel. This honors the purpose and intention of the Lectionary, not as a retelling of the past but rather a proclamation to the present.[28] The dispersion of the four Gospels over the Lectionary's three-year cycle is also a clear indication that the Lectionary compilers were not concerned with history, but rather with meaning.[29]

Assigning Readings to a Liturgical Day

Biblical passages judged to be the most important were assigned to Sundays and Solemnities of the Lord, with complementary texts being assigned to weekdays.[30] The Lectionary adopted three obligatory readings for each Sunday and each major feast, offering a broader representation of Scripture. The first reading, psalm, second reading (on Sundays and major feasts), Gospel acclamation, and Gospel provided in the Lectionary were held to be obligatory. This was decreed in order that the system of readings might accurately represent the unity of the Old and New Testaments, promote universal uniformity, allow priests and laity to know with certainty which Scripture texts would be heard on any particular Sunday, and to fulfil the Council's aim of enabling Catholics to become familiar with a broad range of Scripture.[31]

The first reading, predominantly from the Old Testament, is usually brief and is chosen to harmonize with the Gospel by way of providing context or contrast.[32] In the early church, believers held firmly to the idea of a continuity of God's activity through history, and to the notion that the Hebrew Scriptures (Old Testament) both foreshadowed and came to fruition in the Christian Scriptures (New Testament). This typological approach was influential in selecting Old Testament texts to harmonize with the Gospel.[33]

27. O'Loughlin, "Sharing the Living Word," 13.
28. Lathrop, *Saving Images*, 128.
29. Lathrop, *Saving Images*, 131.
30. GIL 65.
31. SC 51; Sheerin, "Interpreting Scripture," 167; Bailey, "Lectionary," 141.
32. In the Easter Season, however, the first reading is chosen from the Acts of the Apostles on Sundays and weekdays. GIL 99–101; Black, "Journeying through Scripture," 60.
33. Bradshaw, "Use of the Bible," 46.

A responsorial psalm is provided for each Sunday and weekday, putting the words of Scripture on the lips of the assembly and facilitating the people's reception of the first reading as living word in the present.[34] A broad range of psalmody is incorporated into the Lectionary, from psalms of praise and thanksgiving to psalms of lament.

Sunday Masses include a second reading which is constituted by an independent and semi-continuous reading of the epistles of Paul or a text from the book of Revelation.[35] A Gospel acclamation is also provided for each day and, like the psalm, it is designed to be sung. The congregation stands to sing the Gospel acclamation due to its paschal character and its place as preparation for the Gospel.[36] The high point of the Liturgy of the Word on both Sundays and weekdays is a reading from one of the four Gospels, which is read by a priest or deacon.[37]

The order of proclamation of the readings does not reflect the order of appearance of the respective books in the biblical canon, but rather highlights the relative rank of each reading. In the same way as the highest-ranking member of clergy comes last in a liturgical procession, so too the Gospel is the last Scripture reading the assembly hears at any Mass. Despite the primacy of the Gospel, the Lectionary arrangement reveals that the Gospel message does not exist in isolation but necessarily expands backwards to the Old Testament and forwards to the lives of modern-day hearers. The decision to add a reading from the Old Testament to every Sunday and feast (except in the Easter season when Acts is read) strongly affirms the place of the Old Testament in the Christian story, illuminates the unity between Old and New Testaments, and emphasizes the connected relationship of promise and fulfillment. However, the process of selecting Old Testament selections to complement the Gospel of the day reveals the underlying conviction that, for Christians, Old Testament readings reveal their true significance when viewed in light of Christ's death and resurrection.[38] The fact that the Gospels only constitute about 10 percent of the Bible, means that only a small number of Old Testament texts can be matched by way of juxtaposition according to the principle of harmonization.[39] Connections between Old Testament and Gospel readings in the Lectionary are

---

34. Lathrop, *Saving Images*, 132.

35. There is no second reading on weekdays unless that day is a feast or solemnity. GIL 69, 84.

36. GIRM 62.

37. The reading of the Gospel by a priest or deacon dates back to the early church. Donaldson, *Constitutions*, 51.

38. GIL 106; Martimort, *Church at Prayer*, 135.

39. Martimort, *Church at Prayer*, 135.

sometimes tenuous, perhaps based only on one common word or phrase between the two texts.[40]

Harmony of a different kind was used to assign readings to Sundays in Advent, Christmas, and Lent due to their distinctive characters. Gospel passages and Old Testament texts were selected and juxtaposed on the basis of their complementarity with the story of Jesus being recalled in these liturgical seasons.[41] At Vatican II, there were calls for a similar thematic approach to the readings for Sundays in Ordinary Time, suggesting that each Sunday be devoted to a particular theme of Christian life which would then provide direction for the homily. This idea was unanimously rejected by the study group, who found it unhelpful to suggest that the same homiletic theme would be appropriate across the whole world on the same day.[42] They insisted that the focus remain on

> ... the genuine conception of liturgical celebration. The liturgy is always the celebration of the mystery of Christ and makes use of the word of God on the basis of its own tradition, guided not by merely logical or extrinsic concerns but by the desire to proclaim the Gospel and to lead those who believe to the fullness of truth.[43]

Beginning and End of a Pericope

Decisions about where to start and finish a reading have direct implications for the meaning attributed to a Scripture text.[44] At the Mass of the Lord's Supper which marks the start of the Easter Triduum, for example, the assembly hears only four verses of 1 Corinthians 11 (23–26) where Paul recounts the institution of the Lord's Supper: "This is my body . . . this cup is the new covenant in my blood . . . Do this . . . in remembrance of me." While this text about the sacramental body is entirely appropriate for the liturgical day being celebrated, the verses that come before and after it in the biblical narrative provide important context which the assembly does

---

40. Martimort, *Church at Prayer*, 146. Wiener, "Roman Catholic Eucharistic Lectionary," 12. The Revised Common Lectionary attempted to address this criticism by including continuous and semi-continuous arrangements of Old Testament texts as alternative readings, without any requirement of harmonization to the Gospel text of the day. However, the Revised Common Lectionary only encompasses Sundays and major feasts.

41. Black, "Journeying through Scripture," 60.

42. Bugnini, *Reform of Liturgy*, 421–22; GIL 68.

43. GIL 68.

44. Elich, "Word in Worship," 94.

not hear. The text is preceded in the Bible by a verse which denounces those who would let another go hungry (v22), asking the probing question: "Do you show contempt for the church of God and humiliate those who have nothing?" The Bible verse which immediately follows the Lectionary selection (v27) provides: "Whoever, therefore, eats the bread or drinks the cup of the Lord in an unworthy manner will be answerable for the body and blood of the Lord." A key ecclesial reference from Paul's writing has been removed precisely when the text will be proclaimed in a communal worship setting where the final outcome of the liturgical hearing is ideally to do good in the world, thus bridging liturgy and life. Paul's warning would prompt a certain amount of discomfort and would challenge listeners to turn their attention to social justice, rather than being internally absorbed within their own particular sacramental experience.

Brevity of Pericopes

Almost immediately upon publication of the Lectionary, a significant group of liturgical specialists in Washington DC objected to the brevity of the lections.[45] This brevity was the result of the process undertaken by the working group at the Second Vatican Council where initial collections of readings were sent to various churches across Europe for comment. Conscious that worshipers had been accustomed to only two brief readings in Latin, the overwhelming response of pastors was that the proposed readings were too long. In response to this feedback, the subsequent round of revisions saw a significant truncation of some readings, particularly those from the Old Testament.[46]

It has consequently been noted that the Lectionary pericopes "lean heavily towards conclusions"[47] and that "the devisers of the Lectionary appear to love summaries, finales."[48] This is problematic given the narrative nature of Scripture, where stories contain a beginning, middle, and end. Lectionary pericopes taken from Paul's epistles, for example, often present the ethical implications of Paul's thought without the preceding theology that provides the context, or outline his theological assertions without the

---

45. Sloyan, "What Kind of Canon?," 33.

46. Sloyan, "What Kind of Canon?," 33; Boisclair, *Word of the Lord*, 92.
Considering that bishops from all over the world were present at Vatican II, it is surprising that only European pastors were invited to trial the new Lectionary readings.

47. Lowry, *Living*, 17.

48. Willimon, "Lectionary," 336.

corresponding moral implications.[49] In cases where the conclusion of a story is presented in isolation, there is an unfounded assumption that the assembly is familiar with the context or preceding conflict that has led to the resolution. The question of what has been lost in the editorial process, therefore, becomes crucial for preachers.

Selection and Omission

For pastoral reasons, it was decided to omit from the Sunday Lectionary particularly difficult passages that would require extensive explanation. However, it was recognized that some difficult texts could be clarified through their juxtaposition with another reading while others could be expounded through the homily.[50] The compilers included long narrative passages that were capable of holding the attention of the congregation, and texts which were more dense and therefore needed to be kept short due to the profound nature of the teaching. Some longer passages were accompanied by an alternative short form of the reading which retained the essential elements.[51] The General Introduction to the Lectionary reveals that any omissions of verses in readings were carefully considered "to ensure that the essential meaning of the text remained intact."[52] If such verses were not eliminated, according to the General Introduction, certain spiritually important readings would have had to be omitted from the Lectionary because they included "some verse that is unsuitable pastorally or that involves truly difficult problems."[53]

Balancing Written and Communal Memory

Fritz West describes the work of arranging Scripture texts within the framework of the liturgical year as balancing the written and communal memory of the Catholic Church.[54] He notes the inevitable tension between the two integral stories: the canonical narrative (the theocentric Bible) and the

---

49. Willimon, "Lectionary," 338.

50. GIL 76. Some difficult passages were assigned to the Weekday Lectionary or the Liturgy of the Hours.

51. GIL 75.

52. GIL 77.

53. GIL 77.

54. West, *Scripture and Memory*, 7–8.

calendrical narrative (the Christocentric liturgical year).[55] The canonical narrative, according to West, tells the story of God's salvific action throughout history, preserving the unity of the two biblical testaments and setting the life, death, and resurrection of Christ within the broader context of salvation history. The calendrical narrative, however, places Christ at the center and follows the contour of the liturgical year which is constituted by feasts that celebrate events in the life of Christ and the Christian Church.[56]

Clearly an unsatisfactory representation of the Christian story would result from a focus on either narrative alone. If the Lectionary were built solely on the life, death, and resurrection of Jesus (the calendrical narrative) this would ignore pivotal themes of the biblical story (canonical narrative). Similarly, a suitable balance for a Christian Lectionary is not to be found in attempting to represent the entire biblical text since the New Testament constitutes only one quarter of the Bible. West notes that the Lectionary compilers sought to overcome this difficulty by endeavoring to "strengthen the canonical component of the Lectionary's calendrical form."[57] In practical terms, the study group arranged biblical readings within the framework of the liturgical year with primacy given to the Gospel reading (calendrical narrative) and chose readings from both Old and New Testaments (canonical narrative) to adequately tell the story of salvation history.

In his ecumenical study, West distinguishes between the proclamation of Scripture in Catholic and Protestant liturgies.[58] He notes that in Protestant churches, the Bible is physically present, with the presider reading a chosen passage aloud either holding the Bible in his/her hand or reading from a lectern. According to West, this indicates that in the Protestant tradition, Scripture is held in the written memory of the Bible. By way of contrast, the Bible itself is not present in the Catholic liturgy. Rather, Scripture is conveyed through predefined lections bound together in a Lectionary specifically designed for liturgical proclamation. Scripture texts are organized according to the framework of the liturgical year and the ritual shape of the Catholic eucharistic event. West argues that the use of a Lectionary for

---

55. Of course, it must be acknowledged that the biblical canon was constituted by those texts which had already formed part of the church's communal memory in its early liturgical celebrations.

56. It follows that the parameters of the calendrical narrative are defined by the New Testament only. The liturgical year consists of the Advent-Christmas cycle which tells of Christ's birth, the Lent-Easter cycle which presents his death and resurrection, and Ordinary Time which presents the mystery of Christ through his preaching, healing, words, and actions. Catholic Church, "Universal Norms," 43.

57. West, *Scripture and Memory*, 36.

58. West, *Scripture and Memory*, 7.

proclaiming Scripture is a ritual expression of the primacy of the communal memory of the Catholic Church over its normative texts. This communal memory is that of the paschal mystery of Christ's life, death, and resurrection which is celebrated in the eucharistic liturgy, and which serves as the overarching framework of the Lectionary.[59] Thus, in the Catholic paradigm, Scripture is carried by communal and ecclesial memory as expressed in the ritual tradition.

Timeframes Governing Lectionary Structure

Scripture texts have been arranged across two timeframes in the Lectionary. The first timeframe is a synchronic one, with groups of pericopes assigned to a liturgical day, to be heard at a particular point in time. The second timeframe is a diachronic one with a series of readings extending across Sundays and weekdays unfolding over time in a semi-continuous fashion according to their position in the biblical context. Fritz West observes that these mnemonic substructures effectively balance the two forms of ecclesial memory: communal and written memory. The synchronic aspect carries Scripture in the communal memory of the Catholic Church, presenting pericopes within the Christological framework of the liturgical year and assigning them to liturgical days and feasts. In its diachronic aspect, Scripture is carried by written memory (the Bible) whereby epistle and Gospel pericopes are arranged in semi-continuous fashion across weeks and seasons. Some readings may stand only in one time frame, such as an epistle which is not related to the Gospel or first reading of the day; the only mnemonic context for this reading is the diachronic dimension. However, some readings may form part of a synchronic and a diachronic dimension simultaneously. A Gospel may be synchronically related to the first reading on its particular liturgical day and also diachronically related to a series of Gospel readings cast over consecutive Sundays.[60]

Furthermore, texts are then heard in situational time within a liturgical celebration and enter a new timeframe when proclaimed in the liturgy to be word-event for the present day. Scriptural pericopes in the Lectionary are not viewed as constituting a historical book of the past, but are reinterpreted in terms of the historical continuum in which the contemporary situation is located, influenced by the events that have constituted history to the present, and conscious of the future times in which the word will also be heard.[61]

---

59. West, *Scripture and Memory*, 12.
60. West, *Scripture and Memory*, 12–13.
61. Venturi, "Criteri Interpretativi," 231–37.

Assigned to Feasts and Seasons

From Bugnini's account of Lectionary construction, it is evident that the compilers preserved some of the ancient tradition of hearing particular readings on certain feasts and assigning set sequences of continuous readings in certain liturgical seasons.[62] Where biblical passages are heard over many years in association with particular feasts or seasons, the texts thereby become enriched with additional layers of meaning.[63] The Gospel readings of the Samaritan Woman at the Well, the Healing of Blind Bartimaeus, and the Raising of Lazarus which have been read on the three Sundays prior to Easter for centuries, have become imbued with Lenten themes of penance and Christian initiation.

Biblical texts which, in their native context make no reference to the Virgin Mary, take on new layers of meaning when assigned to Marian feasts.[64] On the feast of the Assumption, for example, the assembly hears a text from the book of Revelation which uses mythical images to examine the struggle between good and evil. The book of Revelation is an instance of apocalyptic literature, which sends a message of hope to those suffering persecution using symbols that the oppressed people will comprehend. In the pericope assigned to the Assumption,[65] goodness is symbolized by "a woman clothed with the sun, with the moon under her feet, and on her head a crown of twelve stars . . . And she gave birth to a son, a male child, who is to rule all the nations with a scepter of iron."[66] Evil is symbolized as "a great red dragon, with seven heads and ten horns . . . His tail swept down a third of the stars of heaven and threw them to the earth."[67] Some biblical interpretations have suggested that the female representation of goodness could be a representation of Israel from within whose ranks the Savior was born. The representation of evil in the form of a dragon has been construed as symbolizing the Roman Empire in its persecution of Christians. In this depiction, the woman serves as a symbol of the persecuted church, with the biblical text promising that neither the woman nor her offspring will be destroyed by the dragon.[68] In the Lectionary's arrangement, however, as the people celebrate the feast of the Assumption, the image of the woman in

---

62. Bugnini, *Reform of Liturgy*, 410.
63. Elich, "Word in Worship," 95, 98.
64. Elich, "Word in Worship," 95.
65. Rev 11:19, 12:1–6, 10.
66. Rev 12:1, 5.
67. Rev 12:3–4.
68. Ralph, *Breaking Open*, 214–15.

the sky and the attributes of goodness are inevitably perceived as references to Mary.

Furthermore, when particular pericopes are juxtaposed in the Lectionary to constitute the Liturgy of the Word for a liturgical celebration, and are heard over several years as a unitary sequence, new connections are created between these texts quite independent of their biblical context.[69] For example, the creation story from the book of Genesis, heard at the beginning of Ordinary Time in Year B, gains an entirely new context when it forms part of the complex of readings at the Easter Vigil heralding the new creation of Christ's resurrection, and when it is proclaimed amidst the symbols drawn from the natural world such as the Easter fire and baptismal water. The worshiping assembly is thus able to perceive the dialogue and interaction taking placing between the Scripture texts, notice emerging images which prompt new connections, and join in the interweaving acclamations which provide space between the texts, all of which constitute a profound hermeneutical impact.[70]

II. PRINCIPLES OF LECTIONARY CONSTRUCTION

The Lectionary compilers directed their efforts towards achieving the objectives set out by the Second Vatican Council, fostering a greater "hunger for the word of God" and leading all Christians to regard sacred Scripture as the "perpetual source of spiritual life."[71] The principles adopted in selecting and arranging scriptural passages are set out in the Introduction to the Lectionary.

Principles of Selection and Juxtaposition

Two key principles guided the Lectionary compilers' selection of scriptural pericopes for liturgical days. The first principle of selection, which follows the canonical narrative, gives priority to written memory and is based on the continuous (or semi-continuous) reading of a biblical book thus preserving its inherent unity. The second principle, which adheres to the calendrical narrative, begins with the liturgical calendar and searches for Scripture texts that constitute a thematic harmony with a particular feast or season.[72]

---

69. Elich, "Word in Worship," 94; Power, *Word of the Lord*, 4.
70. Lathrop, *Saving Images*, 129.
71. Paul VI, *Missale Romanum*.
72. Rouwhorst, "Bible in Liturgy," 838.

Some scholars have noted the heavy influence of communal memory in the construction of the Lectionary evidenced by retaining the traditional assignment of passages to particular feasts and seasons. This assignment of pericopes based on the festal occasion constitutes an explicit interpretation of the Scripture text and inevitably leads the assembly to interpret the text from within the perspective of that feast or season.[73]

Arguably, one of the greatest contributions of the Lectionary is the fact that it prompts the interpretation of Scripture by Scripture. The juxtaposition of seemingly unrelated readings from different biblical books results in remarkable cross-fertilizations that could not have been perceived in their native biblical context.[74] The intrinsic intertextuality of Scripture is brought to light by the pairing of Scripture texts in the Lectionary to demonstrate the ways in which the Old and New Testaments illuminate each other.[75] One example occurs in the texts assigned to Sunday 22 Ordinary Time Year C, where the first reading from the book of Ecclesiasticus emphasizes the importance of humility and denounces pride, while the Gospel reading from Luke presents the teaching of Jesus that "all who exalt themselves will be humbled, and those who humble themselves will be exalted."[76]

The juxtaposition of pericopes facilitates the process by which biblical readings reverberate and resonate deeply with one another to generate harmonies, accentuate central themes, and highlight harsh dissonances, shattering any notion of a homogenous interpretation of Scripture. Gerard Sloyan claims that worshipers who listen attentively to the Scripture readings over each three-year cycle will become familiar with established principles of biblical interpretation, thus acquiring a particular variety of scriptural competence.[77] The emphasis given to the homily in the Catholic liturgy is a clear acknowledgement that the scriptural pericopes are rich and polyvalent, capable of speaking to constantly changing situations.

Pastoral Aim

Chapter IV of the General Introduction articulates that the Lectionary "has been composed above all for a pastoral purpose."[78] The cursus of readings is designed to endow worshiping assemblies with a knowledge of the whole

---

73. Rouwhorst, "Bible in Liturgy," 838.
74. Meeter, "Church Tells Time," 41.
75. GIL 66(1).
76. Sir 3:17–20, 28–29; Luke 14:11.
77. Sloyan, "Lectionary as Context," 44.
78. GIL 58.

Scriptures, and, particularly during the seasons of Easter, Lent, and Advent, to foster a more profound insight into the events of salvation history. The hearing and internalizing of these biblical stories foreseeably shapes the minds and hearts of the assembly and invites a faith-filled response in their lives.[79]

Part of a Liturgical Event

The interpretation of each reading from the Lectionary is influenced by the other readings assigned to the same liturgical day, but the Lectionary was not intended to be read or studied privately using strategies of textual analysis. Rather, there is a presumption that readings are to be heard as part of a communal, dialogical, and temporal liturgical event, followed by the celebration of the Eucharist and enhanced with music, singing, and processions.[80] Consequently, the pericopes chosen for the Lectionary are designed to illuminate the primary mysteries being celebrated in the liturgy.[81] The question of how the various multisensory elements of the liturgy create the context in which the Scriptures are heard will form the focus of the next chapter.

Followed by a Homily

In line with the provisions of *Sacrosanctum Concilium,* the Lectionary presumes that the scriptural proclamation will be followed by a homily:

> By means of the homily the mysteries of the faith and the guiding principles of the Christian life are expounded from the sacred text during the course of the liturgical year. The homily is strongly recommended since it forms part of the liturgy itself. In fact, at those Masses which are celebrated on Sundays and holydays of obligation, with the people assisting, it should not be omitted except for a serious reason.[82]

Some have claimed that, despite the aims of Vatican II in striving to open up the treasures of the Bible, the challenge of hearing or preaching on three

---

79. Boisclair, *Word of the Lord*, 11.
80. West, *Scripture and Memory*, 47–52.
81. GIL 59–60; Elich, "Word in Worship," 96. It has also been noted that the brevity of the pericopes reflects the presumption that readings form part of a eucharistic event. Allen, "Common Lectionary," 24.
82. SC 52; See also GIL 80.

readings at any one time is problematic, particularly since connections between passages can be tenuous.[83] The common thread supposedly uniting the readings can also be difficult to identify due to diverse literary genres, cultural origins, authors, and historical times of composition. However, no homiletic instruction indicates that all three readings must be woven together in a homily on any liturgical day.[84] Indeed, while a series of three readings and a psalm may baffle one listener, it may prompt further thinking and reflection in another.[85]

Primacy of Sunday Eucharist

The Introduction to the Lectionary declares that more significant passages have been assigned to Sundays; while there is no clear criteria for assessing which passages are more significant than others, it is evident that the paschal mystery of Christ's death and resurrection is central.[86] The Lectionary cursus leads worshipers through a theological exposition of the paschal mystery not in chronological or sequential fashion, but rather through the framework of the Christocentric liturgical year.[87] Eucharistic assumptions are evident from the brevity of pericopes and the primacy of the Gospel readings within the Lectionary.

To be Proclaimed and Heard

One of the considerations in selecting Lectionary pericopes was the suitability of a text for proclamation. Indeed, ancient writing was intended to preserve the sound of someone's voice so that the words could be re-sounded in another time and place.[88] In the early church, most of the worshiping assembly would not have had access to the texts in written form, nor indeed would they have had the required literacy to read the texts for themselves.[89]

---

83. Sundberg, "Limitations," 17.

84. Provision is made in the GIL that a conference of bishops may make a pastoral decision, on days for which three readings are assigned, that only two readings be proclaimed—the first *or* second reading, followed by the Gospel. GIL 79.

85. Black, "Journeying through Scripture," 61.

86. GIL 65.

87. Allen, "Common Lectionary," 26.

88. O'Loughlin, "Would You Read?," 21–22.

89. This persisted until the advent of mass literacy and education in nineteenth-century Europe. Vincent, *Rise of Mass Literacy*, 115.

THE STRUCTURE OF THE LECTIONARY

The oral performance of the texts was therefore fundamental for passing on the word of God.[90]

While scholars are unable to agree on a precise time at which western society transitioned from predominantly reading aloud to reading silently, an excerpt from Saint Augustine's *Confessions* is evidence that silent reading was still remarkable enough to record in 400 CE:

> But when he was reading, his eyes would scan over the pages and his heart would scrutinize their meaning—yet his voice and tongue remained silent. Often when we were present (no one was ever forbidden to enter, nor was it his custom to have those approaching him announced) we saw him reading like that, silently, but never aloud.[91]

Despite the fact that modern congregations have ready access to the biblical texts either in print or electronic form and are perfectly able to read the texts for themselves, the Lectionary was not designed for personal reading. Rather it was designed for oral proclamation, honoring the ancient Catholic worship tradition. The conviction that "faith comes by hearing" stems directly from the words of Saint Paul in the letter to the Romans (10:17).[92] The Introduction to the Lectionary also affirms that "the congregation of Christ's faithful even today receives . . . the faith that comes by hearing"[93] and insists that the place from which the readings are proclaimed must facilitate the listening and attention of the congregation.[94] Also emphasized is the need for each member of the assembly to acquire the key skill of attentive listening which is identified as the most important element of full, conscious, active participation during the liturgical proclamation of Scripture.[95] Focusing on the person proclaiming the readings instead of having one's attention fixed on a personal copy of the text, emphasizes that the Scriptures are the book of the ecclesial community and encourages a greater awareness of the presence of Christ in the proclamation and in the assembly.[96]

---

90. Sheerin, "Interpreting Scripture," 2.
91. Augustine, *Confessions*, 242–43.
92. This notion has found prominent expression in the monastic tradition as seen in the prologue to Saint Benedict's Rule which reads: "Listen carefully, my son, to the master's instructions, and attend to them with the ear of your heart." Benedict, *Rule of Benedict*, 5.
93. GIL 45.
94. GIL 32.
95. GIL 6.
96. GIL 6; Lathrop, *Saving Images*, 123–24.

III. THE LECTIONARY AS A PARTICULAR INTERPRETIVE STANCE ON THE SCRIPTURES

Early Christians who were tasked with compiling the Bible, selected writings which were regarded as essential to define a canon, or rule of faith.[97] In so doing, a written memory was instituted with a particular structure and content. The compilers of the Catholic Lectionary, however, selected Scripture texts to enable faith to be proclaimed in the liturgy within the framework of the liturgical year, and therefore chose to structure the pericopes with regards to communal memory, or ritual.

The word "pericope" comes from the Greek word Περικοπή meaning "a cutting." West paints the idea of the Bible as a tapestry or cloth from which a pericope is cut to take its place in the Lectionary. It has an identity independent of the biblical tapestry, but it is possible to see the hole in the tapestry from whence it came. "On the edges of the carpet piece one can see, now dangling and disconnected, the cut threads . . . that once held it in the whole."[98] Reinserting a pericope into the biblical tapestry provides a deeper understanding of its original context.

Yet, the pericopes of the Lectionary have a literary and a thematic cohesion which allows them to be organized into an alternative structure, namely the framework of the liturgical year, and to be placed beside other previously unrelated readings sparking the emergence of new and unforeseen meanings. Where the Bible itself constitutes a unified literary composition and tells a continuous narrative from creation until the end times, each set of readings assigned to a liturgical day in the Lectionary constitutes a cohesive unit. West thus refers to the Lectionary as a "creative act of mnemonic composition"[99] which takes the framework of the liturgical year with its Sundays, weekdays, feasts, and seasons, and assigns texts to each according to the structure of the Liturgy of the Word. The semantic independence of extracted Scripture passages permits them to be juxtaposed with other texts in a way that is completely unrelated to their biblical context, allowing new connections to be formed. The individual readings retain their identity

---

97. The formation of the Canon was a complex process. Many existing works detail this historical process; it is outside the scope of this book to revisit such material here. It is sufficient to note that scriptural texts became part of the canon, not due to any privileged status independent of the worshiping community, but due to the extent that they were accepted by and proclaimed in the worshiping community as an expression of their faith. See Casey, "Liturgy Matters," 5–7.

98. West, *Scripture and Memory*, 27.

99. West, *Scripture and Memory*, 28.

but combine in a new context to build a particular meaning, situated in the "today" of the liturgy.

Different emphases can be perceived in the same reading when it appears in different liturgical celebrations, due to the other readings beside which it is juxtaposed, or due to the particular rite. The Gospel story of Zacchaeus from Luke's Gospel, for example, is heard on the Thirty-First Sunday in Ordinary Time Year C. The story of Zacchaeus, the notorious tax collector with whom Jesus chooses to eat and who experiences a change of heart, appears alongside a text from Isaiah about the patient and merciful nature of God, and a letter from Paul to the Thessalonians praying that God might make the people worthy of their call and fulfil their desires for goodness. This can be contrasted with the interpretation that emerges when the same reading is used in the Rite of Dedication of a Church: "Zacchaeus, hurry and come down, for I must stay at your house today."[100]

Fritz West notes that "we tend to contrast the Lectionary to the Bible as that which is partial, selected, and derivative to that which is whole, inviolate, and original."[101] He also observes that a Protestant critique of the Catholic Lectionary revolves around the inadequate quantity of Scripture included when compared to the written memory of the Bible. Proponents of this position argue that the Lectionary fails to present the complete biblical story, and that the selective use of the Scriptures in fact "obscures the way the Bible itself remembers God's relationship to the world."[102] Yet the aim of the Lectionary is not to reconstruct the historical events of the Bible, but rather to re-present the biblical text for contemporary congregations in order to affirm a sense of common identity, and to facilitate a meaningful reception of the texts that will influence their lives. Thus, the primary commitment of the Lectionary is not to the realm of historical-biblical interpretation, but rather to the worshiping assembly in which the texts will be proclaimed and heard; the Lectionary is an inherently contextual entity.[103]

Ecclesiological Dimension

One of the key responses to the question "Why use a Lectionary?" is the promotion of ecclesial unity. In many cases, this unity extends to other Christian denominations who have adopted the Revised Common Lectionary. The pastoral advantage of providing a set of obligatory Lectionary

---

100. Luke 19:5.
101. West, *Scripture and Memory*, 35.
102. West, *Scripture and Memory*, 8.
103. Procter-Smith, "Lectionaries," 95.

readings for each liturgical day is that Catholics hear the same Scripture passages on any given day, regardless of which parish they attend or which country around the globe they happen to be worshiping in. Not only the clergy but also members of the assembly can prepare the readings before the liturgy by exploring commentaries or reflections on the readings, and can thus participate more fully as they hear those readings proclaimed in the ecclesial assembly. Use of a Lectionary thus honors the fundamental premise that "the word of God is always coming to us from beyond ourselves and our own choices and that our local assembly is in communion with a much greater church."[104] The Scripture texts for the day are given to the community, not chosen by the presider, which eliminates the potential for "favorite" passages to be chosen or more difficult texts avoided. While a presider may succumb to "bending" the meaning of texts to suit a particular line of preaching, the Scripture passages set down in the Lectionary nonetheless set the parameters within which the people hear the words of the homilist.[105]

SUMMARY

The profound rearrangement of biblical pericopes in the Lectionary for the purposes of proclamation in a corporate worship event constitutes a particular interpretation of Scripture that requires its own hermeneutic.[106] There are, of course, several points of similarity between Bible and Lectionary. Both contain sacred writings of the Christian Church and are the result of selection processes which retained some texts and excluded others. Both convey a similar message, that of humanity's salvation in Christ, and use a variety of literary forms to express the story of redemption.[107]

Yet, passages read from the Bible are understood within the context of the biblical book to which they belong. In the Catholic Lectionary, however, the context for each pericope is the liturgical day and season to which it has been assigned. Where the Bible constitutes a canonical narrative, the Lectionary is built upon a calendrical narrative. It can be argued, therefore,

---

104. Lathrop, *Saving Images*, 125.

105. Cf. Lloyd Bailey who warns that texts assigned to a particular day in the Lectionary may not necessarily speak to the immediate needs of the people gathered nor seem applicable to their daily lives. According to Bailey, "Lectionary texts come to the congregation tone-deaf to its situation: They may be largely unrelated to it; or they may be supportive when a challenge is needed and vice-versa." Bailey, "Lectionary," 144.

106. Venturi refers to the Lectionary as a "liturgical Bible." Venturi, "Criteri Interpretativi," 230.

107. West, *Scripture and Memory*, 34.

that the Lectionary does not constitute a "canon within the canon,"[108] but is rather a particular interpretation of the Scriptures within the framework of the liturgical year.

Of integral importance is the fact that the Lectionary compilers never intended the scriptural pericopes to be read to oneself or studied in isolation. Rather, the Introduction to the Lectionary insists on the link between the scriptural pericopes it contains and the ritual, communal context for which it was designed. The interpretation of Lectionary texts, therefore, presumes a hermeneutical role for the Catholic liturgical context. It is this Catholic liturgical paradigm to which we now turn.

---

108. Sloyan, "Lectionary as Context," 43.

CHAPTER 4

The Catholic Liturgical Paradigm

The Lectionary's assignment of texts across the particular feasts and seasons of the liturgical year indicates that the intended liturgical contexts must be carefully considered when interpreting the pericopes. The use of a Lectionary is not particular to the Catholic Church, yet it is proposed here that Catholic liturgical practices and traditions lead to a particular experience of worship and place a certain interpretive framework on the Lectionary.[1] In his ecumenical study of the Lectionary, Fritz West noted that "the Catholic liturgical paradigm is marked by weekly Eucharist, a balance of word and sacrament, a sacramental perspective on worship, appreciation for ritual and symbol, organic understanding of church, and veneration of tradition."[2] This chapter explores the hermeneutical impact of hearing the Lectionary pericopes proclaimed aloud in the communal, multisensory context of the Mass surrounded by ritual gestures, hymns, prayers, and other biblical fragments which together constitute the Catholic liturgical paradigm.

I. THE CATHOLIC RITE OF MASS

The Catholic liturgy consists of four key parts: The Introductory Rites, the Liturgy of the Word (within which the scriptural proclamation takes place), the Liturgy of the Eucharist, and the Concluding Rites. While the proclamation of Scripture takes place within the overall shape of the Mass, a more detailed description of the Liturgy of the Word is instructive.

---

1. West, *Scripture and Memory*, ix.
2. West, *Scripture and Memory*, 8; Visentin, "Parola di Dio," 242–43.

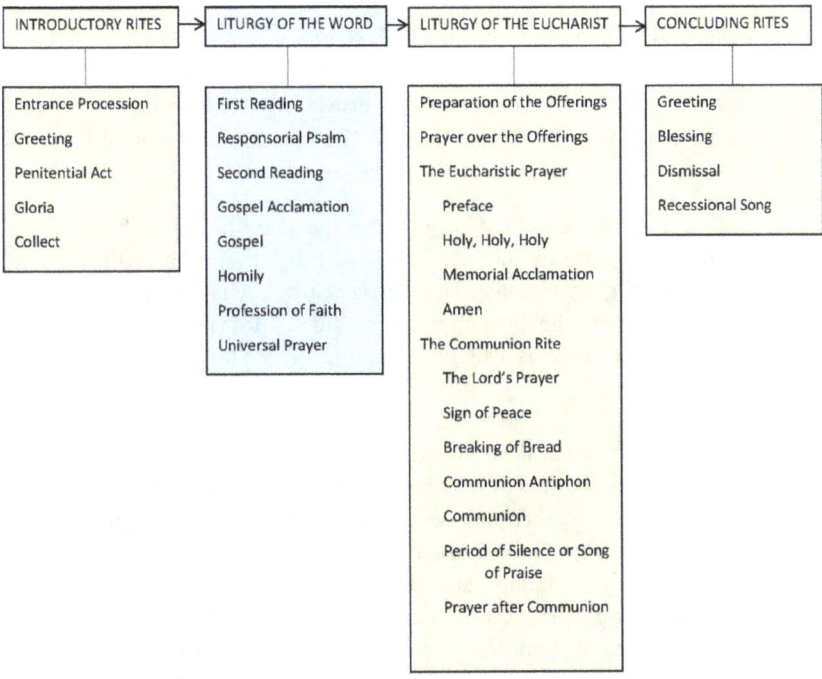

The Liturgy of the Word begins as the reader goes to the ambo to read the first reading; the assembly sits and listens. To conclude the reading, the reader acclaims "The word of the Lord" to acknowledge the sacred status of what has just been proclaimed. Regardless of the fact that some readings are particularly challenging, perhaps even disheartening, the rubrics of the liturgy provide that the assembly's response is always "Thanks be to God."[3] This reflects an underlying premise of the Catholic liturgical paradigm that the proclamation is in fact the word of God resounding in the assembly, which calls forth a spirit of gratitude and receptivity.[4]

The responsorial psalm is then sung by the cantor, with the people singing the response after each verse. If there is to be a second reading, a reader proclaims this from the ambo with the same concluding acclamation and response as given for the first reading. The assembly then rises to sing an acclamation to welcome the Gospel and remains standing for the Gospel as a sign of particular respect.[5] If incense is to be used, the priest puts some into a thurible and blesses it during the Gospel acclamation.

3. GIRM 128.
4. Anderson, "Practicing Scripture," 103.
5. GIRM 131.

The Gospel is read by a priest or deacon. If a deacon is present, he bows before the priest and asks for the blessing. If a deacon is not present, the priest bows before the altar and prays silently, "Cleanse my heart and my lips, almighty God, that I may worthily proclaim your holy Gospel."[6] The General Instruction of the Roman Missal (GIRM) sets out the ritual process surrounding the proclamation of the Gospel:

> 133. If the Book of the Gospels is on the altar, the Priest then takes it and approaches the ambo, carrying the Book of the Gospels slightly elevated. He is preceded by the lay ministers, who may carry the thurible and the candles. Those present turn towards the ambo as a sign of special reverence for the Gospel of Christ.
>
> 134. At the ambo, the Priest opens the book and, with hands joined, says, *The Lord be with you*, to which the people reply, *And with your spirit*. Then he says, *A reading from the holy Gospel*, making the Sign of the Cross with his thumb on the book and on his forehead, mouth, and breast, which everyone else does as well. The people acclaim, *Glory to you, O Lord*. The Priest incenses the book, if incense is being used. Then he proclaims the Gospel and at the end pronounces the acclamation *The Gospel of the Lord*, to which all reply, *Praise to you, Lord Jesus Christ*. The Priest kisses the book, saying quietly the formula *Per evangelica dicta* (*Through the words of the Gospel*).

The richness of this symbolic action emphasizes the primacy of the Gospel and highlights the hierarchical ranking of the readings "according to the directness with which they announce the good news."[7] While Jesus is spoken about in third person at the conclusion of the first two readings, there is a clear change in the ritualized dialogue both before and after the Gospel which involves the assembly's direct address to Christ: "Glory to you, O Lord" and "Praise to you Lord Jesus Christ."[8] The liturgical ritual reflects the presumption that Christ himself is present to the ecclesial community in the scriptural proclamation and honors that presence through the handling of the sacred book and through the ritualized words and gestures of the community provided for in the rubrics.

The placement of the Book of the Gospels on the altar at the beginning of Mass signifies that the same dignity belongs to the word of God as to

---

6. Catholic Church, *Roman Missal*, 558 (hereafter RM).
7. West, *Scripture and Memory*, 48.
8. GIRM 134.

the eucharistic elements. It also expresses the theological presumption that worshipers are nourished by "the bread of life... from the table of the word of God and the Body of Christ."[9] Taking the book to the ambo from the altar, the place where the sacrifice of the Cross is remembered in the Eucharist, reflects the presupposition that the Gospel should always be heard in the context of the paschal mystery.[10] This link is further signified symbolically when the priest or deacon traces the cross on the page from which he will read the Gospel, and when the whole assembly, together with the priest or deacon, traces a cross on their forehead, lips, and chest, indicating their openness to the Gospel's transformative effects on their mind, speech, and will.[11]

II. THE LITURGICAL EVENT: FEATURES WHICH INFLUENCE THE INTERPRETATION OF SCRIPTURE

Sacramental Encounter

The distinguishing feature of the scriptural proclamation in the Mass, which sets it apart from other contexts in which people might engage with biblical texts, is the premise that Christ is sacramentally present and speaking in the midst of the liturgical assembly.[12] Stemming from the teachings of Saint Augustine in the fifth century a sacrament is commonly defined as an "outward and visible sign of an inward and invisible grace."[13] The Catechism of the Catholic Church provides that sacraments are signs that sanctify and are efficacious, producing their desired effect because Christ is at work in them.[14] For example, the cleansing symbolized by the pouring of water at baptism is made effective through the grace of Christ and the Holy Spirit. In the Catholic liturgy, the sacramental quality is attributed not to the sign itself, but to the action associated with it—namely, the breaking, sharing, and eating of bread, the pouring and drinking of wine, the smearing with oil, the plunging into water. The people receive God's action and respond to it.

Similarly, the sacramentality of the word refers not to the Scripture texts themselves, but rather to the proclamation of Scripture in the liturgy

---

9. Vatican Council II, "Dogmatic Constitution, *Dei Verbum*," 21 (hereafter DV).

10. Boselli, *Spiritual Meaning of Liturgy*, 49.

11. GIRM 134.

12. "[Christ] is present in his word, since it is he himself who speaks when the holy scriptures are read in Church." SC 7.

13. Holcomb and Johnson, "Introduction," 1.

14. Catholic Church, *Catechism of Catholic Church*, 1127, 1131 (hereafter CCC).

which constitutes a living event.[15] Worshipers do not hear *about* Christ; rather, they hear Christ *speaking to them* in the present; "the Word comes alive amidst a people, making present a living encounter with the Lord Jesus."[16] This finds expression in paragraph seven of *Sacrosanctum Concilium* and underpins the Catholic approach to the importance of Scripture in the liturgy:

> Christ is always present in His Church, especially in her liturgical celebrations. He is present in the sacrifice of the Mass, not only in the person of His minister . . . but especially under the Eucharistic species. He is present in His word, since it is He Himself who speaks when the holy Scriptures are read in the Church. He is present, lastly, when the Church prays and sings, for He promised: "Where two or three are gathered together in my name, there am I in the midst of them" (Matt 18:20).[17]

The sacramental presence of Christ is assured once more in the General Instruction of the Roman Missal which provides: "When the Sacred Scriptures are read in the Church, God himself speaks to his people, and Christ, present in his word, proclaims the Gospel."[18] These two provisions from the conciliar documents reveal the conviction that Christ is present in an integrated and complex way, and that this presence is located in the dynamic activity of the assembly. Christ speaks to the gathered assembly and enters into a dialogical encounter with them.

Paul Janowiak describes the presence of Christ in the word as "a complex circulation of grace-filled energy whose elements are the Scriptures, the assembly, the preacher, the lectors, and the ritual enactment in which it takes place."[19] In the ritual proclamation of the Lectionary readings, therefore, there is not only an encounter between God and humanity, but also an encounter of faith between human beings.[20] The proclamation of the readings presumes a relationship of faith between the speaker and the listeners which is deemed necessary for the Scripture texts to mediate meaning.[21] In instances where a celebration of the Eucharist is not possible, the assembly is assured of the sacramental presence of Christ and their communion with him through the proclamation of Lectionary pericopes in which they are fed

---

15. De Clerck, "In the Beginning," 12–13.
16. Morrill, "Intimate Connection," 10.
17. SC 7.
18. GIRM 29.
19. Janowiak, *Holy Preaching*, xiv.
20. Elich, "Word in Worship," 97.
21. Irwin, *Context and Text*, 169.

from the table of the word. This has particular theological importance for remote communities who participate in Sunday Celebrations of the Word due to the unavailability of a priest. The sacramental presence of Christ in the word event finds expression in the ceremonies that accompany the procession of the Lectionary or Book of the Gospels and in the proclamation itself.

The Working of the Holy Spirit in the Liturgy

The Catholic Catechism provides that Christ is made present in the liturgy through the action of the Holy Spirit. In each liturgical event, the Holy Spirit moves to draw members of the assembly into communion with Christ, gathering them into one Body.[22] The Spirit facilitates a living encounter between Christ and the worshipers, and prepares the hearts of the assembly to receive the words of Scripture so that they might "live out the meaning of what they hear, contemplate, and do in the celebration."[23]

In the Liturgy of the Word, the Holy Spirit awakens the memory of the worshipers by "giving life to the Word of God"[24] and by granting "a spiritual understanding"[25] of the Scripture texts to the gathered assembly. In the Liturgy of the Eucharist, the priest, who received the gift of the Holy Spirit at his ordination during the laying on of hands and is thus able to act in the person of Christ, lays his hands over the bread and wine during the epiclesis, asking the Father to send the Holy Spirit to transform the gifts into the body and blood of Christ.[26] Thus the Spirit works in co-operation with the ritual words, actions, and symbols of the liturgical celebration, such that "the liturgy becomes the common work of the Holy Spirit and the Church."[27]

With regards to the interpretation of Scripture more specifically, two active roles have been proposed for the Holy Spirit, firstly in inspiring the original composition of the biblical texts and secondly in illuminating the Scriptures for successive generations.[28] *Dei Verbum* (The Dogmatic Constitution on Divine Revelation) promulgated at the Second Vatican Council, clearly expresses the principle that the same Holy Spirit who inspired the original writing of the Scriptures now elucidates the interpretation of

22. CCC 1097, 1108.
23. CCC 1101.
24. CCC 1100.
25. CCC 1101.
26. CCC 1105–6.
27. CCC 1091.
28. Pinnock, *Biblical Revelation*, 216.

biblical texts in modern times.[29] The community is the primary locus of illumination, such that new insights emerge in the liturgy as the People of God reflect upon the biblical text in light of their own experience.[30] It is not proposed that the influence of the Holy Spirit imparts additional information, but rather that it changes the hearts of the interpreters and facilitates a transformative encounter with the Scripture text.[31]

Paragraph twelve of *Dei Verbum* further points to a pneumatological exegesis in providing three factors to be attended to in interpretation: the unity of the Scriptures in Christ, the living tradition of the Catholic Church which has unfolded over time under the guidance of the Spirit, and the analogy of faith.[32] In other words, *Dei Verbum* envisages a participatory role of the Holy Spirit in Scripture interpretation which is at once "christological, ecclesial, and theological."[33] Since paragraph twelve also affirms the principles and processes of the historical-critical method for exegesis, it provides for both reason and faith to be engaged by members of the liturgical assembly as they hear the Scripture texts proclaimed. It is the Holy Spirit that is attributed with bestowing the gift of faith and helping it to grow within the community.[34] Thus, the interpretation of the Lectionary pericopes can be conceptualized within the paradigm of the Catholic liturgy as a co-operative engagement between the Holy Spirit and the worshiping assembly, with both participating actively in uncovering the contemporary significance of the text.[35]

Full, Conscious, Active Participation

Another hermeneutical feature of the liturgical event that impinges on interpretation is the presumption that worshipers are participating actively, rather than listening passively. *Sacrosanctum Concilium* stated in the clearest possible terms that "the full and active participation by all the people is the paramount concern."[36] When the gathered assembly sings, acclaims, listens, and engages in bodily gestures and postures, they are not simply re-enacting a scene like actors in a theatrical production, but are rather

---

29. DV 9–10.
30. Dorman, "Holy Spirit," 431.
31. Pinnock, "Role of the Spirit," 495.
32. DV 12.
33. O'Collins, "Dei Verbum."
34. CCC 1102.
35. Wyckoff, *Pneuma*, 113–14; Thiselton, *Two Horizons*, 148–49.
36. SC 14.

celebrating a current event, participating in the mystery of salvation and experiencing it personally.[37] This means that there is no audience in the liturgy. The conceptualization of the liturgical space as a performance venue where the priest and ministers enact their roles under the observation of an attentive congregation is inaccurate. Rather, each person present at the liturgy is a "doer" of the liturgical action by virtue of their baptism.[38]

Since the Catholic Church teaches that liturgy is an action of the *Christus totus*, those who have been baptized into the Body of Christ are all celebrants of the liturgy.[39] In the liturgy, worshipers manifest their unity as members of the Body of Christ through their common responses to prayer dialogues, congregational singing, listening together to the proclamation from the Lectionary, processing together to receive communion, and by uniting their hearts and minds to the prayers spoken aloud by the priest on the community's behalf.[40]

The incorporation of bodily gestures, postures, and processions in the liturgy draws together the external and the internal, establishing a mutual relationship between thoughts, words, and actions and creating a unique context in which to interpret the scriptural pericopes.[41]

It is important to note, however, that active participation not only encompasses observable movements but also requires an interior attention such that the hearts and minds of the worshipers should correspond to the words that are spoken or sung. Cardinal Ratzinger, later Pope Benedict XVI, argued emphatically that spiritual participation through listening and the receptive engagement of the sensory and cognitive faculties, were just as much "active" forms of participation as speaking, gesturing, or processing.[42] The interactions between the various sensory elements in the liturgical event and the members of the ecclesial community gathered there serves to deepen the sense of involvement and promotes internal participation in the process of making meaning of the Scripture texts.

American priest, author, and liturgical theologian, Kevin Irwin, also points out that active participation means more than "doing something" in the liturgy, and should be conceived as a way of responding to God's

---

37. Maggioni, "Encountering Jesus."

38. Elich, "Word in Worship," 98. *Sacrosanctum Concilium* provides that liturgical participation is something to which worshipers "have a right and to which they are bound by reason of their baptism." SC 14.

39. SC 7.

40. Martimort, *Church at Prayer*, 99.

41. Ratzinger, *Feast of Faith*, 63–64.

42. Ratzinger, *Feast of Faith*, 123–24.

initiative in the liturgical event.[43] Fostering full, conscious, and active participation in the liturgy, therefore, is not about developing new liturgical structures or ministerial roles in order to involve as many members of the congregation as possible. This would be a misguided attempt to manipulate external activity in order to achieve a spiritual end.[44] Rather, the goal is that all those present might interiorize the liturgical action and join in a unified celebration of the Mass through speech, song, silence, posture, gesture, and procession.[45] The words which introduce the opening prayer of the Mass—"Let us pray"—invite the congregation to access the deep recesses of their minds and hearts in a participation which has no external form but which "gives rise to the whole drama of the liturgy."[46]

It is noteworthy that the liturgical books presume the ideal scenario where the readings are proclaimed articulately and audibly, and the assembly is quiet, attentive, receptive, and liturgically educated. However, the reality of many liturgical events is quite different. The congregation may include parents with small children who are distracted for several minutes at a time, people who are absorbed with other concerns, and those who are unfamiliar with the texts and rituals. The volume of the reader's voice may be barely audible due to an ineffective sound system, or a strong accent on the part of the person reading may make the words difficult to decode. The work of active participation required of the assembly during the Liturgy of the Word is a skill which requires practice and nurturing, and which may occur with varying degrees of success in any particular liturgical event.

Liturgical Space

The architectural space in which the liturgy takes place also has a powerful hermeneutical role in drawing the assembly into the sacred text. When a person enters the church building, they pass from their everyday surroundings into a unique space which has clearly been set aside for a particular purpose.[47] The elevated ceilings, arrangement of furniture, lighting, altar, ambo, and baptismal font, all inspire feelings of reverence and create the context within which the Lectionary texts are heard.[48]

43. Irwin, *Context and Text*, 140.
44. Kunzler, *Church's Liturgy*, 156.
45. Kunzler, *Church's Liturgy*, 157. This demands liturgical education and repeated practice which is addressed in chapter 9 of this book.
46. Ratzinger, *Feast of Faith*, 89.
47. Fodor, "Reading the Scriptures," 157.
48. Hughes, *Worship as Meaning*, 155–56.

An important relationship exists between the ambo and the altar in that these physical elements of the liturgical space reflect the ritual structure of word and sacrament. The reference in the liturgical documents to the "table of God's word" and the "table of the Eucharist"[49] is not a literal suggestion that there be two tables in the liturgical space. Rather, a "harmonious and close relationship is achieved through a balance of proportion and a unity of material and design."[50]

The ambo constitutes the location set aside for the proclamation of the word.[51] The ambo is used by those proclaiming the Lectionary readings, the psalmist, the homilist, and the person who leads the Universal Prayer.[52] The ambo is positioned in such a way that the attention of the assembly is naturally drawn towards it during the scriptural proclamation, and the addition of an inconspicuous microphone helps to ensure that the voice of the reader is clearly heard.[53] It is to be a place in the church that is "somewhat elevated, fixed, and of a suitable design and nobility."[54] Reading from this elevated position reflects the theological premise that the Lectionary texts constitute the word of God to be addressed to the people, as distinct from the liturgical prayers, dialogues, hymns, and acclamations which are themselves deeply influenced by the texts of Scripture.[55]

Singing

The words and images of Scripture are not only uttered by the reader or the presider in the liturgy but are also placed in the mouths of the assembly. The responsorial psalm, prayed in response to the first reading, is one such occurrence in the liturgy. Instead of reciting the text of the psalm, however, the GIRM provides that this element of the Liturgy of the Word should be

---

49. GIRM 28; GIL 10; DV 21.

50. Australian Catholic Bishops Conference, *And When Churches*, 70.

51. During the Rite of Dedication of a Church, the first words to be proclaimed from the ambo are: "May the word of God always be heard in this place, as it unfolds the mystery of Christ before you and achieves your salvation within the Church." Catholic Church, *The Rites*, 53.

52. The ambo should not be used for making announcements, providing commentary, or leading singing. Australian Catholic Bishops Conference, *And When Churches*, 72.

53. GIL 32; GIRM 309.

54. GIL 32.

55. Fodor, "Reading the Scriptures," 158.

sung.⁵⁶ When the assembly sings the responsorial psalm, something is happening which is quite distinct from the recitation of a poem or a sonnet:

> The people are not *imagining the psalmist* praying or proclaiming; nor are they *imagining themselves to be the psalmist* praying or proclaiming. Rather than *imagining*, they are themselves *actually* praying or proclaiming, doing so with the words of the psalm rather than with their own words.⁵⁷

Singing is given a particularly special place in the Catholic liturgy, stemming from the words of Saint Paul to the Colossians: "Let the word of Christ dwell in you richly . . . and with gratitude in your hearts sing psalms, hymns, and spiritual songs to God,"⁵⁸ and to the Ephesians: ". . . sing psalms and hymns and spiritual songs . . . singing and making melody to the Lord in your hearts."⁵⁹ In emphasizing the importance of singing, the GIRM cites the ancient proverb, "Whoever sings well prays twice over" and insists that singing be part of Sunday celebrations.⁶⁰ Singing the words of Scripture as a corporate body also "helps to develop the unity of mind and heart which is part of the mystery of the Church" and "carries the liturgical assembly beyond the text into a sense of the mystery of God."⁶¹

The various forms of liturgical song (acclamations, hymns, psalms, processional songs) provide rich avenues for the words of Scripture to be sung by the assembly, and for the themes of the readings to be revisited and meditated upon throughout the liturgy. Singing can also be a meditative engagement with Scripture, requiring the assembly to dwell longer on the words as they befit the melodic contour. The place of singing in the Catholic liturgy cannot be overlooked as a hermeneutical influence on the interpretation of Scripture texts.

Silence

While a common outward expression is integral for the establishment of community, facilitated by liturgical prayers and responses, and the commonality of action and song, it is the aim of the liturgical action that there

---

56. GIRM 61.

57. Wolterstorff, *Acting Liturgically*, 138. See also the writings of one of the desert fathers: Cassian, *John Cassian*, 304.

58. Col 3:16.

59. Eph 5:19.

60. GIRM 39–40.

61. Australian Episcopal Conference of the Roman Catholic Church, "Music," xiii.

also be a shared interiority or a common path inward on a cognitive and affective level.[62] To facilitate this interior active participation the liturgical rubrics expressly provide for the collective silence of the assembly after each reading, and after the homily. Liturgical silence is not a passive stillness but is rather deliberate and active. It is not an interruption of the liturgical action; it *is* the action. These periods of silence allow the gathered worshipers to dwell on the word, reflect on the symbolic ritual actions and sensory stimuli that form the hermeneutical context, and prepare a response in prayer.[63]

Signs, Symbols, and the Multisensory Nature of the Liturgy

In attempting to understand the words proclaimed from the Lectionary, worshipers are subject to the hermeneutical influences of the multisensory symbolic elements that constitute the Catholic Mass. The context of the liturgical event is rich in auditory, visual, tactile, and olfactory elements. The auditory sense is stimulated with words spoken by the presider and the reader, the acclamations of the assembly, instrumental sounds of the musicians, the singing of the cantor and assembly, bells rung at the consecration; even the creaking of pews as the assembly stands and sits, and the cries of infants and small children provide auditory stimulation. Visually the congregation absorbs the arrangement of the architectural space, the appearance of the sacred books, the baptismal font, ambo, and altar, the celebrant's vestments, candles, processions, liturgical colors, sacred vessels used for the Eucharist, works of religious art that adorn the worship space, the gestures, movement, and postures of the presider and the assembly, and indeed the visual impact of seeing a large number of worshipers gathered in one space. The olfactory sense is engaged when incense is used on occasions of particular solemnity, when sacramental oils are used at baptism and confirmation, at the fire of the Easter Vigil, and more generally when worshipers perceive the unique smells that inhabit a particular church building. The tactile sense is engaged in the bodily experiences of sitting, standing, genuflecting, moving in procession, sharing a sign of peace, and receiving communion. The bodily postures which engrave themselves onto the members of the assembly express deep presumptions that are not expressed in words.[64] Sitting after the opening prayer indicates a preparedness for listen-

62. Ratzinger, *Feast of Faith*, 70–71.
63. GIRM 45; GIL 28.
64. Fodor, "Reading the Scriptures," 159; Ratzinger, *Feast of Faith*, 75.

ing as a collective group, and facilitates a meditative recollection and inward stillness in the moments of silence between each reading. Standing to greet the Gospel denotes a degree of heightened reverence and attentiveness. The incorporation of the sense of taste at the reception of holy communion completes the engagement of all five senses.

The sensory dimension cannot be engaged to the same extent during each liturgy and indeed feasts of particular solemnity are intended to engage the senses more abundantly.[65] Decisions are made in Lent, for example, to use less music and to have less elaborate church decoration to emphasize the penitential flavor of the season. The sparseness of the space, the increased use of silence, and the paucity of musical elements, all contribute to the liturgical context within which the Lectionary texts are heard. By way of contrast, the abundance of music and flowers at the Easter ceremonies then impacts the senses of the worshipers more powerfully and creates an atmosphere of triumphant joy within which the liturgical readings and texts are heard.

French theologian, Jean-Yves Hameline, refers to the liturgy as a "space of sensitivity" unparalleled by any other context, constituted by the interaction of a number of co-existing elements which impact upon the senses during the ritual event of corporate worship.[66] Hameline claims that the elements of this defined spatio-temporal liturgical framework result in an "intersensory experience or convergence of sensory modalities."[67] French historian, Eric Palazzo, builds upon Hameline's work, noting that the interaction between elements of the liturgy leads to the "activation" of the sensory dimension and prompts the disclosure of the invisible reality represented by the liturgical signs and symbolic actions.[68] Palazzo's study of the relationship between art, liturgy, and the five senses in medieval culture suggests that meaning is revealed simultaneously with sensory experience in the particular spatio-temporal ritual of worship.[69]

In medieval times, the appeal to each of the senses in the liturgy reflected the conviction that the human person, comprising a body and a soul, was a depiction of both the material and spiritual dimensions of the Catholic Church.[70] Swiss literary historian, Paul Zumthor, notes that the

---

65. Wikström, "Liturgy as Experience," 92; Valenziano, "Vedere la Parola," 68.
66. Hameline, *La Poétique*, 93–103.
67. Hameline, *La Poétique*, 107–10.
68. Palazzo, "Art, Liturgy, and Five Senses," 31.
69. Palazzo, "Art, Liturgy, and Five Senses," 31.
70. Palazzo, "Art, Liturgy, and Five Senses," 27.

medieval liturgy evoked in an exceptional manner the sensory participation involved in the communicative process between humanity and God:

> Spectacular in its most minute parts, it *signified* the truths of faith through a complex interplay of auditory (music, psalmody, readings) and visual (the splendid buildings; the performers, their clothes, their gestures, their dance; the settings) perceptions, sometimes even tactile ones: one touches the holy wall, kisses the statue's foot, the reliquary or the bishop's ring; one breathes the smell of frankincense and of candle wax.[71]

Contrary to the notion that images and objects in the liturgy served as functional items which merely allowed illiterate members of society to participate in corporate worship, medieval writings reveal the importance of concrete, symbolic, ritual elements in intentionally expressing the sacred alongside the Scripture readings and other texts.[72] Hrabanus Maurus, a medieval theologian and Catholic Archbishop of Mainz in Germany, used his homilies to emphasize the various visual and auditory elements of which the liturgy was comprised and exhorted worshipers to allow the truths expressed in the readings, songs, and prayers to permeate their memories.[73] American theologian, Mary Carruthers, highlights the ways in which visual liturgical symbols acted as mnemonic devices that shaped medieval modes of thinking through repeated participation in the liturgy.[74]

The sensory dimension of the liturgical event and the activation of sensory elements during the ritual action, which was of such central importance in the medieval liturgy, continues to permeate the modern Catholic liturgical paradigm in facilitating the human encounter with the divine, alongside the sacramental understanding of Christ's presence in the scriptural proclamation. Human beings can only perceive and understand through their inescapably material and sensory nature.[75] Consequently, through its symbolic, sacramental dimension, the liturgy establishes a connection between that which is visible (the liturgical signs and symbols accessible to human perception) and that which is invisible (the deeper reality of what God is doing and saying amongst the worshipers).[76]

The liturgy, therefore, today as in medieval times, is defined not only by the sacred texts, the gathered assembly, and the physical space, but

71. Zumthor, *La Lettre*, 26–27.
72. Palazzo, "Art and Liturgy," 180.
73. Maurus, "Homilia 39," 275–76.
74. Carruthers, *Craft of Thought*, 275–76; Palazzo, "Art and Liturgy," 180–81.
75. Dulles, "Symbolic Structure," 56.
76. CCC 1131.

also by the variety of multisensory signs and symbolic actions interwoven throughout the liturgical event which contribute to the process of understanding the texts proclaimed from the Lectionary. Some scholars have argued that meaningful participation in the Mass and the ability to uncover meaning in the proclaimed Lectionary texts requires a number of pre-existing capacities. These include familiarity with the flow of the liturgy and its idiosyncratic patterns of speech, literary skills to engage with the various genres of Scripture text, appreciation of aspects of the biblical stories that are "culturally incongruous," and an understanding of liturgical signs and symbols.[77] However, it has also been established that the primary function of language in the liturgy is not to transfer information; participation is far more important than cognitive or cerebral engagement.[78] The hermeneutic importance of the richly symbolic and multisensory context of the liturgy is indisputable not only for its contribution in uncovering meaning in the proclaimed pericopes, but also in alleviating the need for literary competencies.

As a text moves from potentiality to actuality in its proclamation, during what Palazzo would describe as the "auditory activation" of the text,[79] the congregation is immersed in a sensory experience which concretizes and incarnates the story that is being proclaimed verbally. The Lectionary readings which describe the events of salvation history form part of a complex semiotic totality accompanied by images that depict these events, by the homily, prayers, acclamations, and other verbal elements that proclaim these events, and by the visible elements and bodily postures that materialize the congregation's participation in the continuation of that history in the modern-day liturgy. The non-verbal elements promote a profound affective response which facilitates an encounter with the Lectionary readings that goes far beyond the texts themselves. The sensory elements and symbolic actions that form a part of the liturgical event, therefore, not only support and complement the Scripture readings but become a significant part of the message being transmitted.[80]

Swedish educator in the psychology of religion, Owe Wikström, points out that the symbolic language of the liturgical and biblical texts can only survive if it is shared and confirmed by significant others.[81] The ritual words and actions of the liturgical event bear meaning because the individual is part of a social complex with others where all share a common

---

77. Day, *Reading the Liturgy*, 146.
78. Wheelock, "Problem of Ritual Language," 62–63.
79. Palazzo, "Art, Liturgy, and Five Senses," 40.
80. Irwin, *Context and Text*, 185.
81. Wikström, "Liturgy as Experience," 92.

understanding. The symbolic language, gesture, and ritual action of the Catholic liturgical event as it unfolds in the liturgical space, play an important hermeneutical role in establishing the context within which the scriptural pericopes are heard.

Leading to Eucharist

The proclamation of Scripture in the Catholic liturgical event is seen as forming part of a single act of worship with the celebration of the Eucharist which follows.[82] The Introduction to the Lectionary for Mass emphasizes this unity:

> The Church is nourished spiritually at the table of God's word and at the table of the eucharist: from the one it grows in wisdom and from the other in holiness. In the word of God the divine covenant is announced; in the eucharist the new and everlasting covenant is renewed. The spoken word of God brings to mind the history of salvation; the eucharist embodies it in the sacramental signs of the liturgy.[83]

The Liturgy of the Word, therefore, is not merely a preliminary event or a preamble to the main event of the Eucharist. This interconnectedness is further highlighted in *Dei Verbum*:

> The Church has always venerated the divine Scriptures as it has venerated the Body of the Lord, in that it never ceases, above all in the sacred liturgy, to partake of the bread of life and to offer it to the faithful from the one table of the word of God and the Body of Christ.[84]

Although these two parts of the Catholic Mass occur in succession, it is clear that word and sacrament are intricately intertwined as part of the same act of worship. Scholars have noted that hearing scriptural pericopes as part of a eucharistic event guards against the perception of Lectionary readings as a collection of doctrines and beliefs, positioning the listener, rather, to think about how the teachings can be appropriated. Similarly, a celebration of the Eucharist without the Liturgy of the Word is rendered incomplete and

---

82. SC 56: "The two parts which in a sense go to make up the Mass, viz. the liturgy of the word and the eucharistic liturgy, are so closely connected with each other that they form but one single act of worship."

83. GIL 10.

84. DV 21.

indeed "runs the risk of turning into a kind of magic."[85] Pope Benedict XVI in *Sacramentum Caritatis* declared:

> If it is to be properly understood, the word of God must be listened to and accepted in a spirit of communion with the Church and with a clear awareness of its unity with the sacrament of the Eucharist. Indeed, the word which we proclaim and accept is the Word made flesh (cf. *Jn* 1:14); it is inseparably linked to Christ's person and the sacramental mode of his continued presence in our midst. Christ does not speak in the past, but in the present, even as he is present in the liturgical action.[86]

Biblical Fragments throughout the Liturgy

The proclamation of Lectionary readings in the Liturgy of the Word is not the only occasion in which Scripture is heard in the Catholic liturgical event. Indeed, biblical fragments pervade the Catholic Mass from beginning to end and take on new meanings as a result of their position in the liturgical event. Before coming forward to receive Communion, the people say together:

> Lord, I am not worthy
> that you should enter under my roof,
> but only say the word
> and my soul shall be healed.[87]

This prayer is immediately recognizable as the biblical words of the centurion who, trusting in the ability of Jesus to heal his servant from afar, implored Jesus: "Lord . . . I am not worthy to have you come under my roof . . . But only speak the word, and let my servant be healed" (Luke 7:6–7). In the liturgical context, the words of the centurion are placed on the lips of the assembly, reminding them to adopt the centurion's attitude of faith and humility, and to approach the sacrament as personal recipients of Christ's healing. The recitation of this Scripture text by the assembly week after week adds a new layer of meaning which becomes embedded in their minds such that they cannot hear these words of Luke's Gospel without perceiving eucharistic connotations.

---

85. Fodor, "Reading the Scriptures," 166.
86. Benedict XVI, *Sacramentum Caritatis*, 45.
87. RM 704.

Another example of the use of Scripture in the liturgy is the communion antiphon, a brief scriptural verse provided for each liturgical day, which may be recited by the whole assembly, by a reader, or by the presider before communion is distributed.[88] The assembly's hearing of a scriptural excerpt just prior to receiving communion reinforces the unity of the table of the word and the table of the eucharist: "The fragment of bread takes on, so to speak, the flavor of the Gospel."[89] It serves as a reminder that the word should be first heard and accepted before approaching the table of the Eucharist. Finally, the communion antiphon reveals that the word of salvation heard in the Lectionary readings is only fully realized through participation in the eucharistic communion that follows it.[90] In the liturgical event, therefore, the hearing of Scripture texts does not begin and end with the proclamation of the Gospel. Rather, scriptural fragments are heard throughout the eucharistic liturgy and create the context in which the Lectionary readings are heard.[91]

III. THE WORD EVENT: FROM LECTIONARY TEXT TO LIVING PROCLAMATION

Liturgical Proclamation as a Contemporary Event

There is a continual fluctuation in circumstances of time and culture, and in the personal and communal situations of a liturgical assembly. While many of the same texts may be used across different liturgical events, no two celebrations occur in exactly the same way. Consequently, each scriptural proclamation is a unique and non-repeatable event.[92] Ever-changing circumstances in the life of the Catholic Church, the world, the nation, the worshiping community, and indeed the nuances that occur within a particular liturgical event, invite a multiplicity of meanings from the Lectionary readings, since the texts are addressed to each community in their contemporary situation. Three important principles for arriving at an understanding of the scriptural proclamation stem from the words of Jesus after he

---

88. GIRM 87.
89. Boselli, *Spiritual Meaning of Liturgy*, 68.
90. Boselli, *Spiritual Meaning of Liturgy*, 12.
91. The Italian Missal contains a three-year cycle of Collects. These Collects offer a pre-interpretation of the Scripture readings and position the assembly to hear the Scriptures as addressed to them in the present. In the English version of the Missal, there is only one cycle of Collects and hence the text of the Collect does not relate to the Scripture readings of the day.
92. Irwin, *Context and Text*, 267–68; Day, *Reading the Liturgy*, 150; GIL 3.

read from the scroll of the prophet Isaiah in the synagogue: "Today this Scripture has been fulfilled in your hearing" (Luke 4:21). Firstly, the Scriptures are to be received in the "today" of the current liturgical event, at this particular moment in time. The liturgical texts for Christmas, Easter, and Ascension affirm that "Christ is born *today*, he is risen *today*, he ascended to Heaven *today*"[93] (my emphasis). The words of Eucharistic Prayer I for Holy Thursday, prayed aloud by the presider during the consecration of the bread and wine, explicitly remind the assembly of the liturgical "today":

> On the day before he was to suffer,
> for our salvation and the salvation of all,
> *that is today,*
> he took bread . . . [my emphasis].[94]

Secondly, the gathered worshipers receive "this Scripture" as set down by the Lectionary rather than some alternative passage chosen by the presider. Thirdly, "in your hearing" indicates the immediacy of the communication precisely for those who are gathered at that particular liturgy.[95] The acclamation at the end of the reading—"The word of the Lord"—is a declaration that the word event is happening here and now. The focus is not historical or exegetical; worshipers are focused on constructing meaning in the present.

Each liturgical event begins at a defined time, comprises a sequence of elements which unfold according to pre-established rubrics, and then comes to an end.[96] The liturgical greeting is replete with contextual significance in marking the beginning of the worship event for the gathered assembly. The presider's announcement, "The Lord be with you," creates new, sacred temporal conditions.[97] There is a distinct shift in focus as the assembly anticipates a divine encounter due to the theological presumption of the sacramental presence of Christ in the presider, in the assembly, in the words of Scripture, and in the Eucharist.

It could be argued, in fact, that the "reading" of the pericopes from the Lectionary commences long before the voice of the reader is heard. The assembly's engagement with the Scriptures begins when the Book of the Gospels is carried in the entrance procession, elevated above the head of the

---

93. Office for the Liturgical Celebrations of the Supreme Pontiff, "When to Celebrate."

94. RM 340. The Prefaces for Ascension and Pentecost also declare that the feast being celebrated in each case (namely Christ's Ascension into heaven and the coming of the Holy Spirit) is happening "today" (494, 602).

95. Boselli, *Spiritual Meaning of Liturgy*, 40.

96. Hughes, *Worship as Meaning*, 164.

97. Terrin, "Dialogo," 132.

reader, preceded by a cross bearer, and followed by the celebrant and altar servers who will facilitate the worship. The procession is accompanied by music and congregational singing, led by a cantor and/or choir enhancing the unity of those gathered and setting the scene for the liturgical feast about to be celebrated. On occasions of particular solemnity, a thurifer carries a thurible with smoking incense as part of this procession igniting the olfactory senses of the people. Also forming part of the procession are ministers carrying lighted candles to symbolize the presence of Christ in the assembly. The Lectionary is enthroned on the ambo and takes its place in the midst of the community.[98]

The event of liturgy is inevitably a complex interweaving of text and symbolic action. Italian professor of biblical theology, Tommaso Federici, espouses the concept of "celebratory linguistics." He claims that the scriptural proclamation receives illustrations of its latent meaning from the signs and symbols that abound in the liturgy, and that, likewise, the Scripture text, which is itself a "sign" of God, illuminates the meaning of liturgical symbols, thus highlighting the dynamic relationship which exists between them.[99] While Federici acknowledges the place of textual exegesis, he warns that any analysis of the Lectionary texts which does not take into account the rich, complex, and embodied activity of liturgy, may devolve into external literalism and thus be fruitless.[100] The texts of the liturgy, which include greetings, prayers, readings, acclamations, professions, intercessions, and instructional rubrics, find expression in the action and participation of the worshiping assembly who derive meaning in the current moment. The variety of liturgical settings in which a Scripture text may be heard allows its inherent richness to be perceived.[101] This becomes particularly evident in sacramental celebrations, such as the Rite of Baptism, where the introductory prayers, imagery, and symbols position the assembly to hear the Scriptures with a particular focus.[102] Italian theologian, Aldo Natale Terrin, refers to the event of liturgy as the moment where the "ideal" subjects envisaged by the rubrics and provided for by the ritual texts become "empirical" subjects in an actual liturgical event which occurs at a specific point in time and in which meaning is derived in the current moment.[103] The sacred time thus established by the celebration, in which the texts are interpreted by

---

98. Fodor, "Reading the Scriptures," 157.
99. Federici, "Bibbia Diventa Lezionario," 214.
100. Federici, "Bibbia Diventa Lezionario," 214.
101. Irwin, *Context and Text*, 194.
102. Irwin, *Context and Text*, 107.
103. Terrin, "Dialogo," 138.

empirical subjects capable of playing an active role in the worship event, gives rise to the process of disambiguation of the Scripture texts.

A liturgical hermeneutic of Scripture rests on the premise that the text cannot be considered without the context when examining the creative and dynamic process of understanding that takes place when pericopes are proclaimed from the Lectionary in each unique liturgical event. Russian philosopher, Mikail Bakhtin, claimed that any instance of language is a "situated utterance" and that meaning cannot be separated from its surrounding context.[104] Since the liturgical proclamation is a form of situated communication, in which words and texts are "embedded in concretely embodied interactions,"[105] an examination of the contextual conditions is an essential part of the hermeneutical process. Of course, there is some degree of stability in the meaning that can be extracted from the biblical pericopes, yet the ever-changing contexts in which these texts are heard contribute to their polyvalence.[106]

Potentiality to Actuality in Proclamation

Just as a musical score is no more than a series of black marks on paper until the musicians take up their instruments and transform the written marks into musical sound, so too Scripture remains dormant in a state of future potentiality until it is proclaimed and actualized.[107] American priest, philosopher, and professor of English literature, Walter Ong, creates a parallel between living words pressed within the pages of a closed book, and the Victorian art of pressing flowers. The flowers become dry and lifeless, yet all of their details are preserved.[108] Words pressed within a book are not dead, however, but merely exist in a state of potentiality until the book is re-opened. In the Catholic tradition, the liturgical proclamation is the primary context for accomplishing this inherent unity of written and proclaimed word, converting the otherwise dormant letters of the Lectionary pericopes into living words addressed to a contemporary community. Tom Elich describes it well:

> The human eye falls upon the printed word, and the ideas come to life again in the mind, and can find their place again on the

---

104. Bakhtin, *Dialogic Imagination*, 284; Min, "Bakhtinian Perspectives," 2, 14.
105. Gaarden and Lorensen, "Listeners as Authors," 41.
106. Irwin, *Context and Text*, 177.
107. Anderson, "Practicing Scripture," 86–87; Day, *Reading the Liturgy*, 147.
108. Ong, *Orality and Literacy*, 80.

human tongue and in the human ear. This is what happens in the event, the action of the liturgy. The potential of the written is actualized in the spoken.[109]

The proclamation of Scripture facilitates the movement of the texts from potentiality to actuality in the liturgical event, through gestures and postures, acclamations, and responses. While these ritual actions and acclamations take place during a particular liturgy at a definitive moment in time and are therefore not repeatable, such "signifying activities" form part of the Catholic tradition of liturgical discourse and, through their repetition at each liturgical event, come to represent a standardized framework within which interpretation takes place.[110] The proclamation event that takes place in the liturgy is a creative act of tradition, establishing a connection between "the Scriptures fixed yesterday and accepted today, and between the word heard yesterday and proclaimed once again today."[111]

While scholars may provide analyses of the historical world behind the text, and examine literary features of the text itself, their work does not require them to accept these texts as Scripture. In the liturgical proclamation, by way of contrast, the texts are embodied and proclaimed in a community of faith and thus become Scripture for the assembly of worshipers. United Methodist pastor and liturgical theologian, E. Byron Anderson, argues that the meaning of the biblical text as Scripture "emerges in active behavior" as individuals and communities respond to its active embodiment in some interpretive environment.[112] For the purposes of the current investigation, the context of the liturgy serves as that hermeneutical environment with the ceremonials and ritual actions in the Liturgy of the Word elaborating the significance of the public act of reading.[113]

In a highly literate society where people are accustomed to having personalized and immediate access to texts, the assertion that Lectionary texts can only be actualized through proclamation in the midst of an ecclesial community and within a ritual context calls for further investigation. In modern times, scriptural pericopes are no longer confined to black marks on a page but are readily accessible in a variety of translations with associated commentaries, in both printed and electronic formats. An internet search instantaneously displays any chosen pericope of the Bible, while a

---

109. Elich, "Word in Worship," 97.
110. Anderson, "Practicing Scripture," 88.
111. Anderson, "Practicing Scripture," 100.
112. Anderson, "Practicing Scripture," 88.
113. Hughes, *Worship as Meaning*, 157; De Clerck, "In the Beginning," 2–4.

variety of apps can display the Lectionary readings assigned to any given liturgical day.

Yet, existing scholarship on orality and literacy recognizes that when a text is read aloud in a public forum, meaning is conveyed not only through the content of the text, but through the very act of its being proclaimed publicly.[114] Anderson claims that the hermeneutical impact of the liturgical proclamation is pivotal since the Scripture texts can have little meaning unless they are read, practiced, received, and interpreted.[115] The ritual act of proclaiming scriptural pericopes in public not only attributes to the texts a sense of continuity and enduring wisdom, but "is an affirmation of their normative status in and for the Church."[116] The ecclesial action of proclaiming in the midst of the community is as important for creating meaning as the Lectionary text itself.

From Written Biblical Text to Proclaimed Lection

In the Catholic liturgical paradigm, Scripture texts are regarded as the product of an oral tradition, in which writing was simply a way of carrying and preserving spoken words across time and distance until they could be resounded.[117] The Bible is inherently shaped by oral-aural compositions such as poems, songs, myths, prophecies, letters to early Christian communities, and parables. The Gospels contain considerable amounts of direct speech attributed to Jesus and to those with whom he interacted. Furthermore, oral features such as performative language, rhetorical and phonological attributes, graphic imagery, and mnemonic devices such as rhyme and repetition are embedded in the biblical texts. These characteristics were designed to assist in the hearing of the texts, rather than facilitating their comprehension in silent reading.[118]

It is noteworthy that the Hebrew term used to denote the Scriptures is "miqra" which is typically translated as "reading."[119] The work of French linguist, Henri Meschonnic, makes it clear that in biblical Hebrew, "miqra" did not denote a private reading, but rather it signified a socially contingent activity where reading occurred orally. For this reason, the Hebrew verb from which the word "miqra" comes, has been translated as "to read aloud,

---

114. Janowiak, *Holy Preaching*, 63.
115. Anderson, "Practicing Scripture," 88.
116. West, *Scripture and Memory*, 38.
117. O'Loughlin, "Would You Read?," 21.
118. O'Loughlin, "Would You Read?," 34.
119. Boyarin, "Placing Reading," 154.

to call out, to cry out, to proclaim."[120] In Hebrew, therefore, to talk of the Scriptures is to simultaneously refer to oral proclamation of the texts.

Walter Ong sets out some dynamics of textuality and compares these to the features of oral language. He notes that meaning is conveyed in oral speech through intonation, emphasis, and pause, whereas written texts rely on punctuation, typography, and space to communicate meaning. While textual features can signal a tone of voice to some extent, they cannot provide a complete set of clues. Ong notes, for example, that actors spend a considerable amount of time deciding *how* to utter the words in a script and observes that two actors may arrive at entirely different decisions for a particular line; for example, one may decide to shout while another elects to whisper.[121]

Although the Lectionary exists as a written record of scriptural pericopes, it is printed solely for the purposes of public proclamation. Its contents are in fact spoken and aural, rather than silent and visual. Lections, therefore, which constitute the transformation of the printed Scripture texts back into the oral language from which they originated, fall into the categories of both written and spoken text which gives them a distinctive influence. As written text, the lections convey a sense of authority and permanence; as spoken words they embody the qualities of presence, spontaneity, participation, connection, and involvement.[122]

Fritz West has suggested that hermeneutical investigations into the liturgical use of Scripture should focus on the proclaimed lections. West argues that the Bible and the Lectionary "are both one step removed from the liturgical event"[123] and require investigative approaches that are relevant but subordinate to the liturgical proclamation of Scripture. Focusing on the Bible implies that the investigator sets out with literary and historical concerns. Beginning with the Lectionary necessarily imports theological and ecclesiological considerations. A focus on the proclaimed lections, however, permits a focused examination of the liturgical use of Scripture as it is actualized in a liturgical event.[124] It is important to emphasize that the lections do not exist as isolated entities completely unaffected by their trajectory. Rather, the lections accumulate meanings from each of their successive interpretive and linguistic contexts and are the result of the "progressive

---

120. Meschonnic et al., "Poetics," 454; Miller, *Performances*, 76.
121. Ong, *Orality and Literacy*, 99.
122. West, *Scripture and Memory*, 38, 46; Graham, *Beyond the Written Word*, 157.
123. West, *Scripture and Memory*, 19.
124. West, *Scripture and Memory*, 19.

appropriation" of biblical texts for liturgical worship.[125] West summarizes this transition by stating that "lections are drawn from the Bible to float on the communal memory of the Church."[126] The hermeneutical pathway of each lection thus begins in the Bible, moves to the Lectionary where it is extracted from its canonical form for use in the calendrical narrative, and culminates in the liturgical event where it is placed alongside other readings and prayers, and heard within the experiential context of worship.

The Homily

The belief that Christ is actually present in the scriptural proclamation and speaks directly to the people in the Gospel, would seem to render the words of the homilist extraneous and inconsequential in the Catholic liturgical paradigm. Yet *Sacrosanctum Concilium* strongly asserted that preaching should be an element at all eucharistic celebrations even on weekdays.[127]

Although discursive in form, the homily continues the liturgical hearing of the sacred texts, illuminating a focus from the readings and exploring implications for the contemporary assembly.[128] On any particular liturgical day, the same Lectionary text is heard, albeit in the vernacular language, in every parish around the world, and must be mediated to convey meaning to each specific congregation. Since a homily necessarily involves a concrete assembly, the task of illuminating the riches of the Lectionary pericopes for a parish congregation is difficult in cases where a priest does not serve the same community each Sunday or where priests alternate between various churches. The homilist should have a deep knowledge of the assembly, and should feel a part of the community to whom the homily is addressed, in order to identify the features of the pericopes that best speak to their current situation.[129] Indeed, the homilist should spend as much time interpreting the local community and their specific socio-cultural reality as they do interpreting the Scriptures.[130] The pivotal role of the homilist in the Catholic Mass is captured well by Paul Janowiak:

---

125. Irwin, *Context and Text*, 168–69.
126. West, *Scripture and Memory*, 25.
127. SC 52.
128. Irwin, *Context and Text*, 175, 179; United States Conference of Catholic Bishops, *Fulfilled in Your Hearing*, 12.
129. Wiener, "Roman Catholic Eucharistic Lectionary," 136.
130. Cilliers, *Living Voice of the Gospel*, 132–35; Francis, *Evangelii Gaudium*, 142–45 (hereafter EG).

> The dynamic meeting between revealed word and contemporary lives, between comfortable interpretations and alternate ways of experiencing the text, engenders within the community a wider vision and a richer experience of encounter. Reverencing the potential and inexhaustible riches of the biblical texts, the preacher speaks a fresh word to the assembly so God's creative interaction can transform the event of hearing and allow the community to see in a new way.[131]

The preacher thus speaks to the community as one with them, as a "questioning listener" embedded in the same culture and time.[132]

Divine Activity or Human Event

Theologians differ in their views on preaching as either a divine or a human event and on the role attributed to the listener in the homiletic action. The Herald Model holds that preaching is a sacramental act and a kerygmatic event.[133] According to this approach, the homily is not about communicating human experiences or understanding the human psyche, but rather should focus on God's salvific action and elucidate the Scripture as God's word from above.[134] This model is a deductive one, where the listener assumes a passive role in the encounter between the human and the divine.

By way of contrast, proponents of the New Homiletic approach advocate an inductive model where the listener takes on an active role, and a mutual and reciprocal conversation takes place between speaker and listener.[135] This model views the purpose of the homily as the facilitation of an experiential event and emphasizes the importance of connecting the Lectionary text with the concrete life experiences of the assembly. It is not anti-theological yet clearly prioritizes the concept of preaching as an act of interpersonal communication and suggests a turn to discourse analysis. This is not to say that the kerygmatic models ignored the role of the hearer, but rather that "their concern for the hearer was primarily theological and epistemological in nature."[136]

---

131. Janowiak, *Holy Preaching*, 169.

132. Van De Geest, *Presence in the Pulpit*, 116–30; United States Conference of Catholic Bishops, *Fulfilled in Your Hearing*, 30, 34.

133. Immink, "Homiletics," 91–93; Long, *Witness of Preaching*, 28–29.

134. Barth and Marga, *Word of God*, 212–17; Thurneysen, "Die Aufgabe," 113.

135. Immink, "Homiletics," 100.

136. Immink, "Homiletics," 96.

Swiss theologian, Rudolf Bohren, has recognized the interplay between divine activity, as advocated by the kerygmatic model, and the active participation of the human listener. He proposes that the dynamic presence of the Holy Spirit in the midst of the community influences both the preaching and the reception of the word.[137] The hearer selectively identifies elements of the communication which speak to their experience and thereby supplements the sermon.[138]

There is general agreement in modern homiletic research that the listener is an active participant in the homiletic event. Investigations have focused on the role of the hearer's expectations and the extent to which their existing mindset influences the interpretation of the preacher's words. It is acknowledged that each person in the assembly is inevitably a product of their experience, and that reasoning about the sacred texts is deeply dependent on a person's assumptions, experiences, and prior understandings.[139]

Co-Authors in Preaching

Recent scholarship has led to an understanding of preaching as a dynamic, interactive exchange between preacher and worshiper through which the worshiper creates meaning. This stems from a conception of the homily as a dialogical event rather than an instance of unidirectional communication, and an understanding of listening as an "internal dialogue" taking place in the mind of the listener.[140]

The work of Marianne Gaarden, a theologian and bishop in the Church of Denmark, reveals that worshipers experience the preaching act as a polyphony of voices, where the preacher contributes one voice among many in the internal dialogue of the worshiper. An examination of the responses of worshipers who were asked to convey what they had heard in the homily, revealed that the words of the preacher had become inextricably intertwined with the thought processes stimulated by those words such that the two were no longer separable.[141] The preacher did not control the trajectory of the internal dialogue, yet the interpretation of the Lectionary readings expounded in the homily stimulated an internal dialogical interaction for the worshipers and activated the subjective construction of meaning.[142]

137. Bohren, *Predigtlehre*, 74–77.
138. Bohren, *Predigtlehre*, 153; Janowiak, *Holy Preaching*, 26.
139. Gaarden and Lorensen, "Listeners as Authors," 29.
140. Gaarden, "Living Voice," 4.
141. Gaarden and Lorensen, "Listeners as Authors," 30–31.
142. Gaarden and Lorensen, "Listeners as Authors," 31.

Gaarden thus describes the process of listening to the homily as "an inner conversation, where the preacher's voice is critically assessed and evaluated in relation to the churchgoer's own experiences, like an interlocutor in an ongoing internal dialogue about faith."[143]

While the presider cannot control or predict what each listener will recall or understand from the homily, the words of the homily nonetheless stimulate and disturb the internal dialogue of the worshipers. Those listening to the homily create associations to related aspects of their own lives, formulating new questions that the preacher did not foresee or intend.[144] Gaarden refers to this as "the emerging sermon" in which there is a surplus of meaning that is not the same as the presider's intended meaning and is far more than the worshipers' prior experiences. She argues that the emergence of new insight is "activated" by the homilist and the listener in the liturgy but is not controlled by either of them. There is a sense of engagement in and surrender to the homiletic event which gives rise to the emerging sermon.[145]

Worshipers revealed that their reception of the homily was also interwoven with the other elements of the liturgy. They referred to the readings, liturgical texts, music and hymns, the liturgical space, and the rite being celebrated in describing what they were thinking during the experience of the homily. In many cases, the listeners had extrapolated the preacher's words to make the message more applicable to their own personal scenario, leading to the conclusion that the listener was the "co-author" of the homily.[146] It would seem, therefore, that a worshiper's engagement with the homily is not simply an act of understanding the message the presider intends to deliver; rather, the worshiper experiences an internal dialogical interaction activated and stimulated by the words of the homilist and influenced by other elements of the liturgical context, leading them to an "inter-subjective production of meaning."[147]

Homily as Polyphonic Dialogue

The findings of Danish scholars, Gaarden and Lorensen, reinforce the findings of earlier research that the voice of the preacher becomes one voice among others in the internal dialogue of the listener. After interviewing

---

143. Gaarden and Lorensen, "Listeners as Authors," 5.
144. Gaarden, "Emerging Sermon," 3.
145. Gaarden, "Emerging Sermon," 10.
146. Gaarden, "Emerging Sermon," 32.
147. Gaarden, "Emerging Sermon," 2.

worshipers about their experience of sermons, Gaarden and Lorensen identified three key categories of polyphonic dialogue.[148]

Firstly, the most frequent dialogical process reported by worshipers was an "associative interaction," in which the words of the preacher prompted a series of associated thoughts in the mind of the worshiper that incorporated their life experiences and personal reflections. The words of the homilist were not valued so much as answers, but rather for their role in helping worshipers to formulate questions as part of an ongoing search for deeper understanding.[149] The findings suggest that the preacher acts as a "theological reflector" and imply that Mass-goers "seem to project their own presuppositions and life experiences onto the reflector and grasp those associations that return in more or less fruitfully disturbed shapes."[150] Through this process, the thoughts and convictions of the worshiper, as well as the words of the homilist, are transformed to create something new.

Secondly, interviewees reported a process of "critical interaction" in which the homilist's insights collided with the preconceptions of the listener, causing the listener to engage in a critical internal dialogue, thereby identifying incongruities and searching for an alternative meaning. The word "critical" is not used here in a negative sense. Indeed, some Mass-goers revealed a desire to have their thinking patterns disturbed such that they were challenged to adopt new perspectives, and found this to be a key motivator for attending the liturgical event.[151]

The third category of response to the homily was "contemplative interaction." Rather than addressing the production of meaning, this category encompasses the capacity of the homiletic discourse to initiate a contemplative state of being. In contrast to engaging in a *dialogue with* God, participants reported an experience of *dwelling in* God which produced a state of peace and inner calm. This response was not attributable to the words of the homily alone, but rather emerged as a result of its being embedded in the liturgical event enhanced by music, prayers, rituals, holy communion, and being heard within a communal context.[152]

The research of Gaarden and Lorensen reveals that the hermeneutical impact of the homilist in the liturgical event is to act as a theological reflector, an "agent of interruption who enters into and disturbs the inner

---

148. Gaarden and Lorensen, "Listeners as Authors," 33.

149. Gaarden and Lorensen, "Listeners as Authors," 34–35.

150. Gaarden and Lorensen, "Listeners as Authors," 36.

151. Gaarden and Lorensen, "Listeners as Authors," 37–39; Gaarden, "Emerging Sermon," 3.

152. Gaarden and Lorensen, "Listeners as Authors," 41.

dialogue of the listener," and as a dialogue partner with each worshiper who ultimately co-authors the homily.[153]

IV. HERMENEUTICAL IMPACT OF THE ECCLESIAL COMMUNITY

Proclamation as a Communal and Social Event

The hearing of Lectionary texts in the liturgy is not an individual enterprise but takes place within a corporate, ecclesial, and communal framework. Fritz West emphasizes the communal nature of the Lectionary texts:

> Although printed, they are the written expression of an oral reality intended for public proclamation in the community. Their language is spoken not silent, aural not visual; their memory is communal not individual, shared not localized.[154]

In the liturgical event, the scriptural proclamation constitutes a corporate, ecclesial reading of the text in which God's communicative initiative is directed to worshipers gathered at a particular time and place and in which the entire assembly participates in receiving the Lectionary texts and attributing meaning to them.[155] Since each person prays, believes and worships not as an isolated entity, but as part of a community, the liturgical event is therefore held to be the primary context for hearing and interpreting the word.[156] The words of Jesus which promised that "where two or three are gathered in my name, I am there among them"[157] serve to reinforce the sacramental identity of the ecclesial assembly as the Body of Christ.[158]

This stands in stark contrast to the modern concept of reading, where the reader is presumed to be sitting alone and silent before the written text, engaged in an inward, private, and disembodied activity. American professor, theologian, liturgist, and author, Nathan Mitchell, succinctly summarizes the congregational action of reading as being "a collegial action that is simultaneously cognitive and kinetic, spiritual and sensate."[159] In other

---

153. Gaarden and Lorensen, "Listeners as Authors," 45.

154. West, *Scripture and Memory*, 50.

155. Elich, "Word in Worship," 99.

156. Janowiak, *Holy Preaching*, 248. The question of the relationship between personal prayer and liturgical prayer is beyond the scope of this book.

157. Matt 18:20. See also SC 7.

158. Janowiak, *Holy Preaching*, 165–66.

159. Mitchell, "Ritual," 170.

words, the reading and hearing of Scripture in the Catholic liturgical event is inescapably a bodily and communal speech act in which the sacred text is embodied through gesture, movement, and physical space. It is also understood to be an incarnational event, whereby proclaiming the Scripture texts "enfleshes" the words and brings them to life in human form in a particular place and time for a particular community.[160] Anderson argues that those who would separate Scripture texts from the liturgical context thereby "separate them from the very ecclesial practices that are intended to render them intelligible and rightly interpreted."[161]

It is a fundamental premise of this liturgical hermeneutic that the proclamation of Scripture in the communal context of liturgy is a complex social event, and that the community's hearing of a Lectionary reading is influenced by a range of social exchanges, both current and historical. As worshipers gather in the church, an energy begins to build. The chatter of the community is eventually quieted by the commentator who welcomes the assembly and prepares them to understand and participate in the celebration.[162] Based on previous experiences of gathering, there is a sense of expectation as the community stands to sing the opening hymn. The people orient themselves to watch the procession move through the liturgical space accompanied by the voices of the congregation lifted in song. They note the color of the liturgical vestments, the reader holding the Lectionary elevated in a position of honor, and the altar servers walking reverently with candles. After the procession and entrance hymn, the priest greets the people, and as one they join in the Penitential Act, confessing their sins as a community and preparing themselves to "celebrate the sacred mysteries."[163] Music erupts into the liturgical space once more as all sing the Gloria, a hymn of triumphant praise.[164] The priest invites the people to pray and provides a few moments of silence before praying the Collect aloud on the community's behalf. The people all sit, with a sense of anticipation as the reader approaches the ambo. The Scripture texts are proclaimed in a context where there is

> an interconnectedness of time and place and event, the complexity of shared texts and of people with a shared history, ritual varieties of sights and smells, pauses and abrupt beginnings . . .

---

160. Janowiak, *Holy Preaching*, 168.
161. Anderson, "Practicing Scripture," 96.
162. GIRM 105.
163. RM 550.
164. The *Gloria* is omitted in Advent and Lent.

and complex interchanges of social energy. Together they effect what the congregation will soon hear.[165]

The readings are followed by a communal profession of faith, prayers of intercession, and the celebration of the Eucharist which further influence the interpretation of the readings.

The uniformity of word, song, and action has a powerful psychological impact in the formation of a social identity and the establishment of an ecclesial community within which worshipers perceive meaning in the scriptural proclamation.[166] Indeed, theological underpinnings of the liturgy include not only communion with God, but also with others in the assembly, with the ecclesial community throughout the world, and with the entire created order. Thus, the liturgical-theological concept of "communion" is simultaneously personal, communal, and cosmic.[167]

While the social and cultural features of the contemporary community must be considered as significant hermeneutical influences for interpreting Scripture in the liturgy, it is nonetheless acknowledged that the notion of "Christian community" encompasses worshipers of the past, present, and future.[168] The sacred biblical texts which were accepted as canon in ancient times continue to be preserved by the same "People of God" who now embody the texts and are addressed by them in the liturgical event. This continuity of community affirms the polyvalence of the Scripture texts which have spoken to Christian communities in a variety of temporal and situational conditions throughout the ages.[169]

Pope Gregory the Great, one of the greatest preachers and most prolific writers in the early church, acknowledged that the meaning of a Scripture passage became much clearer to him when he heard it in the midst of the community, as opposed to meditating privately on a passage. In a frequently quoted excerpt from one of Gregory's homilies on the book of Ezekiel, he says:

> I know, in fact, that there are many things about the Scriptures that I have been unable to understand on my own; I have understood them only when standing before my brothers ... It is clear, in fact, that this [understanding] is granted to me thanks to the merits of those around me ... The meaning grows and pride diminishes when I know that it is through you that I am learning

---

165. Janowiak, *Holy Preaching*, 69.
166. Jörns, "Liturgy," 26.
167. Schattauer, "Liturgical Studies," 134.
168. Spinks, "Catching Up," 774.
169. Spinks, "Catching Up," 775.

what I teach when I stand before you. It is the truth—much of what I say to you I listen to with you.[170]

According to Gregory, the hearing of the Scripture texts in the midst of the liturgical assembly facilitates the understanding and interpretation of the texts on a communal as well as a personal level, prompting the actualization and the effectiveness of the texts. Acknowledging that the community is involved in the co-creation of meaning when Scripture is proclaimed in the liturgy honors the inspired and sacred nature of the Lectionary texts as well as the sacramental identity of the ecclesial assembly gathered for worship.[171]

Individuals in an Ecclesial Framework

Despite the social nature of the proclamation event, and the shared meanings flowing from the broader Catholic tradition, various different meanings can emerge from a Lectionary pericope as a function of the complex diversity of worshipers and the unique horizons they bring to the liturgical event. In the congregation there may be a recently engaged couple, a high-school student on the brink of final exams, a parent with a terminally ill child. The minds of each of these members of the ecclesial community may wander in various directions during the proclamation of the word, yet as Janowiak notes, "such apparent intrusions feed the interpretation of the text."[172]

The rich and varied meanings that can be attributed to a reading in the liturgical proclamation also result from the creative energy flowing from the interactivity between the texts and the ritual practices engaged in by the worshiping community.[173] Active participation is a necessary precursor to the reciprocal interchange between text, context, and worshiper which incarnates the word in the present time and place. While a particular pericope may be open to a range of possible meanings, the interpretive sphere is not without limits. The *sensus fidelium*, or the authority of the ecclesial community, is the context within which individual interpretations can be tested.[174]

Italian theologian, Luigi Sartori, notes the distinctions between the churches of the East and the Protestant churches of the West with regards to their emphasis on the community or the individual. He observes that the

170. Gregory the Great, *Homiliae*, 10.
171. Janowiak, *Holy Preaching*, 165–66.
172. Janowiak, *Holy Preaching*, 69.
173. Janowiak, *Holy Preaching*, 165.
174. Pinnock, "Work of Holy Spirit," 168. In addition to the *sensus fidelium*, the teachings of the magisterium provide the ultimate safeguard, and serve as parameters against which to validate a particular individual interpretation.

eastern churches prioritize the celestial "we," viewing the current worshipers as one with the members of the communion of saints of the past and the future, adhering to the liturgy's collective prayer and ritual but not giving adequate space to the "I" of individual worshipers either past or present. Conversely, Sartori argues, the Protestant approach minimizes the fixed, communal nature of the ritual and gives most space to the creative freedom of the pastor such that preaching dominates in length and importance; this approach emphasizes subjective prayer and the engagement of the individual "I" summoned to the liturgy.[175]

Sartori highlights a role for the Roman Catholic Church in curing the balance between these two extremes. While the Lectionary texts are heard within a communal, ecclesial framework, within the Catholic tradition, and in the context of the shared ritual, the reception of the texts must also lead each worshiper, as a member of the Body of Christ, to their personal response and the assimilation of texts into their own frame of meaning.[176]

SUMMARY

The Introduction to the Lectionary never considers the Scripture readings as isolated entities but insists on the indissoluble link between the pericopes and the dynamics of the ritual into which they are inserted.[177] Placing the Scripture texts within the richness of the embodied liturgical event invites a range of hermeneutical influences far beyond the words contained in the pericopes. Aside from the message inherent in the Lectionary text, meaning is communicated through the act of proclamation, through the words of the homilist, through music, both sung and instrumental, through the worship space, through liturgical prayers and texts, through symbols and gestures, through a sense of encounter with the divine, and through participation as part of an ecclesial assembly.[178] These hermeneutical features of the liturgical event, which are shaped by cultural traditions as well as theological principles, enable the assembly to "practice Scripture" and awaken the Lectionary texts as word of God in a particular place and time for a particular community. The acknowledgment of Christ's presence, the invocation of the

---

175. Sartori, "Criteri Teologici," 267.

176. Visentin, "Parola Di Dio," 250.

177. Visentin, "Parola Di Dio," 242, 245; Federici, "Bibbia Diventa Lezionario," 213; GIL 3, 4.

178. Hughes, *Worship as Meaning*, 182; Martimort, *Church at Prayer*, 276 where it is noted that prayers, songs, and liturgical rituals "serve as a continuous commentary on the sacred texts."

Holy Spirit, and the corporate ritual action in which worshipers participate, bring the potential of the Lectionary texts into actuality as Scripture, effecting the transformation of "empty sounds and dead letters" into words whose meaning is unsealed in the liturgical event.[179]

---

179. Anderson, "Practicing Scripture," 104.

PART II

HISTORICAL THEOLOGY

CHAPTER 5

The History of Scripture Proclamation in the Mass

A study of the evolution of scriptural proclamation in the liturgy and the development of liturgical books in response to changing worship practices, offers key insights that inform a liturgical hermeneutic of Scripture. The modifications to liturgical texts and rituals surrounding the scriptural proclamation, which took place over many centuries, illuminate the fact that history is constantly in motion and that the present liturgical life of the Catholic Church is inescapably influenced by tradition.

I. JEWISH READING PRACTICES

Liturgical Proclamation

Evidence of the communal reading of sacred texts in the synagogue tradition points to the cultivation of a public reading culture, where the proclamation of passages from the Torah followed a socially scripted pattern and affirmed the identity of the gathered assembly.[1] The first references to the public reading of the Law are found in Deuteronomy 31:10–13 and Nehemiah 8:1–8. The development of liturgical Scripture reading in the synagogue was particularly modeled on the account in Nehemiah which included ceremonial elements such as standing, blessing, and explanation.[2]

Philo, a Jewish philosopher from Alexandria in the first century BCE, refers to the weekly Sabbath reading of the law by a single reader to the

---

1. Graves, "Public Reading," 467; Keith, *Gospel as Manuscript*, 206.
2. Graves, "Public Reading," 469.

assembled congregation at the synagogue. His account includes the subsequent explanation of the law by a priest or elder:[3]

> There, arranged in rows according to their ages, the younger below the elder, they sit decorously as befits the occasion with attentive ear. Then one takes the books and reads aloud and another of especial proficiency comes forward and expounds what is not understood.[4]

First-century Romano-Jewish historian, Flavius Josephus, provides a similar account of the custom in Judea, holding "the Law to be the most excellent and necessary form of instruction," insisting that "every week men should desert their other occupations and assemble to listen to the Law and to obtain a thorough and accurate knowledge of it."[5] The practice of public reading and instruction is also attested in Luke 4:16–19 where Jesus reads the words of the prophet Isaiah from a scroll "as was his custom" in the synagogue on the Sabbath.[6]

Jewish Selection of Liturgical Readings

While the Jewish liturgy included a variety of readings and prayers, the pinnacle of the service was the reading from the Torah. From the synagogue and temple tradition, Rabbis advocated the practice of establishing set schedules to guide the public reading of the Torah.[7] Scholarship reveals that there was initially a great diversity of practice, with some uniformity being established later.[8] By the time the Mishnah was composed in the first and second centuries, it is clear that readings from the Torah had been chosen and scheduled for festivals and other special days, for Sabbath mornings, and for the "days of assembly" which were Monday, Thursday, and Saturday afternoon.[9] A fixed cycle of readings with a specific set of predefined pericopes for each Sabbath can be detected from the time of the Talmud in the fourth century. Prophetic readings were chosen to correspond with the

---

3. Philo, *Every Good Man*, 56–59.
4. Philo, *Every Good Man*, 56–57.
5. Josephus, *Life*, 362–63.
6. See also Acts 13:15 and Acts 15:21 where the Law and the Prophets are read on the Sabbath at the synagogue.
7. Graves, "Public Reading," 472.
8. Heinemann, "Triennial Lectionary Cycle," 42–44; Klein, "Four Notes," 66–67; Büchler, "Reading of Law," 192, 250–52; Stökl Ben Ezra, "Seasoning the Bible," 231–32.
9. Sefaria, "Talmud Megillah," 30a, 30b, 31a, 31b.

Torah readings.[10] The Mishnah also indicates that prayers of benediction were recited before and after the Scripture reading.[11] This complemented the adoption of a fixed reading cycle and revealed the evolution of the public reading of Scripture passages into a liturgical event.[12]

There is considerable agreement in the literature that the principle of *lectio continua* was probably adopted as early as the century before Christ, with the five books of the Torah proclaimed within either a one-year or a three-year cycle.[13] The continuous weekly cycle of readings from the Torah was, however, interrupted by the Jewish calendar of liturgical celebrations (Passover, Pentecost, and Tabernacles).[14] The Palestinian tradition presented the Torah (or *Pentateuch*) over a three-year cycle of Sabbath days in one hundred and fifty-four consecutive sections.[15] Some scholars attempted to identify the original form of the three-year cycle, yet it is now considered improbable that a single original schedule existed. Instead, recent evidence points to the existence of multiple schedules and divisions of readings, with variety rather than uniformity prevailing.[16] The Babylonian tradition, by way of contrast, was arranged according to a one-year cycle of Sabbaths in which the Torah was divided into fifty-four consecutive sections.[17] It is this latter tradition that ultimately prevailed and became the dominant practice in Jewish synagogues from the sixth or seventh century, although there were still instances of the three-year cycle being used as late as the twelfth century.[18]

After the Torah reading, a second reading was proclaimed from the scriptural books known as the Prophets, although insufficient evidence makes it difficult to ascertain the date at which this became normative. The reading from the Prophets was selected to augment the reading from the Torah and was chosen either because it shared a common theme with the Torah pericope, or because there was a linguistic connection between a

---

10. Graves, "Public Reading," 474–75.

11. Sefaria, "Mishnah Megillah," 4.1; Sefaria, "Talmud Berakhot," 21a.

12. Graves, "Public Reading," 84.

13. Reumann, "History of Lectionaries," 119.

14. Jewish Virtual Library, "Tractate Megillah—Babylonian Talmud," 3:5; Stökl Ben Ezra, "Seasoning the Bible," 232.

15. Bonneau, *Sunday Lectionary*, 6.

16. Graves, "Public Reading," 473; Heinemann, "Triennial Lectionary Cycle," 42–44; Klein, "Four Notes," 66–67; Büchler, "Reading of Law," 250–52.

17. Stökl Ben Ezra, "Seasoning the Bible," 231–32.

18. Elbogen, *Jewish Liturgy*, 132–33.

pivotal word in both readings.[19] This second reading marked the conclusion of the gathering and was therefore known as the *haftorah* (conclusion).[20]

The homily was a key element of the Torah reading ritual by the first century and appears to have been inserted after the first reading which was considered the most important.[21] It has been suggested that an early influence for the liturgical homily can be traced to the passage from Nehemiah 8:1–8, where the priests were "teaching" the people from the book of the Law.[22] Philo provides that it was

> customary on every day when opportunity offered, and pre-eminently on the seventh day . . . to pursue the study of wisdom with the ruler expounding and instructing the people what they should say and do, while they received edification and betterment in moral principles and conduct.[23]

Despite a wealth of scholarship, it is not possible to distinguish any common practice with regards to the delivery of the homily in the early centuries. There are diverse reports about how often homilies were given in the synagogue, and by whom. There are, however, two points of agreement. Firstly, the homily was delivered in the vernacular in order to ensure comprehension. Secondly, there was an expectation that the homily would expound the Scripture reading of the day and that there would be considerable effort devoted to its preparation.[24]

It must be noted that much of the evidence from rabbinic literature regarding the liturgical reading of Scripture in the synagogue postdates the New Testament and is best viewed alongside the development of the Christian liturgy during the patristic period between the second and fifth centuries. There is every possibility that influence occurred in both directions, and that the common Greco-Roman culture also exerted an impact on the developing Jewish and Christian traditions.[25]

---

19. Graves, "Public Reading," 475.

20. Reumann, "History of Lectionaries," 119.

21. Graves, "Public Reading," 480. Jungmann, *Mass of Roman Rite*, 392. A point of difference in the Christian tradition is the positioning of the most important text, the Gospel, as the last reading. The homily, however, is still positioned directly after the pivotal reading.

22. Graves, "Public Reading," 480.

23. Philo, *On Abraham*, 556.

24. Elbogen, *Jewish Liturgy*, 157–58.

25. Reumann, "History of Lectionaries," 122. See also Visotsky, "Fathers of the World," 2.

II. CONTINUITY AND DISCONTINUITY BETWEEN JEWISH AND CHRISTIAN READING PRACTICES

The overlap in Jewish and Christian reading practices suggests that early Christians developed their liturgical reading tradition in accordance with the Jewish practices that were familiar to them.[26] The primacy of the Torah was mirrored by the primacy of the Gospel, with these texts being the subject of *lectio continua* and immediately preceding the homily in their respective traditions. Both traditions developed festal calendars and assigned particular readings to certain feasts which interrupted the continuous readings. Just as the *haftorah* was selected for proclamation in the synagogue based on its ability to illuminate the reading from the Torah, so too the Christians adopted this criterion in selecting Old Testament readings to complement the Gospel reading of the day.[27] The process of establishing a cycle of readings in Jewish synagogues was also implemented by the Christians in establishing their cursus of readings for liturgical proclamation.

Although there is no evidence of a direct continuity between Jewish and Christian selection of pericopes for liturgical proclamation, the Christian Church's liturgical appropriation of the biblical psalms was evident from the fourth century. The earliest and most common attestation of this practice across both the eastern and western rites, was the singing of the responsorial psalm between the readings.[28] This seemed to reflect the rhythm of the evolving Christian liturgy which required an interchange between spoken and sung texts. The psalms were not merely inserted into the Christian liturgical event but were interwoven with other liturgical elements and other texts, both biblical and non-biblical. Psalms were sometimes sung at the entrance procession when a bishop was presiding, as a precursor to the Eucharistic Prayer, or to accompany the distribution of communion.[29] The psalms were interpreted through a Christian hermeneutical lens when they were expounded in homilies. Psalms were intermingled with refrains, antiphons, and responses which often led to truncation of the psalm verses. The psalms were used not only in eucharistic celebrations but also in the Liturgy

---

26. It is necessary to acknowledge the complex nature of the early Christian Church, made up of diverse communities. Some were exclusively or largely Jewish, while others came from paganism. Rouwhorst, "Bible in Liturgy," 827.

27. This was particularly so at the Second Vatican Council when the number of Old Testament readings assigned to the Lectionary increased significantly.

28. Tertullian, *Quinti Septimi*, 170; Alikin, *Earliest History*, 219.

29. Gelston, "Psalms in Christian Worship," 835.

of the Hours. The Rule of Saint Benedict (c. 500 CE) attests to the distinctly Christian practice of concluding a psalm with a doxology.[30]

The narratives of the Gospels themselves, composed in the first century, integrated a hermeneutical augmentation of Jewish Scriptures by weaving allusions to and quotes from the Jewish prophets into the accounts of Jesus' life and ministry. It was the aim of the writers to depict Jesus as the fulfillment of the Scriptures, to demonstrate a continuity between Christ and all of God's working in human history, and ultimately to defend the Scriptures as God's revelation.[31] This interpretive usage eventually flowed into liturgical practice, as attested to by early Christian apologist and philosopher, Justin Martyr, in which the Jewish Scriptures were read alongside the Gospel during Christian worship.[32] This juxtaposition was particularly powerful, as the recently composed Gospel narratives were publicly proclaimed along with (and in light of) ancient Jewish Scripture passages already recognized as having authentic scriptural status:

> It would have been a uniquely unaware follower of Jesus in the earliest stages who genuinely had no sense of what was happening when they or someone else inserted the Gospels into a liturgical space in synagogue typically occupied by the Torah and the prophets.[33]

The interconnectedness between public reading and authoritative status was emphasized further in the Muratorian Fragment of the second century, which distinguished between texts that could be received and read, and those that could not. The document then went on to identify which of the received texts could be read in the ecclesial assembly.[34] The dimension of "discontinuity" introduced by the public reading of the Gospels thus took place alongside a dimension of "continuity," namely the public reading of Jewish Scripture.

---

30. Benedict, *Rule of Benedict*, 169.
31. Poe, *Gospel and Its Meaning*, 83.
32. Martyr, *First Apology*, 106–7.
33. Keith, *Gospel as Manuscript*, 188.
34. Hahneman, *Muratorian Fragment*, 89; Thomassen, "Notes on the Development," 19n36.

III. CHRISTIAN READING PRACTICES
Liturgical Proclamation

The early Christian texts clearly envisaged an assembled community rather than an individual reader. Through public reading in liturgical events, these texts were heard by all in a communal context, regardless of educational background.[35] William Johnson, in his study of the sociology of reading in classical antiquity, views reading as "not in fact an individual phenomenon, but a sociocultural system in which the individual participates."[36] In his view, the highly complex nature of reading in ancient cultures involved "the negotiated construction of meaning within a particular sociocultural context."[37] The innovation of embedding public reading of sacred texts within the ritual event of Christian worship in a socially constructed community, is a clear illustration of a "sociocultural system" which, according to Johnson, makes a text comprehensible. The reading practices of the early church, therefore, must be considered within the larger cultural reality of the repeated, ritualistic, and communal liturgical event which shaped reading practices and imbued the texts with additional layers of significance.

The description of the Sunday assembly given by Justin Martyr in his *First Apology* (155–157 CE) views the public reading of sacred texts as a liturgical act with a distinctly Christian identity related to, though quite separate from, the reading events of the Jewish synagogue or the pagan Greco-Roman culture of the time:[38]

> And on the day called Sunday, all who live in cities or in the country gather together to one place, and the memoirs of the apostles or the writings of the prophets are read, as long as time permits; then, when the reader has ceased, the president verbally instructs, and exhorts to the imitation of these good things.[39]

35. Gamble, *Books and Readers*, 39–40; Hurtado, "Manuscripts," 105.

36. Johnson, "Toward a Sociology," 602.

37. Johnson, "Toward a Sociology," 603.

38. The close interrelationship between a group's accepted texts and their sense of identity was held to be true for the Jewish people gathering to hear the Torah in the synagogue, for the Christians assembling to hear the epistles and Gospels, and for ancient philosophers reading their prized Greco-Roman texts in community. Keith, *Gospel as Manuscript*, 26, 184–85.

39. Martyr, *Justin, Philosopher and Martyr*, 259. Tertullian and Cyprian, among others, report the same custom. Tertullian, writing at the beginning of the third century, reports that the Roman church combines the Law and the Prophets with the Gospels and apostolic letters in public liturgical reading. Tertullian, "De Praescriptione Haereticorum," ch. 36.

The writings of Justin Martyr also describe the liturgical context in which the Gospels were heard, comprising a homily, baptisms, Eucharist, the holy kiss, and prayers and thanksgivings followed by the Amen. Of note, is the custom referred to by Justin in which the presider delivers the homily, yet a person other than the presider is appointed to proclaim the readings.[40] Scholars have reflected that this was to ensure that the word being received *from* God was spoken by a different person than the one delivering the words rising from the worshipers *to* God.[41] By the fourth century, according to the Apostolic Constitutions, it was customary for the assembly to stand to hear the Gospel which was read by a priest or deacon.[42] Meanwhile, in the East, lights were lit during the reading of the Gospel as an expression of joy in the Gospel message.[43]

Justin's testimony does not serve as evidence of a set Lectionary in the Christian community at this early time. Indeed the first four centuries seem to have been characterized by a degree of liturgical improvisation, with the bishop or leader of a particular community exercising the utmost flexibility in the choice of readings.[44] However, the sacred texts soon came to be read continuously, to allow the liturgical communities to hear the Scriptures in their entirety.[45] The predominance of *lectio continua* as the typical system for liturgical reading is attested to in the patristic commentaries on the Hebrew and Christian Scriptures and in the homilies of the Church Fathers from as early as the third century.[46] Notably, the epistles and Gospels were much more frequently read in a continuous fashion than was the Old Testament in the early Roman tradition.[47] While Old Testament readings were chosen for their value in illuminating the New Testament readings of the day, it is clear that public readings from both Testaments were intended to be received in the present by each particular community, and were not read simply to witness to previous events.[48]

Irish Catholic priest and professor of historical theology, Thomas O'Loughlin, argues that it is necessary to think of Christian origins in

---

40. The Apostolic Constitutions (ca. 215 CE) provide a prayer of blessing including the laying on of hands for a person being instituted as a reader. Donaldson, *Constitutions*, 148–49.

41. Jungmann, *Mass of Roman Rite*, 410.

42. Donaldson, *Constitutions*, 51.

43. Rebenich, *Jerome*, 112.

44. Rouwhorst, "Bible in Liturgy," 833.

45. Palazzo and Beaumont, *History of Liturgical Books*, 94.

46. Federici, "Bibbia Diventa Lezionario," 196.

47. Rouwhorst, "Bible in Liturgy," 839.

48. Jungmann, *Mass of Roman Rite*, 396.

terms of "communities of shared memories"[49] in which texts came to be used in place of living performers. As there were no apostles of Christ still living at the beginning of the second century, the manuscript containing the revered texts became "a vehicle of virtual presence"[50] which preserved the deposit of faith handed down by witnesses of the apostolic era, enabled the continuation of the living voice, and offered a support to memory in the early Christian communities.[51] The strength of the oral tradition was evident as the communal *sensus fidelium* resisted attempts to replace the four distinct Gospels with one coherent diatessaron.[52] O'Loughlin attributes this resistance to the fact that each Gospel account was a record of the oral performance of one of the four evangelists; each account was valued for its individuality. The four separate accounts of the Gospel were familiar to early Christian communities through repeated liturgical proclamation and ritual practice, and as such, were not susceptible to change.[53]

The Impact of the Christian Liturgical Calendar

The assignment of fixed readings for liturgical proclamation in the Christian tradition emerged with the development of the liturgical year and marked a revolution in the system of liturgical reading.[54] The annual recurrence of liturgical seasons and feast days, including celebrations of the saints, quickly led to a selection of pericopes which complemented the meaning of the feast or season.[55] The cycle of continuous reading was hence subject to interruption.

From the fourth century, the homilies and other writings of Ambrose and Augustine indicate that certain scriptural books were to be read in certain liturgical seasons. For example, the books of Job and Jonah were reserved for Holy Week, while the Acts of the Apostles was read in place of the Old Testament reading during the Easter season.[56] An early example of a book of readings comes from Saint Jerome (d. 470 CE). He reports that

---

49. O'Loughlin, "Sharing the Living Word," 11.
50. O'Loughlin, "Sharing the Living Word," 11.
51. Rush, *Eyes of Faith*, 126, 135, 150.
52. Rush, *Eyes of Faith*, 146; Watson, "Fourfold Gospel," 46.
53. O'Loughlin, "Sharing the Living Word," 11. Distinct memories of each Gospel became the foundation of the Lectionary's arrangement of the three-year cycle of Gospels on Sundays.
54. Federici, "Bibbia Diventa Lezionario," 197.
55. Palazzo and Beaumont, *History of Liturgical Books*, 94.
56. Jungmann, *Mass of Roman Rite*, 398.

Musaeus of Marseilles (d. c.460 CE) had compiled a book of Scripture passages at the request of his bishop Venerius (d. 452 CE), comprising

> passages suited to the various feast days of the year, also passages from the Psalms for responses suited to the season, and the passages for reading. The readers in the church found this work of the greatest value, in that it saved them trouble and anxiety in the selection of passages, and was useful for the instruction of the people as well as for the dignity of the service.[57]

This may of course have been applicable only to the city of Marseilles and may only have included the more important feasts of the year, rather than every Sunday.[58] The homilies of Gregory the Great, delivered between 590 and 592 CE, are the first written attestations of readings arranged according to a set framework for the liturgical year.[59]

In some regions, readings were chosen to reflect specific local or historical events. For example, to complement the agricultural preparations taking place in the fields and vineyards of Italy, the Parable of the Laborers in the Vineyard (Matt 20:1–16) was read on the Third Sunday before Lent and the Parable of the Sower (Luke 8:4–15) on the Second Sunday before Lent in those regions.[60] The range of reasons for which a pericope might be assigned to a given liturgical day led to a wide variety of reading schemes for liturgical celebrations. The selection of pericopes on the basis of thematic coherence with a particular event being celebrated meant that interpretation of those pericopes was colored by the broader festal context.

Overall, a great diversity prevailed in the selection of pericopes, with the number and choice of readings varying amongst geographical regions.[61] Three significant traditions can be identified from existing scholarship. Firstly, in the areas east of Antioch, two readings from the Old Testament (one from the Torah and one from the Prophets) were followed by one reading from the epistles or Acts, and one from the Gospels.[62] This bears witness to the fact that the liturgical tradition in these regions was still tied closely to the synagogue system.

A second custom, which was adopted in Gaul and Spain (and in Antioch in the fourth century), was to have one Old Testament reading (taken exclusively from the Prophets) followed by two readings from the New

57. Jerome and Gennadius, *Lives*, 81.
58. McKinnon, *Advent Project*, 65.
59. Chavasse, "Aménagements Liturgiques," 83–102.
60. Reumann, "History of Lectionaries," 125.
61. Bradshaw, *Search for the Origins*, 14–20.
62. Donaldson, *Constitutions*, 135; Jungmann, *Mass of Roman Rite*, 394.

Testament.⁶³ This arrangement of readings stemmed from a particularly Christian understanding of the Old Testament as a book of prophecies foreshadowing Christ.

The third major tradition included only two readings during a eucharistic celebration, both of which were taken from the New Testament. Such a system is adopted in the Armenian Lectionary which records ancient liturgical practices in Jerusalem between 417 and 439 CE.⁶⁴ Old Testament pericopes were only heard on particular occasions such as commemorations of saints from the Old Testament, or at vigils which were followed by a eucharistic celebration. By the seventh century in Rome, the Old Testament reading had been eliminated from the Sunday Eucharist; two readings from the New Testament were heard, one of which was from the Gospels.⁶⁵

Written Manuscripts in an Oral Tradition

Organizing Scripture passages into any sort of set cursus would not have been possible without the technological innovation of the codex.⁶⁶ While the Christians were using this format to distribute Scripture texts from the second century, technological advances in the manufacture of codices by the fourth century permitted the binding of works as large as the Christian Bible into a single volume. The codex made it possible to force the biblical texts into a predefined sequence, and to create an "intertextual network" within which interpretation took place.⁶⁷ The codex also contributed to the establishment of Christian identity by providing an aesthetic focus in liturgical proclamation, which was distinct from the scrolls of the Jewish synagogue.⁶⁸

After centuries of oral culture, there was an initial suspicion about the written word. In contrast to a situation where the speaker was physically present, the written word could not be questioned or provide explanation to assist the reader's understanding.⁶⁹ Biblical manuscripts were written (*script*) by hand (*manu*) and thus the process of creating a Bible took an

---

63. Rouwhorst, "Bible in Liturgy," 834.

64. Renoux, *Le Codex,* 163, 168.

65. The evolution of the Roman Rite mirrored similar developments in the Byzantine, Ethiopian, and Coptic liturgies. Jungmann, *Mass of Roman Rite,* 395; Hammond and Brightman, *Liturgies,* 118.

66. Aichele, "Canon," 48; Kelber, "History of Closure," 123.

67. Aichele, "Canon," 51–52.

68. Keith, *Gospel as Manuscript,* 228.

69. Aichele, "Canon," 49.

extended period of time, was prone to error, and was subject to considerable variation:[70]

> Numerous variants among the oldest biblical manuscripts provide evidence of rewriting of the Scriptures, both deliberate and accidental, by scribes who were either careless or incompetent or deliberately trying to "correct" what appeared to them to be a defective source text.[71]

The establishment of the canon secured the biblical texts, concretized their authoritative nature, and protected them from further modification. A foray into the complicated history of the formation of the canon is outside the scope of this book, yet it is important to note that liturgical use was a pivotal factor in determining admittance to the canon.[72] The eventual stabilization of the canon in the fifth century was the result of a complex and extended process of discernment within the Christian community.[73] Texts that were ultimately recognized as having canonical status were those that had been received, venerated, and repeatedly used as Scripture in liturgical celebrations over several centuries.[74] The canonical process thus highlighted the intricately interwoven relationships between the *sensus fidelium*, liturgical tradition, and Scripture.[75]

IV. EVOLUTION OF LITURGICAL BOOKS FOR SCRIPTURE PROCLAMATION

Manuscripts as Emblems of Reading Culture

At the core of both Jewish and Christian ritualized reading practices were manuscripts containing the texts that had acquired authoritative status. Manuscripts were objects of "living literature," embedded in particular cultural, social, ecclesiastical, and theological contexts and revised over the centuries in response to changing practices and circumstances.[76] A manuscript or book which was being read functioned as an emblem of the

---

70. Connell, *Hear the Word*, 51.
71. Aichele, "Canon," 49–50.
72. McDonald, *Formation*, 246.
73. Rush, *Eyes of Faith*, 131; Graham, "Scripture," 134.
74. O'Loughlin, "Sharing the Living Word," 12.
75. Rush, *Eyes of Faith*, 152.
76. Bradshaw, "Liturgy," 138; Schattauer, "Liturgical Studies," 111.

reading culture and became a physical artifact to be revered.[77] The established cultural practice of public reading and its ritual incorporation in the Christian worship event displayed the status of the Gospel texts; the manuscript as a physical object became the principal entity through which that status was exhibited. American cultural historian, William Johnson, claims that the use of the text as a focus of the community's activity in the reading event, coupled with the community's subsequent interrogation of the text to extract meaning, "both revalidates the text as worthy and recommends the community as suitable gatekeepers."[78]

Adaptation of the Biblical Texts for Liturgical Proclamation

The historical emergence of a Lectionary for Mass is shrouded in ambiguity. Sources of evidence include homilies of the Church Fathers, marginal markings in ancient Bible manuscripts, lists of pericopes and ultimately, early Lectionaries bound in a single volume. In early Bible manuscripts, marks were made in the margins to indicate to the reader where the proclamation should begin and end.[79] The liturgical day on which the pericope was to be read was also noted in the margin. Such a system was in place from at least the fifth century,[80] and seems to have been the prominent system until the ninth century.[81]

In the eighth and ninth centuries, graphic signs resembling punctuation began to appear in Bible manuscripts with the purpose of facilitating liturgical reading.[82] The importance of observing the textual markings so as to improve proclamation and promote understanding is revealed in these words of eighth-century English scholar and clergyman, Alcuin, intended for inscription on a Bible at Tours between 799 and 804 CE:[83]

> Let any reader who reads the exalted words of God from the sacred body of the book make clear distinctions between meanings, titles, periods, and commas so that he may enunciate the accents with his mouth. May his pleasant voice carry far, so

77. Johnson, *Readers*, 23.
78. Johnson, *Readers*, 202.
79. Reumann, "History of Lectionaries," 123.
80. Federici, "Bibbia Diventa Lezionario," 200; Palazzo and Beaumont, *History of Liturgical Books*, 94.
81. Martimort, *Lectures Liturgiques*, 22–26; Vogel, *Medieval Liturgy*, 314–16.
82. Vezin, "Divisions du Texte," 57–65; Gilles, "La Ponctuation," 116–18.
83. Garrison, "Alcuin's World," 100.

that everyone may hear and praise God through the reader's mouth.[84]

Subsequently, lists of carefully ordered tables, known as *capitulare*, were copied at the beginning or end of a Bible manuscript.[85] These tables provided a list of the readings for each liturgical day along with the opening and closing words (*incipit* and *explicit*).[86] Despite the rise of the *capitulare*, marginal notes continued to appear in Bibles until the fourteenth century.[87] The chapter divisions that exist in modern Bibles were developed much later by Cardinal Stephen Langton, Archbishop of Canterbury, in approximately 1200. Numbered verses were not introduced until 1500.[88] Nonetheless, ancient manuscripts which date from the fourth century reveal that some divisions resembling chapters (*capitum*) were used, aiding the location of pericopes for liturgical proclamation.[89]

One specific example of these textual features from the third quarter of the ninth century, is a manuscript of the four Gospels which originated in Northern France and is now housed in the Cologne Cathedral Library. A series of canon tables are printed in the front of this manuscript (3r–7r) to indicate where similar accounts appear across each of the four Gospels. Canon table references appear in the margins throughout the manuscript, noting the chapter location of similar pericopes in the other Gospels (see Figure 1). This early system of dividing the Gospel texts into chapters not only assisted with comparisons between Gospel accounts, but also facilitated the location of specific pericopes for liturgical proclamation. Also in the margins are notations to enable the reader to identify the lines containing the assigned lection amidst the full Gospel text (see Figure 1). A *capitulare* precedes each Gospel, and a complete *capitulare* for the entire year appears on the final pages. This manuscript is a striking example of the way in which early church communities used the Bible for explicitly liturgical purposes.[90]

---

84. Alcuin, "Carmen 69," 292; Palazzo and Beaumont, *History of Liturgical Books*, 1:97.

85. Federici, "Bibbia Diventa Lezionario," 200.

86. Pages from the eighth-century codex stored at Würzburg include separate lists of epistles and Gospels. (Comes Romanus Wirziburgensis, M.p.th.f. 62, Würzburg Universitätsbibliothek). The mid-eighth-century Comes of Murbach presents a single integrated list of epistles and Gospels for each liturgical day (Besançon, BM, MS 184; fols. 57–75). See Martimort, *Lectures Liturgiques*, 32.

87. Vogel, *Medieval Liturgy*, 314–16.

88. Kelber, "History of Closure," 129.

89. Edwards, "Hermeneutical Significance," 413–18.

90. Archbishop's Diocesan and Cathedral Library (Digital), "Gospels."

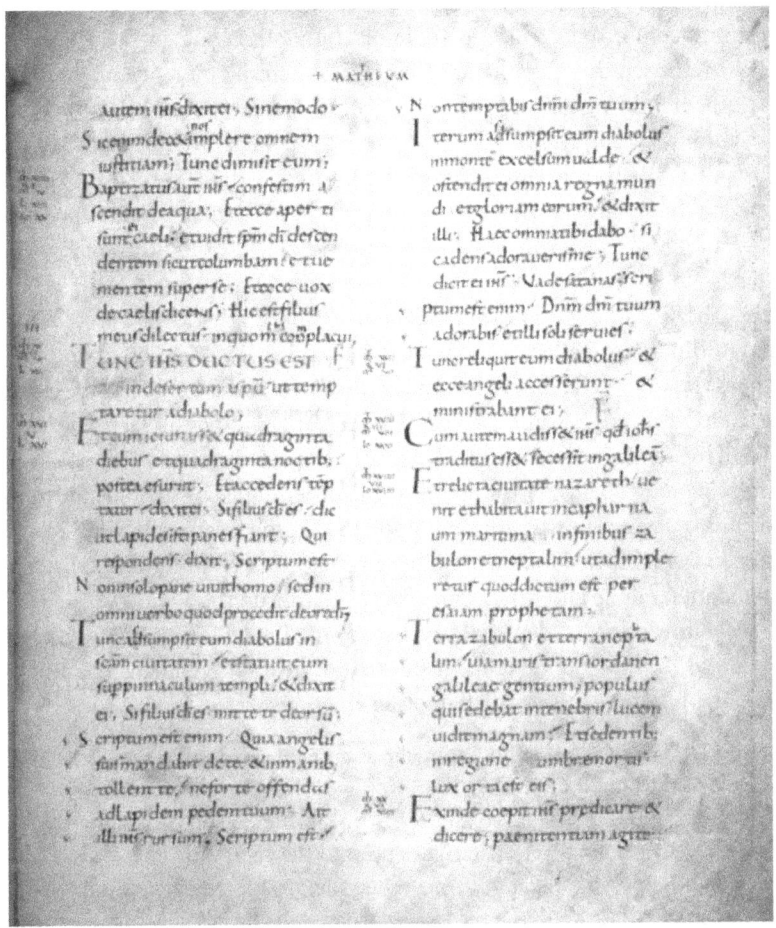

Figure 1: Archbishop's Diocesan and Cathedral Library, "Gospels," Cod. 56 (Dom Hs. 56), Cologne, Germany, 13r

Adaptation of Liturgical Books in Response to Liturgical Ministries

As the liturgy evolved, specific roles were assigned in addition to that of the priest. A cantor sung the responsorial psalm, a reader spoke the words of the epistle, and the deacon proclaimed the Gospel. A book was deemed necessary for each person with an official ministry in the Mass, such that in patristic and early medieval times, the Roman Catholic liturgical-biblical tradition comprised a collection of books rather than one unified volume.[91] The priest used the Sacramentary, a book containing the prayers, prefaces, sacramental formulae, and rubrics for Mass. The directions for the correct execution of the liturgical ministries were given in another book called the *Ordines*, while breviaries contained the Liturgy of the Hours.[92] The cantor who led the singing of the responsorial psalm used a *cantatorium*. The choir used an *antiphonary* which included the chants to be sung throughout the Mass.

The *Ordo Romanus Primus* written in the eighth century provides an extraordinarily detailed account of the liturgical ceremonies undertaken when Mass was celebrated in Rome by the Pope and attended by all clergy and all Catholics in Rome. The ceremonial surrounding the sacred text began in the sacristy when "the reader of the Gospel prepares the Gospel book. The seal being opened at the archdeacon's orders, an acolyte holds the book for him . . . and he finds the place for the Gospel reading."[93] The acolyte carried the Gospel-book before the altar, following behind the subdeacon-attendant, and the latter then placed it reverently on the altar.[94]

Following an in-depth description of the introductory rites, the *Ordo Romanus Primus* goes on to describe the liturgical action during the proclamation of Scripture. It is worth quoting at length:

> [A]s soon as the subdeacon who is going to read perceives that the bishops and presbyters are sitting down after the pontiff, he goes up into the ambo and reads the epistle. When he has finished reading, a chorister goes up into the same with the grail, and sings the respond. And then Alleluia is sung by another singer, if it should be the season when Alleluia is said; if not, a tract; if when neither one nor the other is appointed, only the respond is sung. Then the deacon kisses the pontiff's feet, and the latter says to him in an undertone, *The Lord be in thy heart and on thy lips.* Then the deacon comes before the altar, and after kissing the book of the Gospels, takes it up in his hands; and there walk before him [to the ambo] two district-subdeacons, who have taken the censer from the hand of the subdeacon-attendant, diffusing incense. And in front of them they have two acolytes carrying two candlesticks. On coming to the ambo, the acolytes part before it, and the subdeacons and the deacon with Gospel-book pass between them . . . the deacon goes up to read

---

91. Gy, "Typologie et Ecclesiologie," 12; Kelber, "History of Closure," 127.
92. Jungmann, *Mass of Roman Rite*, 61–65.
93. Griffiths, *Ordo Romanus Primus*, 34.
94. Griffiths, *Ordo Romanus Primus*, 34.

THE HISTORY OF SCRIPTURE PROCLAMATION IN THE MASS 111

> ... When the deacon is come down from the ambo, the subdeacon who first opened the Gospel-book previously takes it from him and hands it to the subdeacon-attendant, who stands in his rank. Then the latter, holding the book before his breast, outside his planet, offers it to be kissed by all who stand [in the quire] in the order of their rank. And after this an acolyte is ready on the step by the ambo with the case, in which the same subdeacon puts the Gospel-book so that it may be sealed.[95]

The ceremonial which took place around the proclamation of the word reveals the honor attributed to the book of the Gospels and the importance of the ambo as the liturgical location for the proclamation or singing of the word. Liturgical books for proclamation of the readings in this rich liturgical context took one of three forms.

1. Evangeliaries contained the Gospels only and were used by the deacon;[96]
2. Epistolaries contained the epistles only and were used by the reader;[97]
3. Full Lectionaries included both the epistle and the Gospel readings and tended to take precedence over the separate Epistolary and Evangeliary from the eleventh and twelfth centuries.[98]

The production of these books not only reflected ecclesiological considerations but also facilitated liturgical proclamation on a practical level. For example, it was much simpler for a reader or deacon to navigate the liturgical year by turning pages in which the readings were arranged sequentially, than to consult the *capitulare* at the back or front of the book and then search for the required pericope.[99] Epistolaries, Evangeliaries, and Lectionaries were, therefore, entirely liturgical books in which the sense of the continuous biblical narrative was broken.

A Gospel Lectionary from the first half of the eleventh century preserved at the British Library contains Gospel passages arranged according to the sequence of the liturgical year. The liturgical day is identified before

95. Griffiths, *Ordo Romanus Primus*, 130–33.

96. The earliest complete Roman Evangeliary dates to approximately 645 CE. Klauser, *Römische Capitulare Evangeliorum*, xxx–xxxv.

97. An early piece of manuscript evidence with pericopes of epistles printed in full is the Epistolary of Corbie c. 770–80 (St. Petersburg, Publichnaya Bibl., cod. lat. Q.v.I, no. 16). For an illuminated Epistolary manuscript, see the Epistolary of the Sainte-Chapelle, Paris from the mid-fourteenth century held in The British Library (MS 17341).

98. A Gallican Lectionary from the early sixth century is preserved at Wolfenbüttel (Herzog-August Bibl., cod. Weiss. 76) and a Lectionary from Northern Italy at the end of the eighth century is stored at the National Library of France (Paris, B. N., lat. 9451).

99. Palazzo and Beaumont, *History of Liturgical Books*, 100.

each reading, along with the Gospel from which the pericope is taken. The red text in Figure 2 declares the reading for Palm Sunday from the Gospel of Matthew and the text of the reading follows in full. There is no marginal notation and no *capitulare* in this manuscript, representing a significant evolution in the usage of biblical texts for liturgical use.[100]

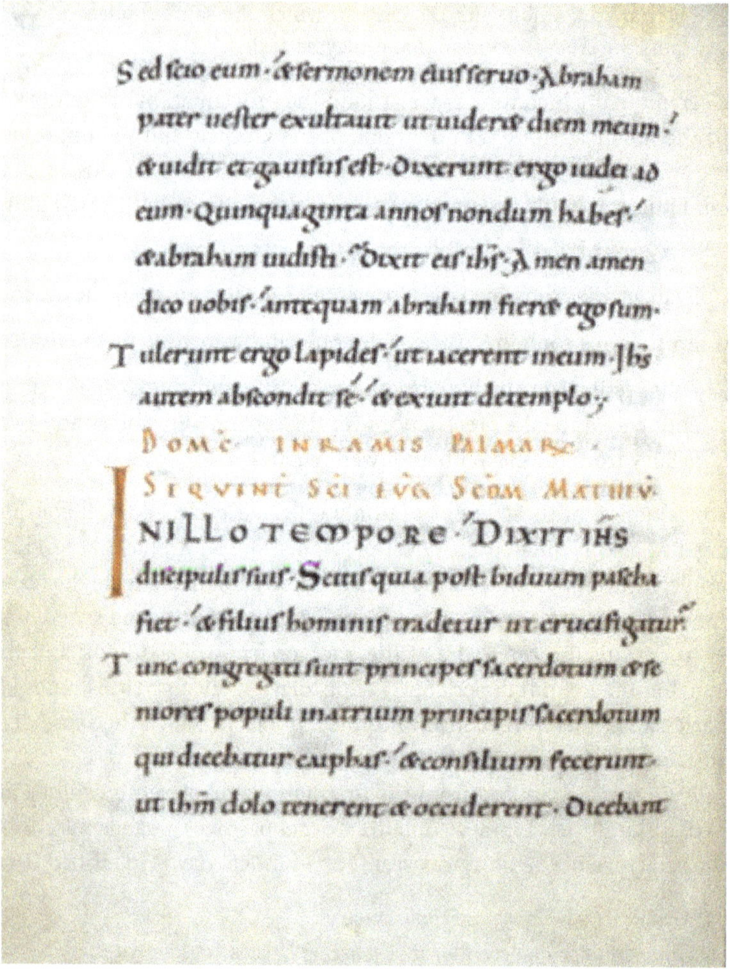

Figure 2: Odalricus Peccator Gospel Lectionary Harley MS 2970 f.22v

---

100. The British Library, *Odalricus Peccator*.

Adaptation of Liturgical Books in Response to Changing Liturgical Practice

In the Middle Ages, notable changes in liturgical practice occurred whereby the priest said Mass without the assistance of other ministers. In these cases, the priest proclaimed the epistle and the Gospel, as well as the prayers of the Mass, in Latin. This change in liturgical practice was reflected in adaptations to the liturgical texts. Beginning in the eleventh century, all the prayers, antiphons, and texts (previously in the Sacramentary) and all the readings of the Mass (previously in the Epistolary and Evangeliary, or in a full Lectionary) were combined into a single liturgical book, the *Missale Plenum*, for the priest's use.[101] This "Complete Missal" which was in common use by 1200, also gave rise to the Private Mass in which a priest celebrated with only a few other people or even perhaps just one altar server. A Cistercian Missal written in England around 1200, now preserved at the British Library, illustrates the positioning of the readings for Mass amidst the other prayers and texts in one single liturgical book for the priest's use (Figure 3).[102]

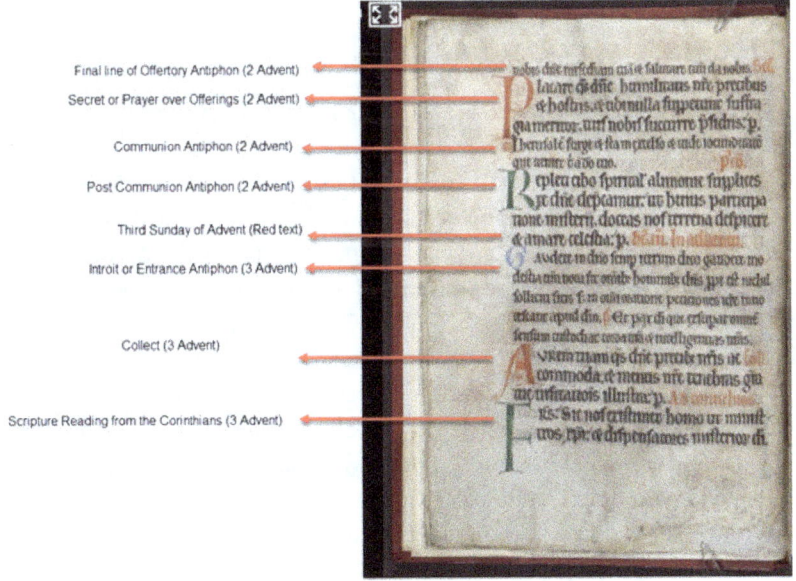

101. Cabié, *Church at Prayer*, 136.
102. The British Library, *Cistercian Missal*.

114　　　　　　　　FROM PAGE TO PROCLAMATION

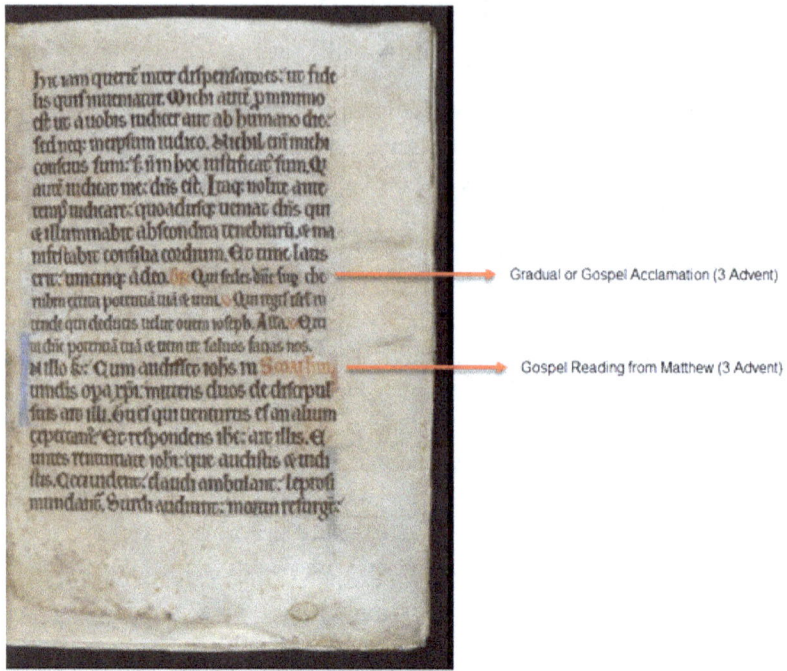

Figure 3: Cistercian Missal, Harley MS 1229, f.3v–4r

The Missal was subject to some variation in subsequent centuries, even in Rome itself. The most popular version was the Missal of the Roman Curia which stemmed from the era of Pope Innocent III (1198–1216). Eventually this Missal prevailed, and the first printed *Missale Romanum* was produced in 1474 in Milan according to the Roman Curia text. It took nearly one hundred years for the Holy See to publish an official copy of the Roman Missal, and in that time several other editions were in circulation.[103] Annotations in a copy of a 1494 Venetian edition of the Missal, shown to be identical to the text of the 1474 Milanese edition, reveal that this version was used as the basis for the official edition of the Missal promulgated by Pope Pius V in 1570 after the Council of Trent which included all the readings for Mass.[104] The system of readings contained a one-year cycle of readings for Sundays and feast days, with only two brief readings assigned to each Mass and a very small percentage of Scripture represented.[105]

103. Ten were printed in Venice, three in Paris, and one in Lyon. Sodi and Triacca, *Missale Romanum,* xv.

104. Celiński, "Per una Rilettura," 401.

105. The two readings were referred to as "The Epistle" and "The Gospel," because

The innovation of the printing press in 1440 made it possible for the liturgical books approved by the Council of Trent to be printed in large quantities with identical text.[106] This marked the first time in the history of the Catholic Church that the same cursus of readings was used so universally; this system of readings continued to be used between 1570 and 1969 until the reforms of the Second Vatican Council.

The Second Vatican Council promoted the rediscovery of Scripture, mandating the creation of a new Lectionary which incorporated a wider selection of biblical texts, to be heard in the vernacular and followed by a homily.[107] While not ruling out the use of Latin, there was a clear acknowledgment that using the vernacular in the liturgy would allow worshipers to participate more fully.[108] The increased role of the laity was further indicated with the recommendation that the altar be detached from the front wall so that the liturgy could be celebrated with the priest facing the assembly.[109] The separation of liturgical books into Roman Missal and Lectionary was restored, such that readers or deacons could once again proclaim the Scripture readings at Mass.[110] The liturgical reforms of Vatican II, only a few of which are mentioned here, established a new hermeneutical context for the reception and interpretation of Scripture texts in the liturgical celebration.

SUMMARY

A study of the origin and evolution of liturgical texts and practices is ultimately directed towards understanding the present, ongoing worship life of liturgical communities:

> Liturgical history . . . does not deal with the past but with tradition, which is a *genetic vision of the present*, a present conditioned by its understanding of its roots. And the purpose of this history is not to recover the past . . . much less to imitate it . . .

---

readings from the Old Testament were rarely used (except for some Feasts, Vigils, and Ember Days). The pre-Vatican Missal included 22.4 percent of the Gospels, 11 percent of the Epistles, and only 1.02 percent of the Old Testament (excluding the psalms). The revision of the *Roman Missal* in 1951 reduced the number of Old Testament passages read at the Easter Vigil from twelve to four, and excised the six Old Testament passages from the Pentecost Vigil. Thenceforth, only 0.39 percent of the Old Testament was represented in the *Roman Missal*. Just, "Missale Romanum."

106. Aichele, "Canon," 53.
107. SC 24, 25, 52.
108. SC 36(1) and 36(2); Elich, "Full, Conscious," 39.
109. Vatican Council II, "Instruction on the Orderly," 91.
110. SC 25, 31.

but to *understand liturgy* which, because it has a history, can only be understood in motion, just as the only way to understand a top is to spin it.[111]

The biblical texts, and later the liturgical books of Scripture, were manuscripts of living literature, adapted over the centuries in response to changing sociocultural and liturgical practice. Of significance, is the degree of flexibility in liturgical practice in the early church, and the diversity that characterized the number and selection of pericopes proclaimed in the worship event. The implication for modern times is that the Lectionary must continue to be viewed as a living text, in recognition of "the importance of the interaction between liturgical texts and their broader cultural, ecclesiastical, political, social—and above all theological—contexts."[112]

The examination of Christian reading practices across the centuries reveals the event of liturgical proclamation to be a complex sociocultural system. This system comprises the repeated, ritual event of Christian worship, the proclamation of Scripture texts, the homily, the ceremonials surrounding the word, and the socially constructed and culturally influenced ecclesial community. The liturgical event, in which the individual participates, makes the text comprehensible and imbues the texts with additional layers of significance. This is as true in modern times as it was for Christians worshiping in early Greco-Roman society.

The value of history is that it liberates us from our immediate past and from the tendency to view either past or present as the absolute and ideal scenario. It illuminates the changing patterns in liturgical texts and practices over time, without mandating what present practice should be. The researcher is then free to examine the current cultural, social, and ecclesial situation and make recommendations for contemporary practice.

In our investigation thus far, Part I has provided a rich description of the Catholic liturgical context within which Scripture interpretation takes place in the Mass, and has offered a detailed analysis of the Lectionary cursus which determines the pericopes proclaimed. Part II has explored the historical evolution of scriptural proclamation in the liturgy and traced the development of relevant liturgical books, establishing that a negotiated interpretation of meaning has taken place within a particular sociocultural, liturgical, and ecclesial context in every age.

The question which naturally arises, is *how* meaning is created in the minds of worshipers when the Scriptures are proclaimed in the liturgy. To

---

111. Taft, *Beyond East and West*, 191.
112. Bradshaw, "Reshaping of Liturgical Studies," 485.

account for the human process of understanding that takes place in this rich context, we now turn to the field of philosophical hermeneutics.

PART III

SYSTEMATIC THEOLOGY

CHAPTER 6

The Event of Meaning: Understanding the Proclamation of Scripture

The critical and dialogical approach to philosophical hermeneutics developed by Hans-Georg Gadamer underpins the current task to develop a liturgical hermeneutic of Scripture. Gadamer does not prescribe methods to be applied when understanding texts but aims to describe what universally happens when people are engaged in the process of understanding. Furthermore, Gadamer holds that any emergent meaning must be critically appropriated and applied in terms of its contemporary relevance in order for authentic understanding to be acquired.

I. GADAMER'S PHILOSOPHICAL THEORY OF INTERPRETATION

Prejudices

Gadamer's hermeneutical approach to textual interpretation is notable for its reluctance to prescribe rules or methods, focusing instead on identifying and foregrounding the preconceptions that motivate an interpreter's questioning of the text. Since every interpreter brings inescapable preconceptions into a hermeneutic encounter, Gadamer emphasizes the importance of examining these prejudices and placing them at risk, so that the researcher might experience the text's claim to truth.[1]

---

1. TM 310; Wink, *Bible in Human Transformation*, 1–2.

Gadamer does not see the temporal distance of a classic text as a hurdle to be overcome. Rather, he values its role in highlighting the foreign nature of the text and provoking the prejudices of the interpreter, thus stimulating a conversation which draws the text along the continuum of tradition into the present.[2] The quality of temporal distance or alienation between the classic text and the modern interpreter is precisely what creates the tension between strangeness and familiarity in which the "otherness" of the text challenges the preconceptions of the modern interpreter.

In contrast to scientific methods which seek to isolate and remove a researcher's prejudices lest the interpretive process be contaminated with subjectivity, such preconceptions are viewed positively as the necessary and productive basis for understanding in Gadamer's philosophical theory. An interpreter is not held captive by existing prejudices; indeed, these prejudices are constantly revised through dialogical and experiential encounters, and those that prove to be unsupported are discarded or transformed into more suitable preconceptions in the movement towards understanding.[3]

Dialogue

Gadamer asserts that human understanding is acquired through "dialogue" or "conversation" where an interpreter's fore-understandings are consciously acknowledged and used to prompt their questioning of a text. Although Gadamer insists on the priority of speech, the task with written texts is "to let speak again" what is transcribed in print and therefore to facilitate a new living conversation between the text and the interpreter.[4] In any encounter with a traditionary text, Gadamer notes that the text puts a question to the interpreter and speaks into the contemporary age. For Gadamer, the hermeneutical experience is a dialectical process, in which the harmonization of familiarity and strangeness is an ongoing process in uncovering truth.[5]

Gadamer, building on the work of German philosopher, Martin Heidegger, claims that truth emerges as an event of *aletheia* or disclosure—an

---

2. "Often temporal distance can solve the question of critique in hermeneutics, namely, how to distinguish the true prejudices, by which we *understand*, from the false ones by which we *misunderstand*." TM 309.

3. Nielsen, "Hearing the Other's Voice," 8; Grondin, "Hans-Georg Gadamer," 399. Gadamer acknowledges the potential discomfort that may result when an interpreter realizes that they have been functioning with unsupportable or distorted assumptions.

4. Gadamer, "Religious and Poetical Speaking," 90.

5. TM 306. Gadamer views hermeneutic distance as a necessary precondition for making possible a complete and authentic participation in the thing being interpreted. TM 308.

experience in which that which was previously hidden is brought into the light.[6] Truth as disclosure occurs within referential contexts and is never final or closed due to the temporal and finite nature of human existence. During an encounter with a text when some truth is revealed, the text simultaneously withholds part of itself in a state of concealedness.[7] An interpreter cannot grasp another entity in its entirety; rather, there are always unforeseen perspectives or contexts beyond one's current horizon that have the potential to disclose new meaning and expand one's horizon of interpretation. Thus, each occurrence of truth is provisional and occurs in the ongoing play between concealment and revealment. Truth is necessarily provisional because the historical, traditional, and linguistic circumstances which prompt its emergence can never be universal or definitive.

When the truth proposed by a text is inconsistent with the presuppositions of the interpreter, a dialogue of question and answer follows in which the interpreter interrogates the truth claim of the text and allows their own prejudgments to be challenged. Due to the fact that the interpreter may not be asking the right questions, any understanding of the subject matter is provisional and limited. Catholic theologian, David Tracy, develops the concept of active dialogue, emphasizing that partners in a conversation risk change as they remain open to the potential revelation of new possibilities that might change their beliefs and shift their horizon.[8] The interpreter revises their initial questions through the dialogical process and progressively asks more pertinent questions in moving towards a more adequate understanding. According to Gadamer, questions come upon the interpreter from two different directions. Firstly, questions arise from and are limited by the subject matter of the text. Secondly, questions occur to the interpreter like a sudden thought or revelation, promoting the openness of the dialogue and increasing the possibility of new insights.[9]

It is the role of the interpreter not only to approach the text with appropriate questions, but also to be open to the questions which the text asks of them. Indeed, an authentic conversation in Gadamerian theory constitutes an interpretive encounter which does not leave a person unchanged, and which illuminates possibilities for self-transformation.[10] To capture the active role of the interpreter in questioning the text and reflecting on their prejudices, Hans Robert Jauss, a student of Gadamer, chooses to speak

6. TM 117; Heidegger, *On Time*, 70.
7. Tatar, *Interpretation*, 55–56; Dostal, "Experience of Truth," 49–50.
8. Tracy, *Plurality*, 93, 103.
9. TM 373–75.
10. Vessey, "Dialogue," 314; TM 366–69.

of a "mediation of horizons." He claims that hermeneutical reflection must consciously preserve the tension between the horizon of the historical text and the horizon of the modern interpreter.[11]

Tradition

Gadamer insists that each interpreter is historically located, a product of their tradition, culture, and experiences, embedded in the tangible and physical world which surrounds them. The perceived distance between the historical and modern context is suffused with the continuity of tradition which has influenced the contemporary culture, and which provides some degree of familiarity. Every interpretation of a text furthers the truth of the text and contributes to its historical continuity. For Gadamer, it is subject matter that serves as the transcendental foundation for the revelation of truth that emerges in the dynamic dialogue between traditionary text and interpreter. Each new interpretation of a classic text occurs by way of an insight into the text which is determined by previous interpretations like a "link in a forward-rolling chain."[12] The content of the text's effect throughout history is referred to by Gadamer as the "tradition" of the text. Tradition is not seen as a rigid entity, fixed in the past and tightly grasping what has been transmitted through time, but rather as an ongoing event. Experiencing the truth of a text implies

> the recognition of the timeless in the temporal. Here one should not assume that the temporal disappears when the timeless is recognized. Rather, temporality is the horizon within which what is timeless reveals itself in its distinctive and original (concrete) aspect.[13]

A text encompasses the historical continuity of its significance, and any encounters with the text in the current moment are influenced by the history of its effects. The historical continuity of a text and its truth is evident when an interpreter recognizes that the traditionary text is directly addressing and engaging them in the present in such a way that the modern interpreter understands it. When engaging with the truth of an ancient text, it becomes apparent that the continuity of the past and its truth is inevitably projecting towards the future.[14]

---

11. Jauss, "Literary History," 23–25.
12. Gadamer, "Continuity of History," 238; Herder, *Ideen Zur Philosophie*, 337.
13. Tatar, "Interpretation," 60.
14. Gadamer, "Continuity of History," 233, 237.

The notion that a person's understanding is always influenced by history, is referred to by Gadamer as *wirkungsgeschichtliches Bewusstsein* which has been translated as "historically effected consciousness."[15] This consciousness that one is affected by history alerts the interpreter to the fact that they are unable to stand outside the situation and are incapable of a purely objective understanding.[16] The purposeful acknowledgment of the tradition of the text and the interpreter's prejudgments are seen to be essential components of the hermeneutic process which allow the interpreter to engage authentically with the "pastness of the past"[17] while gaining insight into a disclosure of truth and meaning in the present. It is important to maintain a simultaneous foregrounding of both past and present to preserve the internal tension that exists between them. Only in this way is the interpreter aware of the limits to their own horizon and able to respond to the challenge issued by the text.[18]

Gadamer regards the traditional text not as a passive object, but rather as an active dialogue partner which contributes both questions and answers to the ongoing dialogue of interpretation and challenges the interpreter with its range of possibilities.[19] The interpreter must contribute actively in order "to keep the conversation open; in order to 'let the truth be revealed'"[20] and must remain open to the truth claims of the historical text as meaning emerges during the experience of encounter.[21] Part of this "being open" encompasses the presumption of faith inherent in the current theoretical model. Worshipers gathered in the liturgical event are not just a random sample of human beings but come intentionally to the liturgy to constitute a community within which the sacred text of Scripture is proclaimed, received, interpreted as part of a worship event, and ultimately related to daily life beyond the liturgy.[22]

For Gadamer, the hermeneutical enterprise comprises the three elements of understanding, interpreting, and applying which operate cooperatively as one unified process.[23] Gadamer draws on Aristotle's concept of "*phronesis*" or "practical knowledge" in developing his concept of

15. TM 312.
16. TM 312–16.
17. Eliot, "Tradition," 37.
18. TM 368–69; Gadamer, "Power of Reason," 11.
19. Thiselton, *Two Horizons*, 87.
20. Feezell, "Thinking About the Aesthetic," 22.
21. TM 366; Vilhauer, "Beyond," 360.
22. Power, *Word of the Lord*, 5.
23. TM 318.

application, describing the interpreter as not merely observing a situation but rather being personally impacted by it.[24] In order to understand a text, the interpreter cannot disregard the tangible situational context in which they exist but must make a connection with that concrete situation. In Gadamer's view, the assessment of whether an interpretation of an ancient text could be considered "correct" is dependent upon whether the text has been correctly applied in a particular situation, rather than evaluating what the text might have communicated in its original context.

Certainly, the Scripture texts were intended to have application beyond the immediate time and place of their composition. They were designed to be read in manifold unforeseeable circumstances and to be applicable in constantly new and diverse situations. The concept of application is particularly salient for Lectionary texts. Such texts do not exist to be interpreted as historical records; rather, they are proclaimed in order to make connections with people's lives. In line with Gadamerian theory, therefore, a Lectionary text proclaimed in the liturgy can only be regarded as properly understood when its life-changing claim to truth, although articulated in a distant time and place, has been assimilated and applied critically in the interpreter's present reality.[25]

Fusion of Horizons and the Emergence of Meaning

While Gadamer's concept of a "fusion of horizons" received a relatively brief explication in *Truth and Method*, it has been affirmed and further developed by subsequent scholars across a range of disciplines. A person's horizon, or current range of vision, constitutes the beliefs and assumptions inherited from their personal experience and tradition. It refers to all that can be seen from one's current vantage point and, by implication, demarcates that beyond which it is currently impossible to see.[26] Although a person moves within their own horizon and must necessarily encounter a traditionary text from their own perspective, this horizon is not fixed or inflexible, but rather fluid and temporal. It is continually shaped, expanded, and reconstructed as prejudices are put at risk through the dialogical process of testing and refining preconceptions in new situations.[27] The goal of the fusion of horizons is not the sharing of subjective states, but rather the disclosure of truth and meaning.

24. TM 324.
25. TM 341; Weinsheimer, *Gadamer's Hermeneutics*, 151.
26. Knotts, "Readers," 236.
27. Knotts, "Readers," 236; TM 315–17; Nielsen, "Hearing the Other's Voice," 5.

Modern interpreters are not required to transpose themselves into an ancient situation or enter into another time and place; nor is it indeed possible to enter the horizon of a historical text and understand it objectively, for it is not possible to step outside of oneself.[28] Instead, authentic understanding preserves the complete historicity of both the interpreter and the text, without destroying either original horizon. A fusion is made possible in the liturgical proclamation of Scripture when the interpreter, aware of their historical consciousness, views their own present situation as well as that of the historical "other" in a way that avoids a hasty assimilation of the past to one's own preconceptions of meaning and rather allows the tradition to speak. Gadamer's theory maintains that there is a bridging or fusing of the present horizon, which the interpreter maintains, and the past horizon of the traditionary text such that a new, common meaning emerges.[29] Gadamer maintains that the fusing of horizons can occur across historical boundaries thus safeguarding the applicability of an ancient text in diverse contexts without compromising the integrity of its particular historical origin.[30]

Conceiving of understanding as a fusion of horizons recognizes that seemingly distant horizons share in a common truth and meaning despite the historical tensions between them. It further recognizes that the understanding one generates is only ever at best a partial grasp of truth. Indeed, it is acknowledged that the meaning of a text is partly formed by the interpreter's "situatedness" in a tradition that reaches the present.[31] Since any interpretation is conditioned by one's history and current horizon, no interpretation can be deemed ultimately correct and final. Rather, the best one can hope for is an *authentic* interpretation which incorporates a conscious reflection on the pre-understanding from which any interpreter inevitably begins; this interpretation is subject to revision over time as the interpreter's horizon shifts with ongoing experiences.[32] A person's current horizon, therefore, is infused with horizons from the past, rises out of a historical tradition, and constitutes an addition to it.

The current investigation extrapolates Gadamer's idea of a two-way fusion of horizons between text and interpreter by proposing that meaning emerges in the liturgical event when four horizons collide: the Bible text, the Lectionary text, the homilist, and the worshiper. It is argued that

28. Ringma, *Gadamer's Dialogical Hermeneutic*, 23.

29. TM 314–15; Grondin, "Hans-Georg Gadamer," 400.

30. TM 316, 322, 382, 406; Gadamer, "Text and Interpretation," 171; Lonergan, "Merging Horizons," 89.

31. Thiselton, *Two Horizons*, 306.

32. TM 307, 313–15, 317; Ritivoi, "Hermeneutics as Project," 69.

a worshiper makes meaning of a particular scriptural proclamation due to the fusion of these four horizons, within the unique context of the liturgical event in the midst of the ecclesial community. This is not to suggest a sense of closure or finality of interpretation, since each horizon remains open to further change and expansion with each new experience of Scripture proclaimed in the liturgy. The variety of potential understandings of a Lectionary pericope are made possible as the truth-claim of the text "relates itself to the unsurpassable otherness of the infinite nows (presents)."[33] The ongoing challenge is to bring together the horizons of the Bible text, Lectionary text, homilist, and worshiper, without eradicating their particular characteristics.

II. THE INTERPRETIVE EVENT AS PLAY

Critics of Gadamer warn that his concept of the fusion of horizons seems opposed to difference and tension, and focuses too heavily on the search for commonality. They reject the idea that one horizon would be assimilated into another in order to produce a unified and homogenous viewpoint, and instead emphasize the "irreducible tension of similarity and difference"[34] as a pivotal part of understanding.

In order to most adequately represent the dynamic nature of an event of understanding as expressed in Gadamer's hermeneutics, therefore, it is necessary to situate the fusion of horizons within the richer concept of "play."[35] The play event is a fundamentally dynamic process involving an interactive, dialogical, back-and-forth movement between the players. It cannot be a solitary event, nor a subjective attitude, but has a spirit of its own that is a product of the activity that unfolds between the players. Boundaries of time and space are marked out and set aside as the arena of play, separate from the real world where the pursuit of aims abounds. The player must voluntarily embrace the play of the game with a profound commitment to comply with the rules of the game and a serious intention to remain open to the shared articulation of truth. The purpose of entering into play is not to achieve a particular goal, but simply to engage in playful behavior within the limits imposed by the game.[36] The movement of responsiveness cannot

---

33. Tatar, "Interpretation," 51.
34. Weinsheimer, *Gadamer's Hermeneutics*, 78. See also Dosse, *Paul Ricoeur*, 358.
35. Vilhauer, "Beyond," 359.
36. TM 107–12; Gadamer, "Relevance of the Beautiful," 23; Williams, "Playing Church," 325–28; Huizinga, *Homo Ludens*, 5–7, 12–13.

be predicted in advance but flows spontaneously, leading British philosopher, Jack Williams, to describe play as an "unintended intentionality."[37]

The event of play has a life of its own that results from the serious engagement of the players. Each player is captivated by and drawn into the game, no longer standing as an outside observer but engaging in a dynamic conversation.[38] The play of language addresses the players, proposes possibilities, asks questions, and offers answers. Gadamer carefully eschews any sense of polarity between the subject and the object, proposing that questions amalgamate in the play of the interpretive event.[39] He holds that the meaning of language is embedded in its context; meaning is revealed through participation in the language event rather than through an objective analysis of the language.[40]

The spirit of play reaches beyond the consciousness of the individual players such that "when we really play any game, it is not so much we who are playing as it is the game which plays us."[41] This lifts the burden from the players, as the play itself takes the initiative and is responsible for revelation.[42] The players choose to participate actively, but they become part of an event that is more than the sum of their individual roles. In this way players are interwoven into the event, belonging to the game and mastered by it, such that self-consciousness is lost and conversation takes over.[43] Gadamer's account of the play event does not exclude subjectivity but rather transcends it.

Play exists only in its presentation and requires active participation by the players in order for truth to emerge.[44] Yet this event of truth is always unfinished. Gadamer envisages an endless circularity of excursion and return to self, yet since each encounter is transformative, it is never the same self that interprets on each occasion.[45] Experience occurs in the movement from an expectation (based on one's preconceptions) to either the fulfillment or non-fulfillment of the expectation. After a new horizon is acquired through experience, a person cannot have the same experience again because they

---

37. Williams, "Playing Church," 330.
38. Gadamer, "Text and Interpretation," 188; Weinsheimer, *Gadamer's Hermeneutics*, 209, 465.
39. TM 505.
40. TM xiii, xvii, 114, 129–30.
41. Tracy, "Creativity," 297.
42. TM 109.
43. TM 109; Tracy, *Plurality*, 18; Vilhauer, "Beyond," 360.
44. TM xiii, 107; Williams, "Playing Church," 325.
45. TM 317; Gadamer, "Aesthetics," 129.

now operate with different pre-suppositions and fore-structures of meaning. That which was previously unexpected is now able to be predicted. This premise has led to the suggestion that the "hermeneutic circle" commonly referred to in the literature could more accurately be viewed as a "hermeneutic spiral."[46] The freedom and variability of movement, along with the diversity of contingencies and concrete circumstances in which the play occurs, result in a game which is never "played" twice in exactly the same way.[47] Yet despite its inherent flexibility, play also becomes structure when its form persists across time. It can be identified as a repeatable and unified whole, with different players yielding a range of correct interpretations, yet it is nonetheless one game.[48] Gadamer argues that play is a transformation into truth, bringing to light what was previously hidden. Something new is revealed which is an event of truth made manifest.[49]

The concept of play reveals Gadamer's belief that understanding is always tentative and reliant upon further dialogue, and it guards against the danger that the interpreter's own pre-suppositions about commonality might go unnoticed and impose themselves on the interpretive process. Furthermore, the notion of "play" supports Gadamer's position that understanding cannot overcome differences between horizons in an absolute sense but can nevertheless mediate distance between the ancient Scripture text and the contemporary interpreter to reveal meaning that can be applied in the interpreter's present reality.

Festival as a Particular Example of Play

For the current investigation of the Catholic liturgy, the concept of "festival" is a pertinent feature of Gadamer's philosophical hermeneutics. A festival is a temporal event into which participants are enticed and which reaches its accomplishment in the celebrating community. Just as the meaning of a Scripture text only exists when it is read, so too a festival only exists when it is celebrated by a community gathered for that specific purpose at a particular time.[50]

---

46. Weinsheimer, *Gadamer's Hermeneutics*, 98.
47. TM 307, 362.
48. TM xiii, 109, 121–22; Williams, "Playing Church," 328.
49. TM 117; Gadamer, "Relevance of the Beautiful," 26.
50. Palmer, "Ritual," 534. Biblical analogues to festival can be found throughout the Old Testament: See Exod 10:9 and 12:14, Lev 23:4, Num 10:10, Isa 30:29, Sir 47:10, Pss 42:4, 149:3 and 150:4.

The temporal nature of the festival event, according to Gadamer, has two discrete but related characteristics. Firstly, a festival is historically temporal, changing from one celebration to the next as time passes. Secondly, a festival is contemporaneously temporal, in that what is being celebrated becomes fully present in the here-and-now, despite its distant origins. When Christians celebrate Pentecost, for example, there is no comparison with the original historical celebration, nor with previous celebrations, but rather a full participation in the liturgical celebration currently taking place. There is a conscious recognition of the historical distance between the original celebration, or horizon, and the present one, yet this distance is acknowledged as the factor that makes participation in the festival possible.[51]

While the festival celebrates something which happened in the past, its primary concern is the present celebration in which the participants are actively taking part. It encompasses both a *re*presentation of the past and a re*presentation* which relates to the present circumstances. A birthday party, for example, celebrates something that happened many years ago, but its primary focus is the celebration taking place this year in this place and time with these people. Each liturgical event celebrates the death and resurrection of Jesus Christ which took place over 2000 years ago, yet the primary focus is on the present celebration taking place within a particular community at a given place and time.

Although a festival is related to previous celebrations, no two celebrations will proceed with identical back-and-forth movements. Indeed, past and present meet in a unique fusion of horizons and a revelation of contemporary truth with each new celebration of the festival. Like a festival, the proclamation of Lectionary texts in the liturgy possesses the particular temporality of celebrating, vanishing, and then returning in a subsequent liturgical celebration. The notion of festival, therefore, emphasizes the fact that worshipers and communities stand in traditions and that past, present, and future are inextricably interconnected.[52]

Those who celebrate a festival are immersed in the event and participate because they want to be with one another. It is meaningful only for those who take part and who fully immerse themselves in the festive occasion. The communicative component of "taking part" is emphasized by Gadamer since he presumes a communality between those who celebrate a festival. The communality is not simply a function of being in the same place; rather, the common intention of gathering for a particular event unites the

---

51. TM 126–27.
52. Grondin, "Play," 47.

participants and guards against individualistic or subjective encounters.[53] Perhaps distinct from its use in everyday parlance, the hermeneutical use of the term "festival" does not simply import notions of joyful or frivolous celebration, but requires serious work and includes lament. Some such examples include the Good Friday liturgy, the gathering of a community to pray in the aftermath of a natural disaster, or the liturgical celebration of a Funeral Mass.

Gadamer does not conceive of someone celebrating alone. He proposes that a person who participates in a festival wants to communicate, not only with words, but also through being with others and taking part in the celebration as part of a community. Gadamer states that a festival "represents community in its most perfect form."[54] It is not only the joyful noise of community, but also the profundity of silence which characterizes the festival celebration. The sense of awe and the pervasive silence that can descend upon a worshiping community as they contemplate a sacred text is one such example of the festive quiet experienced by participants who are gathered together before the thing being encountered.[55]

III. GADAMER'S PHILOSOPHICAL HERMENEUTICS AND THE LITURGICAL PROCLAMATION

The foregoing outline of Gadamer's notions of play and festival contain unmistakable echoes of the liturgical event. Participants arrive at and enter through the church doors to celebrate the liturgy, an event which is set apart in a sacred space and time. The festal character of the liturgy stems from the intentional gathering of a community to participate in a particular celebration and to commit with openness to the rules of the worship event and the truth it expresses.[56]

Within the predetermined rubrics, prayers, and responses of the Catholic liturgy, and the recurrence of Lectionary readings every three years on Sundays (every two years on weekdays), each liturgical event is unique; the assembly is always different as a result of intervening life experiences, and the dialogue with the text is always particular to the current social-cultural-emotional situation. While the ritual is determined and predictable, the spontaneous engagement with the texts and the responsiveness of the community is not.

53. Gadamer, "Relevance of the Beautiful," 39.
54. Gadamer, "Relevance of the Beautiful," 39–40.
55. Gadamer, "Relevance of the Beautiful," 40.
56. Ratzinger, *Feast of Faith*, 63.

THE EVENT OF MEANING

Worshipers are not passive, but rather participate fully, consciously, and actively as celebrants of the liturgy. The players experience the game as a reality that is beyond them, yet they are able to appreciate the significance of the event in which they play their role.[57]

Any member of the liturgical assembly who participates in a self-centered way rather than committing themselves to the corporate action does not participate actively. While it is not possible for the liturgy to "fail," it is nonetheless possible that participants may fail to participate actively or to engage themselves in the liturgical celebration.[58] The result of a worshiper's failure to play properly, is that the full meaning of the revealed truth will not be recognized.

Liturgy, as play, holds a sense of transcendence and points to a truth which lies beyond the social characteristics of the event. It makes present a truth which surpasses a mere description of the activity taking place, and which cannot contain what it produces. The agreed upon rules of the game dictate that the effect of the play does not evaporate with the end of the play itself. Rather the effects of the proclamation of the word take root in the players and continue to influence their lives and dealings in the world until the time of sacred play returns.[59]

Each interpretive context, namely each unique liturgical event, functions as a dialogical partner with the text. The language, ritual actions, gestures, and other "rules" of the sacred "game" of the liturgy are only understood by those who engage seriously and who are open to the emergence of truth. The play, as distinct from the player, carries the onus of revelation.

The meaning of the proclaimed Lectionary text, therefore, cannot be considered in isolation from the event of its proclamation. The Lectionary texts issue a challenge and require a response—a response that can only be made by one who accepts the challenge to be meaningfully addressed by the text.[60] While it can be impossible to determine precisely where the addressing ends and the answering begins, it is clear that a Lectionary pericope poses questions to the worshiper, and that the worshiper sometimes recognizes their own questions in the Lectionary text. Although the exact process of understanding cannot be known, Gadamer would argue that truth is nonetheless experienced and, in the context of the liturgy, it is a truth to which the worshiper belongs. The unutterable and mysterious

---

57. TM 113–14; Vilhauer, "Beyond," 359.
58. Williams, "Playing Church," 327–28.
59. Huizinga, *Homo Ludens*, 14.
60. Grondin, "Play," 45.

quality of the sacred event within which the words are heard, forms part of the hermeneutical context along with the word proclaimed:

> As a practice, liturgy is more than a text to be historically situated and interpreted, an idea to be abstracted and elucidated, or a human psycho-social-cultural dynamic to be researched and explained. It is not reducible to these things as objects of study but must be understood in the fullness and complexity of its doing.[61]

Where there is serious engagement with the liturgy, there can be no evaluation of its success or failure. The goal itself is the activity of "doing" the liturgy; the liturgy is an end in itself. The Catholic liturgy consists of rubrics, texts, and actions in a predetermined order, according to the arrangement of the liturgical calendar, and creates a space within which the soul can wander spontaneously and creatively, actively questioning and searching for an emerging truth.[62]

The Scriptural Proclamation

Each person who hears the Scriptures proclaimed within the communal event of liturgy experiences an encounter not only with the text, but with the community gathered and with Christ present in the word, in the priest, in the Eucharist, and in the assembly. The worshiper is interwoven into the celebratory event and must participate actively or "play along" in order to understand the truth that emerges. Gadamer places significant emphasis on the element of participation in describing the "festival" and claims that people who participate in a festival wish to communicate. It is true that in the scriptural proclamation, the worshipers do not communicate verbally with one another, yet Gadamer makes the important distinction that communication involves a "being with" and a "coming together" and not necessarily an exchange of words:

> Perhaps it is quiet, even more than the festival address, that belongs to celebration . . . one is overcome by an all-embracing festive quiet and one senses how everyone is gathered together before what they encounter.[63]

---

61. Schattauer, "Liturgical Studies," 133.
62. Guardini, *Church and the Catholic*, 177.
63. Gadamer, "Relevance of the Beautiful," 40.

This festive context in the liturgy liberates a listener from their individual perspective which would be dominant in a private reading experience and instead foregrounds the universal perspective of the Catholic Church. It takes the pressure off an individual who struggles to make meaning from a Lectionary text, and rather inserts them into a shared articulation of truth which the assembly takes part in together within the corporate event of worship. This is not to say that each interpreter arrives at precisely the same understanding, but that the movement of the assembly encourages each person to move beyond the parameters of their existing personal horizon towards a more universal perspective.

The notions of "play" and "festival" are models for the liturgical proclamation, since the liturgy "has its own essence independent of the consciousness of those who play."[64] Indeed, it is the "game" of liturgy and not the subjective viewpoints of the individual members of the assembly that constitute the essence of playing. In describing the playful and symbolic nature of the liturgy, Belgian Catholic Cardinal, Godfried Danneels, insisted that "the soul and the body are captured, even when the intellect has not understood everything."[65] In Gadamer's language, the play of the liturgical event has primacy over the consciousness of the worshiper; the meaning that emerges from the proclamation of the word is less the result of what a person does, and more a matter of the liturgy acting upon the celebrating assembly. This can be held in amicable tension with Catholic Church teachings which would attribute such effects to the presence of Christ in the word, the movement of the Holy Spirit, or the initiative of God in communicating with God's people.

The Catholic understanding of the liturgical event is based on a dialogical process comprised of God's initiatory descent to those gathered (catabasis) and the human response or ascent to God (anabasis).[66] Worshipers actively participate in the communication of meaning by opening themselves "to the event of encounter and standing in it in such a way that the being of the work of art shows itself, steps forth, appears."[67] There is an acknowledgment that interpretation of Scripture in the liturgy involves moving beyond the historical or literal and opening oneself to "mystery," namely that which is not discoverable by conscious human reasoning. This is more than just an attitude of faith but stems from an acceptance that the Scripture text, due to its "otherness" will never be fully captured or fully

---

64. TM 107.
65. Danneels, "Comment Entrons-Nous?," 173.
66. Kunzler, *Church's Liturgy*, 15.
67. Palmer, "Ritual," 540.

accessible. The worshipers, including the homilist, and the scriptural pericopes proclaimed from the Lectionary arrangement, relate to one another and walk together towards the truth that surpasses each of them.[68]

The Homily

In the liturgical event, the worshiping assembly hears a series of texts, selected for that particular liturgical day, which have already been the subject of extensive reflection and interpretation through the long tradition of the Catholic Church.[69] This has direct consequences for preachers in approaching the Scripture texts not as static entities but rather as living texts that constitute God's current communication with a contemporary community within the ritual dynamic of corporate worship.[70]

Chapter 4 included a deep discussion of the homily from a liturgical-theological perspective. It canvassed scholarship in which the homily is viewed as a dynamic, interactive exchange where worshipers are co-authors in preaching. Having now explored the philosophical hermeneutics of Gadamer, additional insights into the role of the homily are possible.

The purpose of the homily, viewed through the combined lens of Gadamer's philosophical hermeneutics and liturgical theology, is to illuminate the truth of the proclaimed Lectionary texts so that this revealed truth might prompt a genuine conversion that reaches application in the lives of the gathered worshipers. The homily ideally mediates between the events of God's action throughout history, as preserved in the Scripture texts, and the current demands placed on worshipers to live according to the revealed truth in the present. During this interpretive event, the horizon of each worshiper is ideally challenged and expanded as they are presented with new possibilities.

The homily does not add new content to the proclamation, nor does it supersede the words of Scripture. Rather, the words of the homilist constitute an act of interpretation of the authoritative Scripture texts and contribute an additional perspective to the interpretive process taking place in the minds of worshipers.[71] Of course, there are limits to what could be considered an acceptable interpretation, whether by a preacher or a worshiper. The

---

68. Gargano, "Scriptura Cum Legente Crescit," 163.
69. Power, *Word of the Lord*, 9.
70. Janowiak, *Holy Preaching*, 100–101.
71. TM 339–40, 547; EG 137–39; Congregation for Divine Worship and the Discipline of the Sacraments, "Homiletic Directory," 6–10.

truth of the text cannot be changed or reconstituted as a result of human interpretation. American biblical scholar, Robert Funk, expresses it well:

> The word of God, like a great work of art, is not on trial. The work of art exists in its own right, to be viewed and contemplated, received or dismissed, but not reconstructed. The text, too, although shaped by human hands, stands there to be read and pondered, but not manipulated . . . it is not the text that requires interpretation, but—if the text is called forth by what it says—the interpreter![72]

African American Baptist minister, Henry Mitchell, describes the role of the homilist as "making things available to ordinary persons in their own frame of reference" and in articulating "something from one culture into real meaning and relevance in another."[73] Gadamer would argue further that effective preaching assists the worshipers to enter into an open-ended conversation of hermeneutic questioning, thereby experiencing an encounter with the truth expressed in the sacred text and being prompted to respond to God's invitation to conversion in their daily lives. Thus, in line with Gadamer's hermeneutical position, the horizon of the homilist has a role to play in illuminating for worshipers the perpetual connection between understanding and application.

The Location of Meaning

Throughout the hermeneutical tradition, questions have arisen regarding the location of a text's meaning. Some scholars have argued that meaning resides in the mind of the author, others locate it in the text itself, some situate it in the mind of the reader or listener, and some have proposed that meaning is a social artifact created in the dynamic context of human relationships. Others have insisted that it is necessary to discover the original question that the text was designed to provide an answer to; this position views the understanding of classic texts as a historical endeavor which requires critical thinking and active research.[74]

---

72. Funk, *Language*, 11–12.
73. Mitchell, *Recovery of Preaching*, 27.
74. Hogan, "Hermeneutics," 273.

The Problem of Authorial Intent

The focus on authorial intent as the primary element to be considered in textual interpretation emerged with the Age of Enlightenment and its emphasis on human reasoning, the conscious mind, and the attainment of objective truth. The true and correct meaning of a text was the meaning intended by the author in the moment that the words were uttered or written. In cases where a listener or reader interpreted something in a text other than what the author intended to express, then that listener or reader was said to have misunderstood the text.[75]

In the mid-twentieth century, a more objective approach emerged in the New Criticism, which viewed a text as a self-contained structural unit, and which located meaning within the text itself. American philosophers, Wimsatt and Beardsley, published a ground-breaking paper in 1946 entitled "The Intentional Fallacy" in which they claimed that the intention of the author was "neither available nor desirable"[76] as a standard for understanding a text. They argued that a text "is detached from the author at birth and goes about the world beyond his power to intend about it or control it."[77] Anything not contained within the text itself was considered outside the realm of literary criticism.

Reader-Response theories emerged in the 1960s in response to the New Criticism, shifting the focus away from the text and emphasizing the role of the reader in constructing and completing the text's meaning. Proponents of reader-response criticism focused on the range of responses that a text could provoke in different readers and acknowledged the potential for multiple meanings to be attributed to a single text.[78]

Gadamer's philosophical hermeneutical theory of interpretation, first published in *Truth and Method* in 1960, preserves a pivotal role for both text and interpreter in uncovering meaning. It is important to note that Gadamer speaks of the horizon of the *text*, and not the horizon or intention of the *author*. The difficulty of the intentionalist position for Gadamer, is the assumption that it is possible to suspend one's own horizon and step into a distant point on the historical continuum to extract meaning in an objective sense from the mind of the author. Gadamer would argue that an interpreter does not have pure access to the intentions of the historical author, for in attempting to identify the original meaning, the interpreter's own

---

75. Frank, "Do We Translate?," 656; Vanhoozer, *Is There a Meaning?*, 46–47.
76. Wimsatt and Beardsley, "Intentional Fallacy," 468.
77. Wimsatt and Beardsley, "Intentional Fallacy," 470.
78. Frank, "Do We Translate?," 658. Reader response theorists include Norman Holland, Stanley Fish, and Wolfgang Iser.

horizon has already entered.[79] Gadamer, however, considers the author as "occasional," holding that words are an expression of the intended thing or subject matter, and not an expression of the mind.[80] He argues that once meaning is expressed, particularly in written form, it takes on its own being and direction, and henceforth a new relationship is expressed between the text and its author. Gadamer asserts that, "Not occasionally only, but always, the meaning of a text goes beyond its author."[81]

While the author's intention remains in its subjective state, the author engages in a new relationship with the meaning created by the text; a distinction is created between the "intending I" and the "understanding I." Meaning is detached from its original condition and is able to speak to every space and time; it is not restricted to the original horizon since each reading of the text constitutes an episode in the continuum of meaning:

> Texts do not ask to be understood as a living expression of the subjectivity of their writers . . . What is fixed in writing has detached itself from the contingency of its origin and its author and made itself free for new relationships.[82]

It is language which constitutes the transcendental ground upon which a living dialogue can take place between past and present, and truth may be revealed across historical and cultural boundaries.[83] The historical text is imbued with a surplus of meaning not envisaged by the original author which calls the modern interpreter into conversation with it.[84] Diverse interpretations of a single text are not only possible but unavoidable as each interpreter brings their own unique horizon to the text.

It is important to note, however, that the truth claim of a text transcends any individual awareness of it. The real experience of the text is the recognition that it points away from itself to the subject matter, and reveals to the interpreter *what* the author is writing *about*.[85] The text does

79. TM 306–7; Garrett, "Hans-Georg Gadamer," 395; Goldsworthy, "Moderate Versus Strong," 671.

80. TM 198–99; Tatar, "Interpretation," 39.

81. TM 307.

82. TM 413.

83. Gadamer, "Continuity of History," 238–39. Gadamer only considers the author's intention to be a hermeneutical obstacle in the case of a written text which is read by an unknown person who is physically and/or temporally separate from the author. Conversely, in the situation of a living conversation between two people, Gadamer would hold that the author's intention is essential for promoting understanding of the spoken text. Gadamer, "Reflections," 52.

84. TM 307; Knotts, "Readers," 240.

85. Warnke, *Gadamer*, 7–10.

not contain a record of the historical author's intention or consciousness; rather, it invites the reader into a "dimension of meaning that is intelligible in itself and as such offers no reason for going back to the subjectivity of the author."[86] Meaning does not reside inherently in a text or in the mind of the author, according to Gadamer, but exists only as potential, moving into actuality only in the concrete act of interpretation when a reader encounters a text:

> The real meaning of a text, as it speaks to the interpreter does not depend on the contingencies of the author and his original audience . . . it is always co-determined also by the historical situation of the interpreter and hence by the totality of the objective course of history.[87]

Of course, any purported understanding of a historical horizon will emerge due to the questions asked by the interpreter from their present horizon, and these questions will differ across various interpretive horizons. Gadamer's student, Hans Robert Jauss, insists that the interpretation of a text includes the original horizon of the text, the extended tradition of the text's interpretation from its inception to the modern era, and the horizon of expectations in which the current reader is located.[88] For the purposes of the present investigation, this position affirms the contribution of the historical-critical school of biblical interpretation, incorporates the tradition of the Catholic Church's interpretation of Scripture throughout the ages, and acknowledges the importance of the individual worshiper in the process of interpreting Scripture texts proclaimed from the Lectionary.

The Horizon of the Biblical Text

A deeper perception of the meaning of a text results from an examination of the historical, cultural, and religious contexts in which a passage was written—contexts which are vastly different from the contemporary situation.[89] Examinations of this nature reveal the network of beliefs and presumptions that were operating in the original context and can help to reveal the particular question or situation which prompted the author to write the text.[90] The findings reveal to the interpreter how the texts fulfilled or negated the

---

86. TM 303.
87. TM 307.
88. Jauss, *Question and Answer*, 198, 203–4.
89. Warnke, *Gadamer*, 9; Parris, *Reading the Bible*, 19.
90. Parris, *Reading the Bible*, 24.

expectations of the initial audience and how the text has been received differently over time.

Historical examinations illuminate the "otherness" of the text, and its temporal distance from the interpreter's own horizon of expectation. Invariably, the original questions addressed by the biblical text are quite distinct from the questions brought to the text by modern readers. Considering the importance Gadamer attributes to the dialogical process, the benefits of considering the question that the Bible text was originally designed to answer may illuminate the question of what the text means to the modern reader. Such an examination is referred to as looking "behind the text"[91] and highlights possible alternative readings of the text that may not be apparent when reading the text with a modern Australian frame of reference. A distance is opened up between the contemporary reader and the ancient text, creating a transitional space which invites the reader to acknowledge their own presumptions, and which allows the text to address them in a new way. Such an awareness mitigates the risk that an attempted exegesis of a Lectionary pericope might slip into eisegesis whereupon the interpreter imposes upon the text that which they expect to find.

Of course, the results of any investigation of the Bible text's original horizon will be incomplete and provisional. The quest for a complete or definitive grasp of the presuppositions, beliefs, and values brought to the text by the original audience will always be elusive. The fact that different questions may result in different meanings being revealed by the text accounts for the fact that the same scriptural text may be understood quite differently across the generations. Furthermore, contemporary readers may constantly expand and revise their understandings and applications of the same text as they pose different questions in response to their ever-changing situations and allow the text to address them accordingly.

Thus, Gadamer does not assign a particular priority to the original condition of a text in relation to subsequent interpretive circumstances, but emphasizes the open indeterminacy and transcendence of a text's meaning across historical boundaries. Gadamer's premise is that the meaning which arises when a text addresses itself to an interpreter is always co-dependent upon the interpreter's historical situation, and is the product of a fusion between past and present horizons.[92] For Gadamer, the logic of question and answer, and the resulting fusion of horizons, encapsulate the ceaseless process of human understanding and transformation:[93]

---

91. Parris, *Reading the Bible*, 22.
92. TM 306–7.
93. Kiefer, "Hermeneutical Understanding," 52.

> To be sure, everything that is fixed in writing refers back to what was originally said, but it must equally as much look forward; for all that is said is always already directed toward understanding and includes the other.[94]

The concept of a fusion of horizons implies that the search for meaning in a Scripture text is not to be achieved exclusively by reconstructing the horizon of the Bible text, but rather through an ongoing mutual mediation of past and present which allows a plurality of perspectives to emerge.[95] The enduring identity of a Scripture text, therefore, is revealed in the continuity of its claim to truth despite a multiplicitous array of finite human expressions of its subject matter.

Implications of the Horizon of the Biblical Text for Liturgical Proclamation

The detailed examination of the horizon of the Lectionary text and the context of the liturgical event given in chapters 3 and 4 need not be revisited here. However, a few additional points must be made in the context of philosophical hermeneutics and the emergence of meaning when hearing pericopes proclaimed in the liturgy. The autonomous texts of Scripture have a number of qualifying characteristics that make them a particular kind of hermeneutical partner. Firstly, the texts are addressed to an anonymous audience. Secondly, the scriptural pericopes have the potential to address listeners repeatedly across generations without depleting their surplus of meaning. Thirdly, given the authoritative claim of the text, an interpreter must recognize that the text, and not the interpreter, has the ultimate priority in the disclosure of truth. The worshiper thus finds themselves being interpreted as they submit to the claim of the Lectionary reading being proclaimed.[96]

In the context of Scripture particularly, it is important to emphasize that there is a certain degree of identity by virtue of what is given in the text. The contribution of philosophical hermeneutics, however, makes room for the non-identity which is a function of each instance of interpretation. A parallel can be drawn between liturgical proclamation and the repeated performance of a symphony over time: while the musical score remains the

---

94. Gadamer, "Text and Interpretation," 34.
95. Tatar, "Interpretation," 53.
96. Gadamer, "Religious and Poetical Speaking," 90.

same and gives the work its identity, each performance is unique.[97] Given that each experience of understanding in the liturgy occurs within a particular historical horizon, no interpretation can be exhaustive. "Each generation must read the texts anew and interrogate them from its own perspective and find itself concerned, in its own fashion, by the work's question."[98]

While Gadamer would support the search of each worshiper for an authentic understanding of a Lectionary pericope heard in the liturgy, he does not suggest that a Scripture text can mean anything the interpreter wishes it to mean. A modern interpreter must acknowledge that their understanding will be inevitably influenced by the customs, attitudes, values, norms, and language of their contemporary culture. Authentic interpretation requires a conscious openness to the effects of history which have been instrumental in forming one's own horizon, and a willingness to allow one's current horizon of understanding to be challenged. Thus, it is evident that the authority of the Scripture text itself as contained in the Lectionary, the history of Scripture interpretation through generations of church tradition, and the contemporary church community, together provide the standards for appropriate interpretation.

SUMMARY

According to Gadamer, understanding is not an event that can be objectively verified and methodically evaluated. Rather, it is an ongoing revelatory experience that began in the past, unfolds in the present, and continues into the future. Gadamer's theory is powerful in the context of the current investigation, as it affirms the integral effect of the tradition in which the worshipers stand, the dynamic process of understanding that takes place in the modern liturgical event, and the necessary openness to future experience. It recognizes that the contemporary interpreter stands in a particular historical-cultural context in the same way that the Lectionary pericopes are situated in a unique historical milieu, and it preserves the historicity of both the Lectionary text and the contemporary worshiper in attributing meaning to the texts proclaimed in the liturgy. It recognizes that each worshiper arrives at the liturgy with pre-existing assumptions that stem from both within and without the religious tradition. The dynamic disclosure of meaning and truth, mediated through the fusion of horizons, awakens the Lectionary text as a persuasive, relevant force, whereby every experience of

---

97. Ricoeur, *Interpretation Theory*, 75.
98. Jauss, *Aesthetic Experience*, xii–xiii.

truth that is revealed in a liturgical celebration contributes to the ongoing tradition of Scripture interpretation.

CHAPTER 7

Corporate Memory and Tradition

This chapter endeavors to provide a synthesis of the hermeneutical impact of memory and tradition from the perspectives of both liturgical theology and philosophical hermeneutics as they pertain to the understanding of the scriptural proclamation in the liturgy. The terms "memory" and "tradition" are often used interchangeably in the literature. Irish poet, theologian, and philosopher, John O'Donohue, asserts that "tradition is to the community what memory is to the individual."[1] Tradition is not conceived as a static collection of doctrines, rules, and ritual practices, but rather as a dynamic process of transmission which keeps communal memory alive, and which is continually renewed in negotiation with the ecclesial community's present horizon. The liturgy is viewed as essential for keeping alive the corporate memory of being church by virtue of its unique capacity to actualize the living memory through ritual and narrative. Each liturgical proclamation of the word is viewed as an event of living tradition which mediates past and present and in which the corporate memory has a contemporary frame of reference. It is argued that the anticipation of meaning which guides the assembly's understanding of the pericopes is influenced by the commonality that binds worshipers to the tradition.[2] Understanding is neither objective nor subjective, but rather results from an encounter in which tradition, truth, and preconceptions are viewed dialectically.

I. THE NATURE OF MEMORY

There are many ways to define memory. Some definitions have particular relevance in a psychological or medical context, emphasizing the capacity

---

1. O'Donohue, "Inner Landscape of Beauty."
2. TM 305.

of the mind to store and recover thoughts, knowledge, emotions, and sensations. It is commonly accepted that memory is a highly malleable and constructive process, where the storage and retrieval of experiences proceeds in line with the needs and motivations of the person remembering.[3] In religious studies, memory is conceptualized as part of the time continuum, relating past events to present and future, unraveling and exposing the meaning inherent in life experiences, illuminating patterns which have provided guidance in the past, and encapsulating future expectations.[4] According to Saint Augustine, "the time present of things past is memory; the time present of things present is direct experience; the time present of things future is expectation."[5]

American Protestant minister and scholar, Thomas Best, proposes a threefold structure through which individuals make meaning of experiences that strongly incorporates the role of memory. He claims that events are anticipated, experienced, and then remembered. Experience is viewed as the process of transforming anticipation into memory, and the present constitutes the pivot point whereby that which was anticipated is converted into that which is remembered.[6] Each stage requires active participation:

> In *anticipating* an event, we participate through expectation and hope; in actually *experiencing* that event, we participate through direct engagement with the reality of what is happening to us; in *remembering* that event, we participate through an active recall which can bring the event, once again, into the present and give it power to shape our future.[7]

Best claims that communities also make meaning of events through the same threefold process of anticipation, experience, and remembering. In this case, it is corporate memory which enables the assembly to actively recall past events and appreciate the meaning of those events in light of the community's present reality. The structure proposed by Thomas Best is by no means a linear or unidirectional model. Remembering a past event creates a sense of anticipation about future experiences, and the actual experience of an event simultaneously creates memories and colors further anticipation of similar events.

---

3. Cockayne and Salter, "Feasts of Memory," 284.
4. Hervieu-Léger, *Religion as Chain of Memory*, 125.
5. Augustine, "Confessions, Book XI," 259.
6. Best, "Memory and Meaning," 60.
7. Best, "Memory and Meaning," 61.

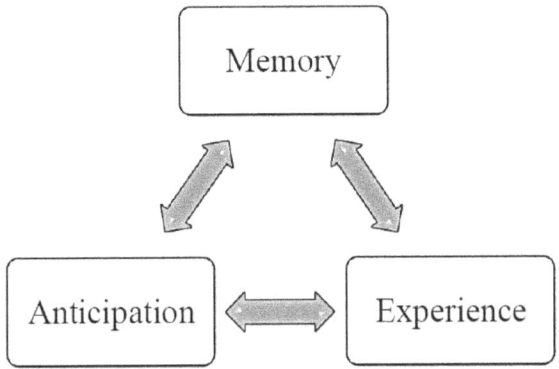

Memory has a powerful function in the liturgy, as it enables worshipers to relate a particular experience of liturgical proclamation to the whole of their experience; no single hearing of a Scripture reading exists in isolation. This interweaving and connective function of memory illuminates patterns and reveals an understanding not only of the text itself, but of who the worshiper is in the present moment and how they might best shape their future. Memory has a key role in highlighting the meaning of Scripture texts proclaimed in a particular liturgy within the wholeness of human life and allows interpreters to move beyond a unidimensional present. "Memory and meaning thus go hand in hand."[8] It is through corporate memory that the Christian community can identify the meaning of a current scriptural proclamation and articulate possible applications of that meaning for the past, present, and future.

While the concept of memory does not feature in Gadamer's *Truth and Method*, American philosopher, James Risser, integrates a discussion of memory with Gadamer's thoughts on understanding and tradition which has a particular resonance for the Catholic theological paradigm. Risser claims that Gadamer's concept of *Bildung* parallels the idea of a "community of memory."[9] The German word *Bildung* refers to education, knowledge, and formation in an ongoing process of development and maturation. In encountering and interpreting a sacred text, the worshiper encounters the absent voices of the past as part of the content of tradition and is educated or formed (*gebildete*).[10] Yet the worshiper does not just experience an increase in their own knowledge and understanding but participates in the ongoing process of tradition. The *sensus communis* of the community is also shaped

---

8. Best, "Memory and Meaning," 62.
9. Risser, *Life of Understanding*, 55; Herdt, *Forming Humanity*, 2–4.
10. Risser, *Life of Understanding*, 56.

and developed. Indeed, in later writings Gadamer speaks less of tradition and more of "solidarity."[11]

II. SOCIAL FRAMEWORKS OF MEMORY

Collective Memory

French philosopher and sociologist, Maurice Halbwachs, proposes that memory is a "present-oriented function of the group rather than a past-oriented function of the individual."[12] He insists that individuals appropriate words and ideas from their society to create a "collective memory" and that they remember according to social frameworks of memory.[13] Memories are formed by shared experience, and individual recollections find meaning in social settings; individuals only remember by locating themselves within the perspective of a particular group, and within one or more "currents of collective thought."[14] The argument proposed by Halbwachs, that memory is formed and recalled according to a corporate framework, is relevant to the task of developing a liturgical hermeneutic of Scripture which incorporates the role of memory in constructing meaning during the liturgy.

Halbwachs also shows that the act of remembering is itself a hermeneutical process in which memory images are integrated into a coherent present day arrangement.[15] The liturgical celebration is one example of what Halbwachs calls a "commemoration," namely a mnemonic strategy for localizing and anchoring corporate memory. The function of the commemoration is to fortify the structure of mnemonic imagery and thus improve the stability and coherence of collective memory. The vividness of a particular memory is closely connected to the influence and authority of the collective group it embodies.[16]

Halbwachs argues that in order for a truth to be established in the memory of a group, it must be present in a concrete event.[17] Worshipers at a liturgical event form a memory image of hearing a text proclaimed from the ambo in the midst of the parish community and within a particular visual-spatial location. Halbwachs would argue that each worshiper composes a

---

11. Gadamer, *Gadamer in Conversation*, 33–35, 80–83.
12. Keith, *Gospel as Manuscript*, 27.
13. Halbwachs, *On Collective Memory*, 22–49.
14. Halbwachs, *On Collective Memory*, 33.
15. Halbwachs, *On Collective Memory*, 45–49, 77–78, 103–5.
16. Hutton, "Halbwachs-Aries Connection," 314.
17. Halbwachs, *On Collective Memory*, 200.

memory of a particular pericope which is socially mediated and relates to the ecclesial community to which they belong. Memories are constructed by individuals in communication with other worshipers with whom they are united through their baptism and through a common understanding of their tradition. The resulting communal memory exists and endures because it contains meaning for the group who remembers.[18] In terms of the liturgical proclamation, therefore, communal memory emerges as the interpretative framework within which the Lectionary texts are to be understood.[19]

Halbwachs, in developing his theory of collective memory, was "not questioning the existence of individual memories, but rather their meaning apart from the social settings that give them their integrity."[20] He claims that memories arise from the imagery of a communal experience and therefore reflect the common understanding and conceptual framework of that social group. American sociologist, Jeffrey K. Olick, builds on the insights of Halbwachs in emphasizing the intersubjective nature of memory. He claims that "there is no individual memory without social experience, nor is there any collective memory without individuals participating in communal life."[21] Despite the acknowledgement of a corporate memory, it is nonetheless individuals, as members of a particular group, who remember.[22] Thus the phenomenological nature of personal memory and the sociological construct of collective memory, must be held in dynamic tension.

Cultural Memory

While Halbwachs was primarily interested in the influence of the contemporary social group upon those who remember, German historian, Jan Assmann, focused on the survival of group identity across generations. He introduced the term "cultural memory" to refer to commemorative practices that ensure the coherence and identity of a social group across generations. His use of the term "cultural memory" equates to what biblical scholars have referred to as "tradition" and is a particular example of corporate memory. Of course, it is acknowledged that the cultural memory formed by a religious group does not exist in isolation, but necessarily incorporates other

---

18. Fentress and Wickham, *Social Memory*, 73, 97.
19. West, *Scripture and Memory*, 51.
20. Hutton, "Halbwachs-Aries Connection," 314.
21. Olick, "Collective Memory," 346.
22. Ricoeur, *Memory, History, Forgetting*, 121–24.

kinds of collective consciousness; there are multiple and overlapping cultures to which worshipers belong.[23]

Assmann highlights two key features of cultural memory that are pertinent for interpreting Scripture in the liturgy. Firstly, he argues that cultural memory operates by reconstructing and relating knowledge to an actual contemporary situation. He insists that memory cannot preserve the past, and claims that what remains in the collective memory is only that which a particular social group can reconstruct from its modern standpoint.[24] Furthermore, Assmann issues a caveat that cultural memory, like individual memory, is also capable of forgetting, distorting, inventing, or embellishing past events.

Secondly, this cultural memory preserves the knowledge, rituals, and understandings from which a group acquires its identity and becomes consciously aware of its unity and distinctiveness.[25] Memory is not merely the storage of historical texts or interpretations, but a continual process of mediation and "reconstructive imagination."[26] The Catholic cultural memory is constituted by the use of sacred texts, liturgical books, and ritual practices which stabilize and communicate the self-image of the ecclesial group.

Assmann identifies the formative principle of cohesiveness in a cultural group across time as "repetition" of the common foundational experiences that give rise to cultural memory. He emphasizes the importance of a regular pattern that "weaves the individual actions into a meaningful, understandable, and clearly laid out whole."[27] In addition, Assmann claims that cultural identity also depends on the "representation" of those experiences or "represented memory" which involves the interpretation of tradition. This leads Assmann to conclude that ritual is the "primary organizational form of cultural memory"[28] as it holds these two poles of repetition and representation in dynamic tension. In relation to the Catholic liturgical event, it is argued that the primary connective structures are not "imitation and preservation," but "interpretation and remembrance."[29]

---

23. Assmann, "Collective Memory," 127.
24. Assmann, "Collective Memory," 130.
25. Assmann, "Collective Memory," 130.
26. Brooke, *Reading Dead Sea Scrolls*, 60.
27. Wils, "Ritual to Hermeneutics," 267.
28. Assmann, *Das Kulturelle Gedächtnis*, 56.
29. Assmann, *Das Kulturelle Gedächtnis*, 17.

Fallibility of Memory

Through a highly flexible and constructive process, memories may be encoded, stored, and retrieved not as pure reflections but according to the motivation of the person or group remembering.[30] This may lead to an inaccurate perception of events or texts based on existing expectations or aspirations, suggesting a meaning that aligns with the expectations of the person or group rather than the actual reality; memory is susceptible to distortion as a result of the present needs of the community. There is a risk that an individual or community may be overcome with memories that are too distressing or confronting to be consciously remembered. There also exists the ever-present risk of dwelling too comfortably in the past, looking backwards to more flourishing times rather than facing current and future challenges. Since corporate memory is not infallible and is susceptible to distortion in the same ways that individual memories are, it is important that the community's memory be supported and corrected if necessary.[31]

III. CONTINUITY AND DISCONTINUITY OF MEMORY AND TRADITION

Active Engagement in Transmitting Tradition

Gadamer insists that interpreters always stand in the river of tradition, captives of its current, and that this situatedness in tradition and culture determines a person's horizon. The interpretation of a classic text constitutes a merging of the horizon of the text with the horizon of the interpreter, whereby the interpreter is "participating in an event of tradition, a process of transmission in which past and present are constantly mediated."[32] Gadamer does not assert that people are merely passive participants in tradition, but that they are actively engaged in arriving at a contemporary understanding of a classic text:

> Tradition is not simply a permanent precondition; rather we produce it ourselves, inasmuch as we understand, participate in the evolution of tradition, and hence further determine it ourselves.[33]

---

30. Laney and Loftus, "Truth," 162.
31. Best, *Memory and Meaning*, 63.
32. TM 302.
33. TM 305.

While the gradual unfolding of the meaning of Scripture texts can be conceptualized as a function of question and answer over time, it is nonetheless true that the Christian tradition does not preserve all the questions which have contributed to the interpretation of scriptural pericopes. Instead, it preserves those elements which are relevant for subsequent generations and which address them in a compelling way.[34] Belonging to a tradition thus "determines in advance both what seems to us worth enquiring about and what will appear as an object of investigation."[35] The transmission of tradition requires a receiving mind which is conscious of the temporal distance separating it from the horizon of the sacred text—a mind which actively engages with a text, and asks questions arising from the current situation or experience.[36]

Sublation and Questioning

The notion of sublation advanced by German philosopher, Georg Wilhelm Friedrich Hegel, and the logic of question and answer espoused by British philosopher and archeologist, Robin George Collingwood, were utilized by Gadamer to account for the possibility of both continuity and discontinuity in an interpretive tradition.[37] Sublation accounts for the process by which each new interpretation of a pericope assimilates previous ones with which it is associated, and in so doing, refigures the understanding of the text. The logic of question and answer reveals that any interpretation of a pericope is not only dependent upon the subject-matter of the text but is a function of the horizon in which the questions arise. As new questions emerge with each generation of Christian believers, new avenues of meaning are recognized in the texts and become incorporated into the tradition.[38] Some interpretations prove to be stable and valuable, and are granted a normative status; however, this status falls away when the questions being asked by contemporary Christian communities are no longer answered by that particular interpretation.

Through the processes of sublation and questioning, along with the application of successive understandings to new situations, the potential meanings of Lectionary texts are continually shaped and expanded. Therefore, it is to be expected that the history of a pericope's interpretation should

---

34. TM 293–94.
35. TM 311.
36. Jauss, *Towards an Aesthetic*, 65.
37. TM 378–87.
38. Parris, *Reading the Bible*, 164.

not resemble a linear aggregation of understandings, but rather a meandering path with features of both contortion and continuity.[39] The potential for diverse understandings across time and culture does not imply that successive interpretations are increasingly better understandings, or conversely, that they are no longer correct interpretations. Rather, Gadamer argues that whenever a person understands they understand in a different way, and that new understandings assist in the formation of future horizons.[40]

Chain of Memory

French sociologist, Danièle Hervieu-Léger, views religion as a "chain of memory," in which individual worshipers become members of an ecclesial community and are thereby united with past, present, and future members of that group. This chain of memory is a particular example of collective memory based on consciously preserving and drawing upon a sacred tradition for the continued nourishment of its members in the present.[41] It must be acknowledged that the modern fascination with personal identity and self-fulfillment has fragmented this continuity and has presented the community with significant challenges in sustaining the chain of communal memory and meaning.[42] Yet this continuity between past, present, and future underpins the dynamic understanding of memory and tradition in a Catholic context. The liturgy is the central event which preserves the continuity of the tradition by providing the context for experiencing and participating in the collective memory. Tradition, as embodied in the liturgical event, is like "the principle of identity which links one generation to another; it enables them to remain . . . the same people as they go forward throughout history."[43]

The memories formed through repeated exposure to the Lectionary texts in the liturgy are pivotal for the continuity of tradition, enabling access to the past, informing the making of meaning and the creation of tradition in the present, and suggesting possibilities for the future continuation of this historical process.[44] For regular Mass-goers, readings come to be imbued with a sense of familiarity as they are heard repeatedly across the yearly

39. Parris, "Reception Theory," 67.
40. TM 307.
41. Hervieu-Léger, *Religion as Chain of Memory*, 4, 101.
42. Hervieu-Léger, *Religion as Chain of Memory*, 166.
43. Congar, *Tradition and Life*, 4.
44. Copeland, "Weaving Memory," 137–38.

cycles.⁴⁵ The bearer of tradition, however, is not the Lectionary itself; rather it is the continuity of memory through which tradition becomes present, and in which new experiences are filtered through the lens of previous ones.⁴⁶ Despite the historical "otherness" of the scriptural pericopes, they have continued to be interpreted through the ages without exhausting the plurality of meanings or the fundamental truths they contain.

IV. THE ROLE OF LITURGY IN CREATING A LIVING TRADITION

Preserving and Creating a Corporate Memory

All societal groups are communities of memory to some degree, but this is particularly so for the Christian community whose identity and beliefs are attributed to the works of God throughout history and to the paschal mystery of Christ's life, death, and resurrection which is celebrated in each liturgical event. The invariance and repetition of the ritual structure of the liturgy contributes to the stability and continuity of memory; potentially countless creative individual expressions are suppressed in order to preserve the enduring ritual patterns and behaviors which contribute to the gradual formation of the corporate body.⁴⁷

Memory and understanding emerge together over time through the worshipers' dialogue with the very tradition that has shaped them. Where worshipers are open to hearing the Lectionary pericopes within the ecclesial tradition, the truth contained in the sacred text speaks directly to the gathered assembly and reveals itself as understanding. The disclosure of truth revealed in the scriptural proclamation is so compelling that it becomes assimilated into the memory and preconceptions of worshipers and enters the tradition through the history of its effects on the horizons of the listeners.⁴⁸ The faith, worship, memory, and ministry of Christian communities dating back to the early church is reactivated in the proclamation, with each liturgical event contributing to the ongoing creation of tradition.

In the same way that individuals form memories as members of a social group, so too worshipers in the liturgy are not present as isolated individuals but as part of the corporate ecclesial body that is participating together in the same experience. While memories formed by worshipers are

---

45. West, *Scripture and Memory*, 37.
46. Ritivoi, "Hermeneutics as Project," 70.
47. Bell, *Ritual*, 151–52.
48. Tracy, *Analogical Imagination*, 103–15.

innately private, the liturgical event is experienced from multiple perspectives and consequently the memories of it do not belong only to an individual.[49] Memories formed in this corporate event are undeniably socially constructed, and the ecclesial community forms a shared identity reflective of the collective memories chosen for the Lectionary and the ritual way in which these memories are shared in the liturgical proclamation.

The use of the Lectionary has made the communal memory more resistant to decay or modification over time. The sacred text as proclaimed by a human voice in a present-day liturgical event actualizes the tradition and connects a potentially infinite number of reception contexts allowing the tradition to be passed down through time and space. The Lectionary pericopes, therefore, function as connective threads that provide continuity to the ecclesial tradition.

Horizon of Expectations

The Lectionary texts, in their particular arrangement, have been experienced by generations of worshipers and have become incorporated into the church's corporate memory to form a particular "horizon of expectations."[50] Despite this ancient tradition, it is noteworthy that worshipers have heard the readings proclaimed in their vernacular language only since the Second Vatican Council. Prior to this, when readings were read by the priest in Latin during the liturgy, the corporate memory of the church with regards to the use of Lectionary texts in the liturgy was being established quite independently of any personal understanding on the part of worshipers. In more recent generations, as the Lectionary's three-year cycle of readings has been heard repeatedly in the vernacular and been the subject of interpretation by worshipers in the liturgy, this horizon of expectations is now more clearly perceived by those who participate in liturgical celebrations. An abundant offering of written commentaries on the readings are readily accessible and have played their part in illuminating the various meanings that have been attributed to the pericopes over the church's history.

Members of contemporary worshiping assemblies are able to compare their current perspectives not only with the horizon of the Lectionary text but with successive horizons in which the meaning of that pericope has evolved throughout the stream of tradition. Individual worshipers present at the liturgical event are recognized as historical beings, who bring their knowledge and experience to the encounter with the Lectionary pericopes

49. Cockayne and Salter, "Feasts of Memory," 289.
50. Jauss, "Literary History," 37.

and make sense of these texts in light of how they have been shaped by their secular, cultural, linguistic, and religious traditions.

It has been noted previously that Gadamer does not see prejudices as tyrannical by nature, but indeed as a necessary condition for understanding. Gadamer argues that prejudice stemming from one's tradition is not only inescapable but indeed formative, and that understanding commences with a provisional meaning projected from one's relationship with the tradition in which they stand:[51]

> Hermeneutics must start from the position that a person seeking to understand something has a bond to the subject matter that comes into language through the traditionary text and has, or acquires, a connection with the tradition from which the text speaks.[52]

Encounters with Scripture texts and images are often indirect in the liturgy by way of music, artwork, prayers, and the homily, and these also enter deeply into corporate memory and form predispositions. These memories influence, to some degree, what a worshiper will perceive in the scriptural proclamation and function as criteria for the appropriateness of an interpretation. The faith, intention, and preconceptions of worshipers emerge as vital components of engaging with their tradition and thereby coming to a clearer understanding of the Scriptures in the liturgy.

The Sensory Nature of Memory and Liturgy

Ancient and medieval descriptions of the neuropsychology of memory and recollection provide interesting insights into the role of memory in Scripture interpretation in the liturgy. Fundamental themes emerge in the writings of Aristotle (384 BCE–322 BCE) and subsequent philosophers regarding somatic-aesthetic features, the role of images, and the importance of place.[53] The reliving of a past experience was recognized as involving contemplation, discernment, imagination, and emotion. Indeed, the relationship of the medieval reader to their texts consisted of ruminating on or digesting the texts, turning over the words so that they formed part of memory. The re-experiencing of a text, in retrieving it from memory, involved a process not of interpreting the text, but of re-authoring it.[54] Aristotle held that

---

51. Culpepper, "Value of Hans-Georg," 100.
52. TM 306.
53. Carruthers, *Book of Memory*, 56–57.
54. Carruthers, *Book of Memory*, 205–10.

memories are presently existing images of things or events that are past, and are a way to make the past perception present.[55] He also spoke of a "deliberative" imagination in which the human mind joins several memory images together into a unified image which constitutes a new composition.[56] This has implications for the ways in which the Lectionary arrangement of readings for a particular day binds previously unrelated pericopes together in people's minds to form new memory-images.

The key characteristic of a memory-image is that it is inherently affective—it is derived through the senses and imbued with emotion.[57] Successful memories do not take the form of algorithms or abstractions but are tagged according to both emotional and schematic features. Every memory is infused with sensory and affective qualities and can never be neutral or merely factual.[58] Religious rituals have also been shown to have the capacity to "trigger emotionally-charged remembering."[59] It follows from this reasoning that a scriptural pericope proclaimed in the liturgy is stored in a worshiper's memory according to how it affected that person at the time, incorporating emotional connotations such as peace, fear, joy, or discomfort. These not only affect current interpretations of pericopes but also influence subsequent recollections of that Scripture text. Where affective qualities are socially pervasive, such as those induced by natural disasters or pandemics, the corporate memory is unavoidably influenced. Furthermore, as demonstrated by Swedish researchers, Willander and Larsson, memories which incorporate the sense of smell and taste produce stronger and more vivid experiences of past events and are "associated with a higher emotional arousal that could not be accounted for by the perceptual stimulation alone."[60] The entire process of experiencing an event through the sensory organs, responding to it, and forming a memory of that event, becomes not only a cognitive but also a physiological process.[61] Clearly, the multisensory features of the liturgical event influence not only the present interpretation

55. Aristotle, *De Sensu*, 101–3.

56. Aristotle, "De Anima," 434a.

57. Carruthers, *Book of Memory*, 75.

58. Aristotle emphasizes the emotional aspect of memory in *De Memoria* 453a. His description is similar to the modern neuropsychological notion of episodic memory as distinct from semantic memory, a separation not recognized in medieval times. Aristotle, *De Sensu*, 117.

59. Cockayne and Salter, "Feasts of Memory," 286.

60. Willander and Larsson, "Olfaction and Emotion," 1662.

61. Thomas Best conceives of memory as a "sensory organ" which relates people to their own experience and brings past events into the present. Best, *Memory and Meaning*, 61.

of Scripture readings, but also the storage and subsequent retrieval of memories of Lectionary passages.

Liturgical Time

For corporate memory to be retained, both repetition and significance are required. Yet, the contemporary assembly does not assimilate the Lectionary texts through repeatedly experiencing the texts as they were in the past, but rather through encountering them in the present. American Catholic priest and professor of historical and liturgical theology, John Baldovin, has noted that

> in liturgy it is the repetition of the pattern, a ritualized form, that molds people's lives as a community of faith. This is precisely what happens with the reading or proclamation of Scripture. We do not read Scripture to find out about what we don't know or have forgotten but rather to let the pattern of the biblical story continue to form us.[62]

It is important for worshipers to be familiar with the concept of liturgical time, the "*hodie*" of the liturgy. Theologically, the liturgy rests on the premise that Christ is speaking to his people "today," that the saving action of Christ is made present "today" in the midst of the assembly. This feature of liturgical time is expressed in the Entrance Antiphon of Christmas Dawn: "Today a light will shine upon us, for the Lord is born for us."[63] Another example occurs in the Preface of Epiphany: "Today you have revealed the mystery of our salvation in Christ as a light for the nations."[64] Memory therefore in the context of the scriptural proclamation in the liturgy is not a question of connecting worshipers with past events, but rather with challenging them to draw meaning from and live out the truth of that which is actualized presently in their midst.

Ritual

The Catholic liturgical event not only preserves and embodies collective memory through linguistic transmission, but also through the postures, gestures, and ritual actions that surround the proclamation. Such bodily practices have been recognized as essential in the transmission of the

---

62. Baldovin, "Bible and Liturgy," 3.
63. RM 196.
64. RM 578.

collective memory of a group.⁶⁵ Fritz West argues that the actions, acclamations, processions, postures, and songs of the liturgy are the "containers of communal memory" through which the Scriptures are safeguarded and passed on to successive generations. He claims that "ritual carries Scripture and memory interprets it."⁶⁶ In identifying liturgy as the memory of the Catholic community *par excellence*, it must be emphasized that liturgy is always a concrete and unique event which occurs in a particular time and place; liturgy is not an abstract construct. Remembrance in the case of the liturgical proclamation is participating with the mind, body, and senses in the process of actualizing the ancient texts of Scripture in the present.

Tradition takes place each time a member of the assembly walks towards the ambo, opens the Lectionary, and transforms the written text into living word.⁶⁷ Tradition is also created when the contemporary application of the word is illustrated in the homily, furthering the ongoing process of Scripture interpretation that began in the early church. The homilist can facilitate the "memory" of worshipers by illuminating the range of ecclesial and individual circumstances in which a text has found application throughout an evolving cultural tradition.⁶⁸ Memory for the Lectionary pericopes is also promoted when biblical fragments are reflected in liturgical hymns, prayers, or responses, promoting a worshiper's assimilation of the texts. This dynamic process of tradition continues beyond the liturgy as the assembly disperses to put the word into practice in their daily lives.

V. TRADITION AND AUTHORITY— CATHOLIC THEOLOGICAL PARADIGM

The Second Vatican Council significantly renewed official Catholic teaching on Scripture and tradition, naming these as the two sources of divine revelation, each having God as their ultimate source. In *Dei Verbum*, the Council declared:

> Sacred tradition and sacred Scripture, then, are bound closely together, and communicate one with the other. Flowing from the same divine well-spring, both of them merge, in a sense, and move towards the same goal . . . Hence both Scripture and

---

65. Connerton, *How Societies Remember*, 72–104.
66. West, *Scripture and Memory*, 37.
67. De Clerck, "In the Beginning," 10–11.
68. Dingemans, *Als Hoorder*, 50; Immink, "Homiletics," 90.

> tradition must be accepted and honored with equal devotion and reverence.[69]

Tradition is presented not as a secure deposit of the Gospel message to be safeguarded by the magisterium but rather as a dynamic entity in which the laity make an ecclesial and spiritual contribution through reflection and worship.[70] This is consistent with Gadamer's conviction that "even the most genuine and pure tradition does not persist because of the inertia of what once existed. It needs to be affirmed embraced, cultivated."[71] The Council supported and promoted the work of exegetes in illuminating the meaning of Scripture to "help the church's judgment to mature."[72] The development of tradition over time is not only a function of its treatment by the magisterium, or the scholarly analyses arrived at by exegetes, but rather is also achieved

> through the contemplation and study of believers who ponder these things in their hearts . . . It comes from the intimate sense of spiritual realities which they experience.[73]

The Council clearly valued not only the preservation of truth claims handed down through apostolic succession and divine revelation but also the provision of avenues for continued inquiry, both personal and communal, in the face of new experiences. This ongoing interpretation of Scripture and tradition, according to Catholic Church teaching, is inspired by the Holy Spirit.

Holy Spirit

Standing alongside contemporary theories of memory and tradition, paragraph twelve of *Dei Verbum* attributes the transmission of tradition and the continuity of memory to the ongoing dynamic activity of the Holy Spirit in contemporary ecclesial communities. The hermeneutical approach advocated in *Dei Verbum* views the Holy Spirit as the pivotal link between past understandings of Scripture texts and their modern interpretation, and maintains a view of tradition "that respects both reason and faith, that is both rational and pneumatological."[74]

69. DV 9.
70. DV 10.
71. TM 293.
72. DV 12.
73. DV 8.
74. O'Collins, "Dei Verbum."

The Holy Spirit has always been present, inspiring the original writing of the Scripture texts and continuing to guide interpretation of the Scriptures in every generation. Using the language of memory, the Holy See has declared:

> The liturgy is the "memorial of the mystery of salvation" while the Holy Spirit is the "Church's living memory" because of its recalling of the mystery of Christ. The first way by which the Holy Spirit recalls the meaning of the event of salvation is by germinating life from the Word of God proclaimed liturgically so that it can become a scheme of life for those who hear it. Liturgical proclamation calls for a "response of faith" indicative both of "consent and commitment" and built up by the Holy Spirit who instils into the members of the assembly "a remembrance of the marvelous works of God" in a developing anamnesis.[75]

The creative work of the Holy Spirit in contemporary times can inspire new insights, but fresh perception of meaning always stands in continuity with previous interpretations that were also guided by the same Spirit.[76] The implication for Scripture interpretation in the liturgy is that three aspects of the Holy Spirit's work must be held in balance: the inspiration of the original Scripture text (Lectionary), the activity of the Holy Spirit throughout history (Tradition), and the current activity of the Holy Spirit in the contemporary church (Community).[77]

People of God

Another pivotal document of the Second Vatican Council, *Lumen Gentium*, describes the Christian Church as the "People of God," as a sacrament of communion by which unity is achieved with God and among its members.[78] Further, it is through the eucharistic event, the source and summit of the Christian life, that the unity of believers is most clearly expressed and actualized.[79] This mindset of being present as part of the unified People of God situates worshipers within the Christian tradition and elevates to consciousness the role of corporate memory in the interpretation of the scriptural proclamation. Each individual worshiper is thus compelled to arrive at

---

75. Office for the Liturgical Celebrations for the Supreme Pontiff, "Liturgy, Work of Trinity."
76. O'Collins, "Dei Verbum."
77. Wright, "How Can the Bible?," 26.
78. Vatican Council II, "Dogmatic Constitution, *Lumen Gentium*," 1 (hereafter LG).
79. LG 3, 7, 11; SC 10.

a responsible interpretation through their participation in the authority of the ecclesial community.

Connecting Memory and Tradition

While the documents of Vatican II did not make a direct connection between memory and tradition, an important work emerged during that time written by French Dominican priest and theologian, Yves Congar, claiming that "tradition *is* memory and memory enriches experience."[80] Further reading of Congar's work reveals his view that tradition is not only memory, but also actual presence and creative experience. Tradition can be viewed as a deeply dynamic process of passing on not only Scripture texts and their interpretations but handing on the life of the ecclesial community which flows from the sacred texts.[81]

Furthermore, in exploring the impact of tradition, with particular reference to the liturgy, Congar pointed out that "the Church not only possesses self-awareness; she keeps and actualizes the living memory of what she has received."[82] While he acknowledges unequivocally that what flows through the channel of transmission has Christ and the Gospel as its unique source, Congar concludes that the active reality of the text, expressed in the liturgy and incorporated into the lives of its members through the action of the Holy Spirit, means that tradition is creative development as much as it is memory.[83]

Twenty years after the Council, Canadian theologian, Jean-Marie Tillard, referred to tradition as a "function of remembrance" and, in his writings on ecclesiology, included a section on the "memory of the church."[84] Referring to the scriptural proclamation in the liturgical event, Tillard proposed that "as the memory of the Church, tradition represents the permanence of a Word which is always alive, always enriched, and yet radically always the same, where the Church never ceases to nourish its faith."[85]

The eucharistic liturgy carries the "memory of the church" in a particular way, as an ongoing response to the command of Christ: "Do this in remembrance of me" (Luke 22:19–20). The Mass thereby constitutes an event of *anamnesis*, a word often translated as "remembrance" or "memorial."

---

80. Congar, *Tradition and Life*, 8.
81. Congar, *Tradition and Life*, 26–28.
82. Congar, *Tradition and Life*, 8.
83. Congar, *Tradition and Life*, 72.
84. Tillard, *Church of Churches*, 140–44.
85. Tillard, *Church of Churches*, 141–42.

These translations are less than satisfactory in the sense that they denote "something absent which is only mentally recollected."[86] However, the notion of *anamnesis*, both in Christian theology and in the New Testament, is imbued with a sense of "'recalling' or 're-presenting' before God an event in the past so that it becomes here and now operative by its effects."[87] The proclamation of the Lectionary texts constitutes a pivotal part of the ongoing play of the eucharistic rite; it does not simply call past happenings to mind, but makes these paradigmatic and primordial events effective in the present life of the church. As the Scriptures are proclaimed in the liturgy, the contemporary worshiping community experiences past events anew, engages in a communal act of memory (*anamnesis*) and thereby preserves its tradition.[88]

VI. RECEPTION OF TRADITION

Through the ages, successive receptions of biblical pericopes have produced interpretive trajectories resulting in standards of appropriateness which guard the fundamental truths of the Scripture texts. The reception history of a Scripture text can therefore operate as a hermeneutical bridge between the ancient text and the contemporary understanding of it. Classic interpretations have become part of the text's history of influence and form part of the horizon of expectations for future listeners. Indeed, when assigning pericopes to liturgical days, the Lectionary compilers considered how these texts had been used throughout history and acknowledged the new layers of meaning which had already taken shape in corporate memory.

Exponents of reception theory would argue that in addition to the dialogue typically associated with interpretation, namely that between the text and the interpreter, the dialogue should be expanded to include the tradition of the text's interpretation and application. The effective history of a scriptural pericope includes literary, musical, political, and economic applications of the text, as well as the appropriation of Scripture in the lives of Christians.[89] The place of reception history in arriving at an interpretation of a text according to Gadamer's hermeneutical position can be summarized as follows:

---

86. Dix, *Shape of Liturgy*, 161.
87. Dix, *Shape of Liturgy*, 161.
88. Irwin, *Context and Text*, 171; Douglas, "Anglican-Roman Catholic," 351–67.
89. Evans, *Reception History*, 126.

> One's interpretation of a particular subject matter stands in traditions of previous interpretations of the same subject. The totality of such "effects" and ultimately the whole historical process linking subject and object constitute the hermeneutical situation of the knower. Effective history is the chain of past interpretations through which the preunderstanding of the interpreter is already linked with his object.[90]

The corpus of Catholic tradition and reception history continually incorporates reinterpretations emerging from present contexts, but these new insights take their place within the existing stream of tradition. Engaging with the heritage of Scripture interpretation provides an interpreter with insights into how they have been shaped by tradition and how their active participation contributes to the continuing development of the living tradition. Only in this way does the worshiper become aware of their situatedness in the stream of tradition and employ the reception history of the text as a standard for verifying their present interpretation. The aim is not simply to collect past interpretations of Lectionary pericopes and seal them for later reference, but rather to engage the tradition of Scripture interpretation in an open dialogue such that one's own understanding of a passage might be expanded, corrected, affirmed, or modified.[91] Indeed, it has been suggested that individuals belonging to a tradition have a "responsibility" to enter into that creative dialogue through which the tradition can be preserved, altered, and passed on.[92]

In considering the tradition of the text's application, the worshiper is able to measure their interpretation of a Lectionary pericope against the broader community perspective and that of the Christian tradition, thus activating their historically effected consciousness—the consciousness that they are "standing within a still operant history"[93] and that there is still something to learn from tradition. In contrast to the view that the effective history of a Scripture text is predominantly determined by authoritative voices of the Christian tradition, this position makes it clear that the historical effect of a scriptural pericope is more evident when observing its impact in the lives of worshipers.[94]

---

90. Mendelson, "Habermas-Gadamer Debate," 55.
91. Parris, *Reading the Bible*, 89.
92. Mitscherling, "Resuming the Dialogue," 132.
93. Hoy, *Critical Circle*, 63.
94. Bockmuehl, "Commentator's Approach," 62.

Limitations in Engaging the Tradition During the Scriptural Proclamation

While there are indisputable benefits of engaging with the heritage of Scripture interpretation, it must be acknowledged that worshipers typically have a very limited knowledge of the history of interpretation of a Lectionary reading they hear proclaimed in the liturgy. Furthermore, worshipers cannot draw on ancient sources or consult scholarly commentaries as they listen to a fleeting proclamation in the liturgy. This highlights the pivotal role of the homilist in making worshipers aware of the diverse ways in which pericopes have been interpreted and applied throughout history. By expounding the tradition of biblical interpretation and illuminating the reception history of a pericope, the homilist assists the worshiping assembly to arrive at criteria for judging whether or not an interpretation is appropriate.[95] The role of the preacher is thus to connect worshipers to the tradition of a pericope's interpretation and application by introducing perspectives from sermons, commentaries, treatises, and spiritual writings which can be incorporated into each worshiper's horizon.

VII. "BELONGING TO" AND "PARTICIPATING IN" TRADITION

In examining Gadamer's position that people both "belong to" and "participate in" tradition, it is instructive to examine the German word *gehören* (to belong to). The root of this verb, *hören*, means "to hear." This semantic range facilitated Gadamer's argument that people not only belong to a tradition (*gehören*) but must also listen (*hören*) through a process of active dialogue, in order to achieve insights beyond their own horizon and experience the truth claims of the text.[96] This continual conversation or task is expressed as the active German verb, *Überlieferung*, which translates into English rather unsatisfactorily as "tradition." It is important, therefore, to keep in mind that Gadamer's notion of tradition imports an expectation of active questioning, and an effort-filled endeavor to overcome one's limited horizon of understanding.

What results from an experience of understanding is not the original meaning of the text, but a new creation—a reconstruction which takes place within the interpreter's horizon, influenced by their culture and the history of the text's tradition. To have had an "experience," according to Gadamer,

---

95. Parris, *Reading the Bible*, 95.
96. TM xv.

a person must confront a sense of negation or provocation, for it is only through the non-fulfillment of one's expected meanings that new insights and understandings are acquired. This confrontation of new perspectives is necessary in order to illuminate what is not known, and to prompt a process of questioning thus leading to the growth and development (*Bildung*) of individuals and communities.[97] Because understanding emerges in the mediation between the horizon of the text and the horizon of the interpreter, it is necessarily a productive activity rather than simply a reproductive one. In the Catholic tradition, as in any tradition, the fusion of horizons is a continuous process as "old and new are always combining into something of living value, without either being explicitly foregrounded from the other."[98]

Might it be possible, however, for a person to understand a text from a tradition in which they do not participate? Since a person can become conscious of the prejudices that govern their own understanding, it is arguably possible for a scholar to arrive at an understanding of a Lectionary text without possessing the Christian faith, for example. Yet this may be a very different interpretation of meaning than that perceived by a worshiper who participates with faith in the liturgy, with the mindset of the People of God, and who experiences the text as addressed to them in an encounter with Christ. The Lectionary texts can be seen to constitute a specific case whereby understanding the text adequately "presupposes a relationship to what it says."[99] Indeed, Gadamer presumes that only those who allow themselves to be addressed by the tradition—whether they believe or doubt—will understand.[100] This reflects what Jauss would call the "social function" of the Scripture texts, in which the literary experience of the worshiper enters into their lived practice, influences their understanding of the world, and impacts their social behavior.[101]

Balancing Continuity and Contingency

Gadamer claims that the historical, cultural, and religious traditions to which a person belongs, form the basis for their presumptions about the world and their anticipation of meaning. At the same time, Gadamer highlights the importance of experience that introduces an element of surprise and undermines expectations, causing an interpreter to reassess the possibilities of

97. TM 309–10, 362, 370, 375.
98. TM 317.
99. Evans, *Reception History*, 248.
100. TM 341.
101. Jauss, *Towards an Aesthetic*, 39.

a situation. American political scientist and philosopher, Georgia Warnke, claims that these features of Gadamer's hermeneutics appear to move in opposite directions. She questions how people can belong to traditions and be oriented to the world through them, yet simultaneously experience those same traditions in ways which challenge and surprise.[102] She refers to a "peculiar oscillation" in Gadamer's hermeneutic position, claiming that he attempts to simultaneously avoid the subjectivism of interpretation according to current circumstances and the conservatism of conforming to tradition; in other words, she questions the ability to affirm both the continuity in the tradition and the historical contingency of an interpretation which leaves the tradition open to critique.[103]

Warnke also challenges Gadamer's claim that the interpreter experiences a transformation when encountering a text or artwork from their tradition. Warnke suggests that the closeness of the interpreter to that element of their tradition may preclude such transformations or alternatively place the bond of their belonging together at risk.[104] If it is the tendency of believers to assume the truth of the Lectionary texts which have been handed down through tradition, the question naturally arises, "How can we ever learn to reject the truth we have assumed?"[105]

It is acknowledged that Catholics present at the liturgical event "agree" with the message proclaimed in the Lectionary pericopes to the extent that worshipers are part of the tradition, and the tradition is part of them. Yet, this is counterbalanced by the range of other traditions to which contemporary Catholics belong, and by the role of genuine dialogue in the liturgy where various perspectives are engaged dialectically. New insights and meanings inherent in the Lectionary pericopes emerge as worshipers engage with the tradition and apply the text to their present reality. In this way, the tradition continues to evolve.

In developing a liturgical hermeneutic of Scripture, it is presumed that people can both belong to tradition *and* experience it. Looking to the tradition and becoming immersed in the Lectionary texts within the liturgy

> can remind us of the commitments we share with it . . . can help us correct practices that fail to accord with these commitments . . . can lend a perspective on our current practices and aspirations.[106]

102. Warnke, "Experiencing Tradition," 347.
103. Warnke, *Gadamer*, 99.
104. Warnke, "Experiencing Tradition," 355–56.
105. Warnke, *Gadamer*, 106.
106. Warnke, "Experiencing Tradition," 369.

A worshiper can be close enough to the tradition that their predispositions are guided by that tradition and simultaneously distant enough that its truth claims can be experienced, leading to a new perspective through a fusion of horizons. The dialogue with the Christian scriptural and ritual tradition can lead worshipers to reconsider their assumptions, or to realize that they had previously failed to appreciate the truth claims embodied in the sacred text, such that new bonds are created.

In the liturgy, worshipers gather with the expectation that the truth claims expressed in the scriptural proclamation will be intelligible in their current reality. They come not to blindly preserve an ancient text, but with openness to have their views challenged, and their assumptions about themselves and their tradition disclosed. Their assembling as the ecclesial community of the People of God with an awareness of their tradition in no way precludes their openness to be surprised or confronted by the current proclamation of the Lectionary readings.

Nonetheless, Warnke's observations point to the complexities of balancing the continuity of interpretive tradition with the contingencies of reception in a particular era. Any tendency to consider reception history or tradition as the measure of interpretation is balanced by the dialogical interplay between interpreter and tradition, whereby through a fusion of horizons, a new consensus of meaning emerges.[107] The potential exists for a transformation of each initial horizon and a new addition to the tradition of interpretation.

VIII. THE PLACE OF TRADITION IN A LITURGICAL HERMENEUTIC OF SCRIPTURE

Since tradition is experienced as a dialogue partner, and meaning is said to emerge from the shared conversational experience, it is instructive to reiterate which parties are involved in the hermeneutical conversation when Scripture is proclaimed in the liturgy. The model presented at the beginning of this book proposes that four conversational entities, represented by their four respective horizons, are present in the liturgy: the Bible text, the Lectionary text, the worshiper, and the homilist.

The aim of the dialectical process which takes place in the scriptural proclamation is to prompt a fusion of the four horizons such that truth, or meaning, emerges for contemporary worshipers. Experience acquired through active questioning does not result in absolute knowledge but fosters

---

107. TM 316-17.

ongoing openness to the truth claims of the Scripture texts and promotes an infinite dialogue between worshipers and their tradition.

As the temporal distance between the original text and the contemporary interpreter widens with successive generations of interpreters, there is a danger that tradition may have a homogenizing effect on the text, such that "the original negativity of the work has become self-evident and has itself entered into the horizon of future aesthetic experience, as a henceforth familiar expectation."[108] The Lectionary texts must continue to be experienced by successive generations in a way that safeguards their "sacredness" or "otherness" such that the continued reception of these pericopes does not diminish their provocative power. The ritual surrounding the proclamation in the Catholic liturgical event has an important role in highlighting the ancient origin of the texts and promoting the active engagement of worshipers so that they might perceive a text's relevance for their own lives. Modern Catholics may fail to perceive the relevance of the Scriptures if they read the texts privately, separated from the ecclesial community with whom they form the People of God, unassisted by the contemporary perspective of the homilist, and in the absence of the multisensory liturgical experience whereby Scripture is illuminated through prayer, song, and ritual. Without the contextual influence of liturgy and ecclesial community, the transmission of the scriptural tradition may be in jeopardy.

SUMMARY

Memory is, without exception, an activity in the present; it takes on different forms as each liturgical celebration comprises a new act of remembering and contributes to the dynamic stream of tradition.[109] In the liturgy, worshipers participate as members of the ecclesial community in the event of liturgical proclamation in the present, conscious that the word is held in readiness for the future, while drawing on the tradition of the continuous past.[110] The protective function of tradition conserves the corporate memory so that it can be applied to new situations over time in response to ever-evolving historical circumstances. Historical distance is not an empty void between modern interpreters and the text, but is imbued with the continuity of

---

108. Jauss, "Literary History," 15. For example, the parable of "The Good Samaritan" fails to shock modern readers in the same way as it did its original audience; indeed, with the passage of time, the word "Samaritan" has acquired a connotation of one involved in good works.

109. O'Loughlin, "Sharing the Living Word," 12.

110. Gadamer, "Aesthetics," 131.

tradition, memory, and ritual, which influence the thoughts and understandings of contemporary worshipers. It is essential that tradition remain connected to its roots as it inevitably extends and develops.

Any tendency towards using tradition as the sole measure of interpretation is balanced by the dialogical interplay between interpreter and tradition whereby, through a fusion of horizons, a new consensus of meaning emerges, and a new addition is made to the tradition of interpretation. The meaning of any text for Gadamer is "always co-determined also by the historical situation of the interpreter."[111] Thus, there is a balance to be struck in avoiding the opposing dangers of either dwelling in the past or advancing too independently with disregard for earlier positions. Indeed, tradition is "equally continuity and progress, conservation and development."[112]

Tradition is in a state of dynamic adaptation as it incorporates new communal experiences into the existing corpus of corporate memory. The interpretation of a scriptural pericope can be conceived, therefore, as a gradual unfolding of meaning during the progressive trajectory of its reception, in which the horizon of expectations for a particular text is expanded with each new act of understanding.[113] The ongoing re-interpretation of the Lectionary pericopes and the application of these interpreted meanings in the liturgical life of the Catholic Church, constitute the continuity of the tradition.

---

111. TM 307.
112. Congar, *Tradition and Life*, 94.
113. Jauss, *Towards an Aesthetic*, 59.

CHAPTER 8

Liturgical Proclamation as Social Event and Personal Encounter

As participants in a dynamic tradition, worshipers in the Catholic liturgical event engage personally with the Scripture texts they hear proclaimed, yet they do so within a corporate ritual structure and in the social context of the ecclesial community. While a sense of personal autonomy is exercised in choosing to enter into the worship event and participate actively, and while a deeply personal encounter may be experienced by each worshiper, the interpretation of Scripture in the liturgy ought not be viewed as an individualistic enterprise. Indeed, there is a sense of interconnectedness between worshipers such that they become socially embedded in the liturgical event and experience the scriptural proclamation within an embodied and interpersonal paradigm. Although personal autonomy and relational autonomy can seem to be a "philosophical dichotomy," it is proposed in this chapter that both are essential when considering how Scripture texts are interpreted in the liturgical event. There is reciprocity between the individual worshiper and the assembly during the liturgy such that each person individually, as well as the assembly collectively, is an active subject in a dynamic social event.

I. PERSONAL ENCOUNTER AND RELATIONAL SELF

Personal Encounter and the Effectiveness of the Word

The early church, as reflected in the Scriptures, resisted notions of individualism, detachment, and separation; instead covenant language was adopted with promises of salvation for a group of people rather than a select number of individuals.¹ Decisions and actions were evaluated from a community perspective, and punishment for disobedience or sin involved exclusion from the worship assembly or exile from the community.²

Yet, in modern society, individualism is the dominant cultural pattern with personal autonomy and independence being highly prized. British-based anthropologist, liturgist, and theologian, Martin Stringer, suggests that before worshipers hear the stories of Scripture, they bring to the liturgical event a collection of their own life stories which may be conscious to varying degrees. He draws upon Gadamer's fusion of horizons in arguing that the emotional content of a proclaimed pericope merges with the emotional content of an individual's story in order to produce a third story within the liturgical event.³ The worshiper is viewed as a collaborator in the effectiveness of the word with a responsibility to co-operate in God's action. Meaning is constructed not simply by decoding the words or symbols of the liturgical proclamation; rather, worshipers make meaning by "engaging intuitively with the experience."⁴

While the Catholic Church teaches that the proclamation of God's word is effective and efficacious in itself,⁵ and that liturgical celebration prompts the transformative power of that word within the individual and the community,⁶ it is nonetheless true that worshipers often experience the *in*effectiveness of the word. Despite strong personal commitment and valiant intention, the proclamation of the word may fail to produce transformation or growth in individuals or in the community. Such failure may sometimes be attributed in part to the manner in which liturgical ministers carry out their function, to music which is poorly chosen or executed, to ineffectual preaching, or to inadequate liturgical space. Yet these are not the only factors.

Italian psychotherapist and presbyter, Giuseppe Sovernigo, claims that in determining the effectiveness or otherwise of the scriptural proclamation, personal psychological factors play a pivotal role in the communal context

---

1. Hebrew Scriptures: "At that time, says the Lord, I will be the God of all the families of Israel, and they shall be my people" (Jer 31:1).
Christian Scriptures: "But you are a chosen people, a royal priesthood, a holy nation, God's own people, in order that you may proclaim the excellence of him who called you out of darkness into his marvelous light" (1 Pet 2:9).

2. Konigsburg, "Worship as Compatible," 135.

3. Stringer, "Gadamer," 11; Gaarden, *Third Room of Preaching*, 107–30.

4. Stringer, "Gadamer," 15.

5. Isa 55:9–11; Heb 4:12–13; Synod of Bishops, "Word of God," 23.

6. Benedict XVI, *Verbum Domini*, 52–59 (hereafter VD).

of worship.⁷ He argues that the content of the message, the modality in which it is delivered, and the psychological motivations of the person listening work together to facilitate understanding when they are in harmony, but inhibit the derivation of meaning when they conflict.⁸ In line with Gadamer's concepts of fore-understandings and effective history, the argument follows that the starting point for understanding is not the act of listening or the participation in the celebration *per se*, but rather the lived experience of faith. Sovernigo identifies four listening perspectives as being present and interconnected within each person, yet claims that one will emerge as most dominant, and will significantly influence that person's interpretation of the Scripture in a particular liturgical event.⁹

1. A person may listen from the *emotional and aesthetic sensitivity* of their lived experience which determines their tendency towards positivity, pleasure, vulnerability, fear, or inhibition. Listening from this perspective tends to produce spontaneous, superficial impressions with only transitory effects.

2. A person may listen from a place of *intellectual familiarity*, having already heard and learned the texts previously. This may result in an apathetic sense of not needing to listen, preventing the text from penetrating into the realm of decision-making.¹⁰

3. A person may listen according to their *immediate life circumstances*, with the expectation that the text will have something to say with respect to their current concerns. This results in a selective, functional listening, where certain aspects of the text are favored and others ignored or rejected, based on personal needs.

4. Finally, a person may listen from a place of *authentic self-identity*, conscious of their gifts and limitations, informed but unimpeded by previous emotional, intellectual, or experiential influences. There is a peaceful sense of closeness to God and detachment from distractions. This results in open, transformative listening which prompts thoughtful decision-making and gives energy for new directions.

The prevalence of one listening perspective over another is a function of the intrapersonal dynamics operating in a person as an individual and as a

7. Sovernigo, "L'efficacia della Parola," 295.
8. Sovernigo, "L'efficacia della Parola," 296.
9. Sovernigo, "L'efficacia della Parola," 299.
10. One who is intellectually familiar with the text may listen with the expectation that the word will speak in a new way, yet Sovernigo warns that where this perspective is dominant, the tendency is towards a comfortable sense of apathy.

member of a community and cannot be explained by the words proclaimed or the liturgical context alone.[11] The motivations and modalities of listening are as central as the content of the scriptural pericopes when considering the process by which an individual makes meaning in the proclamation.[12]

It is noteworthy that "understanding" in a liturgical hermeneutic of Scripture suggests more than an intellectual or cerebral process. Gadamer's notion of prejudices, when applied in this context, includes expectations of what the liturgical event will involve, who else might be present, how affirming or confronting the readings might be, and how engaging and relevant to daily life the homily might be.

Of course, this is not to suggest that worship exists primarily to satisfy individual psychological needs. Nor does it imply that the work of effective listening resides only with individual worshipers. Indeed, Catholic Church teaching provides that it is the Holy Spirit who summons each person to a place of deep listening and makes possible a personal transformation in accordance with the Scripture text.[13] However, each person listens from the place of their predominant intrapersonal dynamic and this has an undeniable impact on the effectiveness of the words proclaimed.[14]

In some instances, there may be little or no engagement at all, and at other times a profound encounter may be experienced. Any attempts to predict the catalyst for engagement in advance are naturally futile, since there is a complex interrelationship between what the worshiper brings into a particular liturgical event, and what happens during the liturgy. A spark of meaning may stem from a Scripture passage itself, from the homily, or from a prayer later in the liturgy that illuminates the Scripture text in a new way. It may be a liturgical action, symbol, or sensory experience that calls forth meaning from the proclamation for a particular worshiper. That moment of challenge, according to Stringer, activates the presuppositions of the individual and prompts more than "simply" understanding; rather, it results in personal growth or expansion of that person's horizon.[15] This encounter may be experienced as an intellectual awakening, or felt in a dimension that cannot be adequately expressed with words.

Repeated dynamic interactions between the Scripture texts proclaimed in the liturgy and the experiential history of the worshiper result in the continued growth of the individual and the ongoing derivation of both

---

11. Wikström, "Liturgy as Experience," 86–89.
12. Godin, *Psicologia*, 182–88.
13. VD 52.
14. Aždajić, "Externalizing Faith," 98.
15. Stringer, "Gadamer and Hermeneutics," 13.

intellectual and emotional meaning for each worshiper.[16] Sitting alongside a theological perspective of what is happening in the liturgical proclamation, it can be proposed that an individual's openness to have their horizon expanded can lead them to experience an encounter with the divine that may produce a sphere of meaning that transcends words.[17]

Personal and Relational Autonomy

Despite the overwhelming cultural and societal trend towards individualism, there is a pervasive tension between the desire for independence and the yearning for relational connection with other people.[18] It is particularly important in the context of the liturgical event to conceive of an autonomous self which acknowledges the basically relational nature of a person's motivations, the embeddedness of their self-concept, and the fundamentally social nature of being.[19] The notion of "relational autonomy" is a helpful construct when envisaging the worshiper participating in the liturgy, as it encapsulates what it means to be "a free, self-governing agent who is also socially constituted and who possibly defines her basic value commitments in terms of inter-personal relations and mutual dependencies."[20] The fundamental principles of liturgical ministry reflect the notion of relational autonomy; an individual should do *some*thing but not *every*thing to ensure that they do not prevent themselves or others from participating. It is a matter of personal autonomy to select which gifts to share with the community, yet relational autonomy would restrict a person's choice to "contributions that enhance rather than detract from worship."[21]

Of course, the decision to enter into worship is a personal one, as is the choice to participate actively and engage with the Scripture readings within the broader ritual context of the Mass. Yet the corporate nature of liturgy imports a sense of relationality, where interconnected associations with others in the shared activity of worship influence perceptions, judgements, and the meaning attributed to Scripture texts.[22] Each individual contributes to the community and, in so doing, enters into relationship with

---

16. Stringer, "Gadamer and Hermeneutics," 14.
17. Fortin, "Christian Rationality," 342–43.
18. Hornsey and Jetten, "Individual Within," 250; Baumeister and Leary, "Need to Belong," 497.
19. Christman, "Relational Autonomy," 143.
20. Christman, "Relational Autonomy," 143.
21. Konigsburg, "Worship as Compatible," 144.
22. Konigsburg, "Worship as Compatible," 140–41.

other worshipers. In Gadamerian terms, persons choose to participate and then commit to the rules of the game, namely the corporate, ritual structure.

Within the liturgical event, participation thus has both an individual and a communal connotation, an internal and an external expression. There is a common outward ritual expression including speech, singing, symbols, and gestures according to agreed ecclesial norms, but there must also be a corresponding internal movement whereby each person enters into the liturgical realm and encounters Christ in the silence of their own heart.[23] This tension between the public, communal, ritualized proclamation of the Scripture texts, and the inward movement towards interiorization and silence must be preserved. In this way, the hermeneutical experience of receiving the proclaimed Scripture texts in the liturgy is profoundly personal, without being individualistic. It is also deeply communal and unavoidably formative of both personal and communal identity.[24]

Interconnectedness: The Relational Self

Scholars often use the words "relational" and "social" interchangeably when speaking of human connection, yet there is a distinction to be made. The term "social" refers to a broad association between people who belong to particular cultural groups or societal institutions.[25] The "relational" self, however, denotes a sense of close interpersonal, dynamic connection with a commitment to the ideals, practices, and values of a community, and a sense of "reciprocal relatedness of individual and community."[26]

In the liturgy, individuals cannot be viewed as isolated entities, extracted from their contingent relationships with other people. Participation in worship and engagement with the liturgical proclamation of Scripture is an outward-focused activity, not an introspective process of solitary, passive reflection.[27] The event of communal worship invites people into community and situates them physically in the midst of that community. Instead of being solely subsumed with individualist concerns about what the Scriptures are saying on a personal level, members of the assembly gathered for

---

23. Ratzinger, *Feast of Faith*, 69–70.
24. Hoffman, *Beyond the Text*, 3, 172.
25. Baumann, "Reconsidering Relational Autonomy," 447; Christman, "Relational Autonomy," 161n15.
26. Bujo, *Foundations*, 14; Hopkins, *Being Human*, 100.
27. Strawn and Brown, "Liturgical Animals," 12.

worship as a unified body experience their attention turned outwards to issues in the community and the wider world.[28]

From a hermeneutical perspective, it can be argued that "no individual's interpretation is individual; it is what it is because the individual lives within and is profoundly affected by a historical community."[29] Worshipers are physically situated within the faith community for whom the texts were written and thus the dialogue incorporates not only the worshiper and the Lectionary's pericopes but also the community in dialogue with its tradition.[30] Similarly, while the Catholic Church recognizes and celebrates the individual person, made in the image of God, it nonetheless holds that individuals are connected as members of the Body of Christ.[31] Consequently, "separation of the individual and social aspects is not possible; the personal union with Christ also involves incorporation into the collective Christian society."[32]

Irénée Henri Dalmais, OP, formerly professor at the Institute Catholique de Paris, speaks of the power of the collective psyche which operates when a worshiping assembly comes together with a shared purpose and a common collective memory:

> In such situations the sense of human companionship reaches a depth rarely achieved elsewhere, for here community can become communion, that is, it can reach a level of intimacy and exchange in which the dialoguing "I" and "thou" become a "we" that is one in heart and mind.[33]

Dalmais cautions against the situation in which such a strong sense of communion may evolve into a "social monolithism or an affective and even sensual rapture."[34] While this eventuality would pose a threat to the independence and individuality of each worshiper gathered, it is argued that hearing the Scripture texts as a "relational self" during the corporate liturgical event highlights the reciprocal relatedness of the individual worshiper and the communal assembly.[35] Viewing each worshiper as a relational entity points to the primacy of the liturgy as a hermeneutical context

---

28. Brunk, "Consumerism," 62, 65; Mackenzie and Stoljar, *Relational Autonomy*, 16–17; Friedman, *Autonomy*, 82–87.

29. Dean, "Challenge of New Historicism," 267–68.

30. Parris, *Reading the Bible*, 66–67.

31. 1 Cor 12:27: "Now you are the body of Christ and individually members of it."

32. Schnackenburg, *Church in New Testament*, 67.

33. Dalmais, "Liturgy as Celebration," 233–34.

34. Dalmais, "Liturgy as Celebration," 234.

35. Hopkins, *Being Human*, 100.

for Scripture interpretation because "only through healthy collectivity can creative individuality arrive at singular being, productive knowledge, and self-consciousness."[36]

II. PROCLAMATION AS A SOCIALLY EMBEDDED AND PHYSICALLY EMBODIED EVENT

Social Embeddedness

Philosophers, theologians, and sociologists agree that individuals are "socially embedded" and that identity formation occurs within the sphere of social relationships.[37] The very nature of the Catholic liturgy as a corporate form of worship entails a shift in focus from personal autonomy and independence to relationships with others and a consciousness that one is deeply embedded in the Christian community and its tradition.[38]

What takes place in the corporate scriptural proclamation is "a bodily engaged and socially embedded set of practices into which the faithful are inducted and according to which they are regularly exercised."[39] The liturgical proclamation is to a people, not to solitary individuals. Members of the assembly gather not as a "loose association of independently spiritual persons,"[40] but as members of the Body of Christ who experience a sense of physical and social embeddedness while listening to the scriptural proclamation which is addressed to them:

> To the extent that Scripture reading embodies itself in specific gestures, spaces, and habits, it is incarnational; reading "enfleshes" the Word; reading gives human form to the Word in space and time.[41]

Just as the language of a culture is embedded in networks of sociocultural relations, so too the Lectionary is "shared property" which belongs to and is shared by the ecclesial community.[42] Of course, there are situations in which

---

36. Hopkins, *Being Human*, 82.
37. Mackenzie and Stoljar, *Relational Autonomy*, 4.
38. It can be argued that a Christian, even when reading the Bible alone, would rarely approach the text as an isolated individual, since the ecclesial community to which that reader belongs shapes their expectations of the text. Thiselton, *Two Horizons*, 65.
39. Fodor, "Reading the Scriptures," 157.
40. Strawn and Brown, "Liturgical Animals," 12.
41. Fodor, "Reading the Scriptures," 168.
42. Frank, "Do We Translate?," 654.

there may not be a sense of real community amongst those gathered for worship in a particular place. Yet the context of the ecclesial community in the present model of a fourfold fusion of horizons does not depend on a sense of personal familiarity between worshipers. Rather, it is baptism which unites those gathered, not only with each other but with those worshiping around the world and with those who have gone before. The words proclaimed in the liturgical event become the living language of a community,[43] and serve to incorporate worshipers into a universal community far beyond the limits of their particular parish church.

The transformative potential of the text lies in the social context which surrounds its proclamation. It is commonly accepted that group dynamics influence the behavior of individuals such that they behave differently in a group than when alone. Similar effects can be observed when people listen in a group context, as the perceptions of each listener are influenced by and interact with those of other group members.[44] Walter Ong further observes that listening to the spoken word as a group produces a sense of unity between listeners and speakers due to the physical constitution of sound which all experience together.[45]

The Scripture texts operate through the structure of the social event of liturgy to open out potentialities of meaning such that the experience of hearing the pericopes entails a dynamic and negotiated construction of meaning within the context of the ecclesial community. Each individual undeniably arrives at a meaning of their own, but the socio-cultural elements of the liturgy inevitably impact upon this construction of meaning. It can be argued, for example, that an individual's emotional response to hearing the pericopes proclaimed is not only an inner phenomenon; rather such emotions are ongoing brain-body adaptations to their current social situation.[46] Thus, what is being reflected in an individual's emotional state is a response to their interpersonal and physical situation, the result of encountering others in a social and connected context. The structure of Catholic liturgy as a fully embodied and communal event which facilitates the full, conscious, and active participation of all in a collective activity, thereby engages the whole person and encourages a profound engagement with the

---

43. Sartori, "Criteri Teologici," 262.

44. Colburn and Weinberg, *Orientation to Listening*, 17–23.

45. Ong, *Orality and Literacy*, 72. This weighs against the practice of following along with the readings in a Missal or other printed worship aid while listening to the scriptural proclamation.

46. Strawn and Brown, "Liturgical Animals," 12.

Lectionary texts as they become actualized in the contemporary context of the community.[47]

Ecclesial Community in its Broader Context

Embodiment as a hermeneutical influence is seamlessly connected to the continuous daily life of worshipers beyond the confines of the liturgical event.[48] From Gadamer's hermeneutical perspective, the ultimate application of meaning derived from the proclaimed scriptural pericopes is completed not with the final spoken words of the Mass, or with the last verse of the recessional hymn, but in the activities of daily life. Members of the assembly take the sacramental presence of Christ, experienced in the liturgical proclamation, into their families, workplaces, schools, and sports clubs.

The establishment of community as a fundamental element of liturgical worship, therefore, is not confined to the ritual event itself. Achieving unity requires active effort and participation, and some of this work in creating communion necessarily originates outside of the ecclesial environment in the sphere of social action.[49] The identity and mission of the Body of Christ can only be fully realized beyond the bounds of the liturgical event, within the broader context of continuing God's work in the world.[50] The context of the ecclesial community in which the Scripture texts are heard in the liturgy thus encourages not only an internal transformation on a personal or even communal level, but rather an all-encompassing sense of being drawn into participation in Christ's mission beyond the liturgy.[51]

In gathering to be nourished and transformed through the scriptural proclamation and through the Eucharist, the worshiping community indeed opens itself to critique; there is an expectation of some evidence of this transformation permeating the wider world. The ritual activity of the community in the liturgy is seen to be paradigmatic for the work of that same community in the world, fulfilling the words of Scripture by feeding the hungry, visiting the sick, sheltering the homeless.[52] The closing words of the liturgy always send the assembly forth on mission, issuing the challenge

---

47. The Prayer of the Faithful which follows the readings and homily subsequently focuses attention outward in praying for the needs of the community and the world.

48. Strawn and Brown, "Liturgical Animals," 13.

49. Heinz, "Celebration of the Sacraments," 160.

50. SC 9; Kenneson, "Gathering," 61–62.

51. Anderson, "Liturgical Reform," 13; Vatican Council II, "Decree on the Apostolate," 10.

52. Meyers, "Missional Church," 46–47; Kenneson, "Gathering," 60–61.

to take the fruits of their encounter with Christ in word and sacrament to the world. Hearing Scripture proclaimed from the Lectionary as an embodied member of the ecclesial community thus positions each worshiper to interpret the Scriptures with an outward, socially-oriented focus.

Sensus Communis

The search for practical, authentic meaning for each interpreter is of prime importance for Gadamer, yet his emphasis on tradition, as the accumulated *sensus communis* of a group, prevents interpretations of a text from sliding into "subjective relativity."[53] The ancient philosophical concept of the *sensus communis*, which refers to the concrete and universal wisdom of a community, supplies the presuppositions from which a worshiper projects the potential meaning of the scriptural proclamation and the standards of appropriateness by which a newly formed horizon may be tested.[54]

Individual worshipers and the ecclesial community are mutually formative—the individual is formed by the *sensus communis* of the Christian Church, and the church in turn is re-formed and shaped through the development of its individual members.[55] The *sensus communis* is not a fixed series of rules and boundaries, rather it changes in line with historical circumstances and is best described as practical wisdom or "*phronesis*" rather than abstract, universal reason.[56] This practical knowledge accounts for an infinite variation of human situations and recognizes that successful interpretation is not reached through disconnected contemplation, but rather through application and deliberate action in concrete circumstances.[57] Each worshiper seeks to understand what a pericope, as a fragment of the Christian tradition, is saying to them at a particular point in time, and then tests the legitimacy of that emerging understanding against the *sensus communis*. This concept emphasizes that the interpretation of Scripture is not a private enterprise for an individual or scholar, but rather that interpretations must be tested and validated in the faith community.[58]

Acknowledgment of the *sensus communis* does not denote an uncritical acceptance.[59] Corporate knowledge and memory do not stand opposed

53. Culpepper, "Value of Hans-Georg," 282.
54. TM 21, 292–93, 303–7.
55. Parris, "Reception Theory," 60.
56. Weinsheimer, *Gadamer's Hermeneutics*, 72–73.
57. TM 19–20.
58. Pinnock, "Work of Holy Spirit," 162–63.
59. Thiselton, "Knowledge," 76.

to critical thought, but rather comprise a necessary precondition for it, serving as a framework within which individuals come to interpret the Scriptures for themselves within the context of the liturgical event and the ecclesial community.[60] In reality, individuals may not agree with one another, nor with the accepted communal meaning. It stands to reason that the diversity of past experiences and current circumstances belonging to individual worshipers may lead to a variety of meanings being attributed to the readings proclaimed from the Lectionary. However, each interpreter is bound to some extent to the truth claims of the community stemming from Christian tradition and the authority of the magisterium.[61] Corporate and individual knowledge and experience are therefore viewed as positive, complementary, and interwoven relationships that contribute to the overall hermeneutical conversation.[62]

The *sensus communis*, which incorporates the ecclesial community and the tradition in which it stands, thus affirms the polyvalence of the Scripture texts and the individuality of interpretation while upholding the role of ecclesial tradition and guarding against entirely subjective meanings. In the context of the Catholic liturgy, each worshiper will interpret a Lectionary pericope in line with their experiences, beliefs, and cultural background, but will also be influenced by the "centrality of interests" of the ecclesial group which ultimately constrains the diversity of interpretations.[63]

Presence and Physical Proximity in Creating an Ecclesial Interpretive Context

Often the fundamental importance of an entity or phenomenon is most profoundly revealed in its absence. During the COVID-19 pandemic, churches were closed suddenly, and communities forced into lockdown for weeks on end. Almost immediately, some of the larger churches and cathedrals were able to live-stream Mass celebrated by the priest. Some Catholics deeply appreciated this ability to connect to their parish church, to see their pastor on screen, to hear the familiar liturgical texts, and to pray the Scriptures from their homes. For others, viewing Mass being celebrated in their empty church only heightened their sense of isolation from the parish community.

Serious liturgical, theological, and philosophical questions emerged regarding the difference between physical and virtual presence, the nature

---

60. Thiselton, "Knowledge," 59.
61. Day, *Reading the Liturgy*, 162.
62. Thiselton, "Knowledge," 72.
63. Colburn and Weinberg, *Orientation to Listening*, 20.

of liturgical participation, and the necessary prerequisites for experiencing sacramental reality.[64] Hearing the voices of the whole assembly joined together with one's own in prayer and song cannot be recreated when sitting alone or in a small family group around a computer screen. If it had not been clear before, the experience of live-streamed Mass demonstrated powerfully that proclamation is fundamentally a work of the assembled community; not the solitary action of one person.[65]

One of the key challenges identified with the live-streamed Mass is the loss of the predominant liturgical symbol—namely, the assembly. It is the assembly, the Body of Christ who celebrates the liturgy, and this active liturgical participation is the right and duty of all the baptized.[66] Those who watch a live-streamed Mass, however, are not able to engage in the communal "celebrating" or physical "doing" of the liturgy together; rather the impression is given that the liturgical action belongs entirely to the priest with the community sidelined as spectators.[67]

Furthermore, the online liturgical environment does not fit the criteria of an event of "play" or "festival" where participants can enter totally into the hermeneutical arena and become immersed in the interpretive event. Instead, two realities are necessarily co-existing. Firstly, there is the physical reality of the room in which the person is sitting. This reality includes the tactile experience of the chair, the taste of the coffee one is drinking, the sensation of the sun streaming through the window, and sounds coming from nearby locations. The second salient reality is the online environment where the unfolding liturgical action can be seen and heard. The sense of unity with others taking part in the virtual liturgy can be broken at any time with a retreat into personal experience as attentional demands coming from the immediate physical environment prevent a complete engagement with what is happening on the screen.

It is true that "real" presence does not necessarily require physical proximity. Reading a letter from a loved one, engaging in a conversation via text message, or conducting a business meeting over Skype can indeed make people present to one another in a very "real" way, but this kind of presence is not sufficient for the purposes of creating community to celebrate the liturgy. To answer the question of whether "virtual presence" is a suitable substitute for "physical presence" in the liturgy, one must turn not

---

64. Grayland, "Liturgy is an Act"; Just, "Real Presence"; Elich, "Discussing Eucharist," 3–4.

65. Carvalhaes, "Word Became Connection," 32.

66. SC 14.

67. Elich, "Discussing Eucharist," 3.

to the realm of digital engineering but rather to theology since the liturgical event is a theological entity.[68] The liturgy involves sacramental reality which is anchored in the physical realm; it depends on bodies present in the same physical location and tangible symbols to serve as sacramental signs.[69] While Christ's sacramental presence in the proclaimed Scriptures and in the Eucharist is not the same as his physical, historical presence with the apostles in the early church, it nonetheless constitutes a sacramental reality that requires tangible symbols and physical actions with stable notions of time and space.[70]

Predating the pandemic, the Pontifical Council for Social Communications in "The Church and the Internet" acknowledged a complementary role for technology and social media platforms, primarily for purposes of communication, but also clearly asserted that "the virtual reality of cyberspace cannot substitute for real interpersonal community, the incarnational reality of the sacraments and the liturgy, or the immediate and direct proclamation of the Gospel."[71] The pandemic experience, which caused people to retreat into their homes, unable to enter their places of worship or assemble in community, highlighted the hermeneutical impact of hearing the Scriptures proclaimed as part of an embodied liturgical action in which worshipers gather to form the tangible Body of Christ and experience sacramental communion in real space and time.

III. RELATIONAL AND CELEBRATORY DYNAMICS OF THE SCRIPTURAL PROCLAMATION

Liturgy as Festival

The primacy of the communal over the solitary in the liturgical event reflects one of the key features of Gadamer's concept of play. The community which gathers to "play" often becomes permanent even after the instance of play has concluded. The experience of being "apart together" in a unique context, having withdrawn from the world temporarily to share in something important, persists beyond the bounds of the game and stays with those who have participated.[72] Yet the context of the liturgical event requires not only participation, but celebration. Catholic Church documents refer to the

---

68. Grayland, "Liturgy Is an Act."
69. Parish, "Absence of Presence," 276.
70. Carvalhaes, "Word Became Connection," 34.
71. Pontifical Council for Social Communications, "Church and Internet."
72. TM 111–14; Huizinga, *Homo Ludens*, 12.

celebration of the liturgy in the sense of gathering to worship God with solemn ritual.[73] Yet the modern use of the word "celebration," with its connotations of festivity and joyful social gathering, also finds expression. The Catholic liturgy embodies the fundamental elements of any human celebration and can be viewed as an example of Gadamer's philosophical concept of "festival" for several reasons.

Firstly, the essence of festival, and indeed of the liturgy, is the transformation of a particular temporality and locality elevated to a celebratory state by the occurrence of the event—the time is made festive with the commencement of the liturgy and not the other way around.[74] Gadamer viewed participation as the cornerstone of any festival, with those present joining in and being immersed in the communal encounter.[75] Similarly, to experience the Mass fully, one must recognize the festive temporality and become completely engaged in the celebratory mood.

Secondly, in the liturgy, as in any other celebration, people gather to express what is important to them and become actively involved in preparing the celebration. In the liturgical event, people come to encounter each other and to be transformed through their encounter with Christ, not to engage in cerebral learning or the acquisition of knowledge. A celebration is only possible when people gather together, and, "transcending their natural separation and isolation from one another, react together as one body, as indeed one person, to an event."[76] To celebrate a festival is an intentional pursuit; likewise it is not the physical state of being gathered together in the church building, but rather the *intention* that unites the gathered assembly and ensures that individuals do not retreat into personal, subjective experiences.[77]

Thirdly, Catholics present at liturgy engage in a festive dialogue through word and song, joining in the corporate expression of worship. In the liturgical event, the moments of silence belong to the celebration as much as the moments of scriptural proclamation or the lifting of voices in song. It is in these moments of festive silence that a worshiper becomes aware of their situatedness in the midst of the assembly gathered together as they encounter Christ in word and sacrament.

Fourthly, the celebration of the scriptural proclamation imports a sense of unity or communion through its symbols and ritual action. The

73. SC 35(4), 102, 112, 113; CCC 1136, 1140, 1141, 1144.
74. Williams, "Playing Church," 327.
75. TM 126–27; Grondin, "Play," 46.
76. Clark, "Lenten Celebration."
77. Gadamer, "Relevance of the Beautiful," 40.

routine return of the festival (the weekly Sunday celebration of Mass) reminds worshipers of their standing in tradition but also simultaneously in the fleeting present whereby past, present, and future connect through a fusion of horizons. This unifying power of the scriptural proclamation, conceived as an instance of festival, temporarily overcomes the modern tendency towards individualism, such that "one truly loses oneself in the celebration and one finds the others in a unique way."[78] The liturgical assembly, like any group gathered to celebrate a festival, is a representation of community in its most perfect embodiment, where there is no separation between one person and another.[79]

Circulation of Social Energy

The vibrant circulation of social energy between events and texts, as expounded by American literary historian, Stephen Greenblatt, provides a helpful vantage point for situating the Liturgy of the Word as a component part of a sacramental encounter while preserving the integrity of the Lectionary text. Conceiving of the Lectionary text as a social event, and the proclamation event as a social text, is the context in which Greenblatt's concept of the circulation of social energy finds clear application.[80]

Paul Janowiak builds on Greenblatt's notion from the perspective of liturgical theology, suggesting that the dynamic circulation of energy in the Mass illuminates the hermeneutical interaction between God, the assembly, the Lectionary text, the individual and shared history of gathered worshipers, and the liturgical ritual.[81] He identifies an exchange between the current life experiences of worshipers and the cultural energy encoded in the ancient Scripture text, noting that the living text of sacred Scripture has the capacity to reach into the present lives of gathered individuals and into the shared life of a worshiping assembly.[82] Gadamer would view this passing back and forth as a dialogical process, while the sacramental theologian might express it as a dynamic encounter. The liturgical hermeneutic of Scripture proposed here does not conceive of a simple two-way interaction between text and hearer, nor does it view the interpreting community as exerting a dominant or overly creative influence such that the Scriptures yield to meanings that may be assigned by an individual or group. Rather,

78. Schmemann, *Great Lent*, 81.
79. Gadamer, "Relevance of the Beautiful," 39.
80. Greenblatt, *Shakespearean Negotiations*, 6–7.
81. Janowiak, *Holy Preaching*, 91.
82. Janowiak, *Holy Preaching*, 104.

the situation is one in which worshiper, homilist, Bible text, and Lectionary pericope encounter one another in a tradition of faith, in the context of the ecclesial community, in the complex and multisensory liturgical event.[83]

The full, conscious, and active participation of the worshipers draws them into the hermeneutical arena such that they themselves mediate and shape the meaning of the proclamation of the Lectionary texts and the preaching that follows. The transformative power of the scriptural proclamation is situated in the context of the worshiping community, where Lectionary pericopes are recognized as alive and permeating, due to the social energy circulating in the community. Locating this energy in the community has clear implications for understanding the hermeneutical impact that the liturgical proclamation can have on the assembly, both collectively and individually. Indeed, the context of the liturgical event and the community within which the sacred texts are heard result in the emergence of meaning in the minds of the gathered assembly—both individually and collectively—in a way that is far more difficult to discern than in the scholarly, controlled environment of textual analysis.[84] It becomes apparent that the hermeneutical focus is not the text alone, or even predominantly, but rather the complex network of interrelationships that draw together people, symbols, texts, actions, and sensory stimuli in the liturgical event.[85]

In establishing a liturgical hermeneutic of Scripture, the recognition of this circulation of energy as part of a social event makes it clear that the liturgical proclamation is not designed to allow the assembly to simply hear *about* God but rather to *reveal* God in their midst. God's self-communication to humanity is channeled through the social community of the assembly and through the liturgical expression of communal identity.[86] The ancient Scripture texts thereby resonate in a particular way in the liturgical event due to the shared faith and common experience which the contemporary community detects in them.[87]

Dynamism of Grace

Greenblatt's notion of a circulation of social energy finds a strong parallel in the theological concept of a sacramental dynamism of grace which is held to be circulating in the liturgical event, facilitating communication

---

83. Fowler, "Who Is 'The Reader'?," 14.
84. Day, *Reading the Liturgy*, 162.
85. Hoffman, *Beyond the Text*, 173.
86. Anderson, "Liturgical Reform," 13; Searle, *Called to Participate*, 23.
87. Janowiak, *Holy Preaching*, 104.

between God and humanity within the social and ecclesial community.[88] Such a complex and multidimensional circulation of energy can be identified as the location for the dynamism of grace occurring in the sacramental encounter between Christ and the worshiping community who hears the word proclaimed. Such dynamism allows for the possibility that fresh insights may emerge as worshipers contemplate the Scriptures in light of their experience.[89] Far from any approach which would assign a didactic function to the Liturgy of the Word, the scriptural proclamation viewed as Christ's self-communication with the gathered worshipers is regarded as an energy-filled event in which "the reality itself draws nigh and announces itself and constitutes itself present."[90] In speaking of the liturgical proclamation, Janowiak argues that

> the proclamatory energy—what sacramentality calls the "dynamism of grace"—circulates throughout the shared tradition of the Church, the concrete lives of believers who have passed it on in faith, and the social context of a particular time and congregation that gathers to hear this proclamation in new and unforeseen ways.[91]

The vibrant energy which circulates during the scriptural proclamation is made possible because Christ's relationship with the worshiping assembly is active and immanent at each point in time through the power of the Holy Spirit. Correspondingly, the work of Scripture interpretation is conceptualized as a co-operative enterprise in which both the Holy Spirit and the worshiping assembly are active participants.[92] Some scholars have referred to this as the Spirit's "activity of actualization," allowing the Scripture texts proclaimed from the Lectionary to be heard through a contemporary lens and applied to contemporary situations, thus remaining relevant across each generation.[93] The inclusion of the Spirit's role in the hermeneutical framework, as an integral part of the liturgical event, thereby guards against "a lifeless repetition of the Word by the tradition."[94]

Of course, the Spirit does not operate with unrestricted freedom as it moves within the interpretive community, but coheres to the Scriptures

---

88. Janowiak, *Holy Preaching*, 96.
89. Dorman, "Holy Spirit," 431.
90. Rahner, *Theological Investigations*, 255.
91. Janowiak, *Holy Preaching*, 96.
92. Pembroke, "Spirit-Word-Community Hermeneutic," 5–6; Johnson, "Ethics of Preaching," 427.
93. Johnson, "Ethics of Preaching," 429; Congar, *Tradition and Traditions*, 22, 39–42.
94. Yong, *Spirit-Word-Community*, 314.

and sheds new light on the enduring word.[95] Rather than receiving new information, listeners are drawn more deeply into the world of the Lectionary text as they engage in dialogue with it. The Holy Spirit also operates at the level of personal encounter in the liturgical event, changing the hearts of individual interpreters so that they might become more open to welcoming the message revealed in the Scriptures.[96] However, this work is not individualistic.[97] The Spirit moves to bring the gathered assembly together and unite them as the Body of Christ, such that each person receives the Lectionary pericopes as a member of the community standing in the stream of Christian tradition.[98] The spirit of openness to the interpretations of others, facilitated by the dynamic circulation of grace, promotes a relative consensus on the meaning of a Lectionary pericope according to the *sensus communis*, without quashing differences of opinion. The interpretation arrived at by each worshiper, therefore, is not a process of perfunctory submission to an ancient text, but rather "an in-depth engagement of its subject matter within the contemporary faith context."[99]

Incorporating the ongoing and grace-filled movement of the Holy Spirit in a liturgical hermeneutic of Scripture recognizes that interpretation is not simply an intellectual activity. Indeed, worshipers making meaning of Scripture texts in the liturgy are "not so much intellectually persuaded as spiritually converted."[100] The scriptural pericopes proclaimed from the Lectionary have both a universal meaning and a personal application, both of which are illuminated by the Spirit through a dynamism of grace, as they co-exist in vibrant and dynamic tension.

SUMMARY

The dynamics of the scriptural proclamation in the liturgy lead each worshiper, as both a personal and relational entity, to experience a sense of social embeddedness in the liturgical event in which the transformational potential of the Scripture text resides in the social context surrounding its proclamation. The celebratory dynamic of the liturgical proclamation finds expression in Gadamer's concept of the festival, where a common intention

---

95. Pinnock, "Work of Holy Spirit," 162; Dorman, "Holy Spirit," 427; DV 9–12; CCC 1101.
96. Fuller, "Holy Spirit's Role," 91–95.
97. Klooster, "Role of the Holy Spirit," 465.
98. Dunn, "Role of the Spirit," 157; 1 Cor 12:13; Eph 4:4.
99. Pinnock, "Role of the Spirit," 496.
100. Pinnock, *Scripture Principle*, 167.

and a commitment to participate unites those gathered and prevents them withdrawing into subjective experiences.

While the possibility of individual interpretations is affirmed, Gadamer's notion of the *sensus communis* safeguards the consciousness that one is deeply embedded in tradition and provides a framework for testing one's interpretations of the Lectionary pericopes within the ecclesial community. The embodied ritual practices in which worshipers participate create a sense of sacramental communion positioning each worshiper to hear the Scripture texts as a member of the Body of Christ.

The social energy circulating in each liturgical event, conceived theologically as the dynamism of grace, illuminates the hermeneutical interplay between the Scripture texts proclaimed from the Lectionary, the words of the homilist, the personal and shared history of the gathered worshipers, the multisensory liturgical ritual, and the movement of the Holy Spirit. Furthermore, the vibrant circulation of grace-filled energy, which involves the Spirit and the community in a co-operative enterprise of Scripture interpretation, results not only in personal or community transformation but prompts an outward orientation and the application of the scriptural message to contemporary situations.

PART IV

STRATEGIC PRACTICAL THEOLOGY

CHAPTER 9

Identifying Issues in a Liturgical Hermeneutic of Scripture

The liturgical hermeneutic of Scripture proposed in this investigation does not attempt to define a method; neither does it articulate a procedure for understanding Scripture in the liturgy. The hermeneutic is not a formula that one can choose to apply or not. Rather it attempts to make sense of the ways in which the Scripture texts are understood in the liturgical event, to elucidate the circumstances in which understanding takes place, and to account for the ways in which the meaning of Scripture is uniquely influenced by its arrangement in the Lectionary and by the liturgical context in which it is received. In line with Gadamer's philosophical hermeneutics, the scriptural proclamation in the liturgy can be seen as one example of an experience in which a truth that cannot be methodologically verified emerges and makes itself known.[1]

I. SCRIPTURAL PROCLAMATION AS AN EVENT OF MEANING

The Emergence of Truth

Truth as experienced in the liturgical proclamation, in line with Gadamer's position, is not something a person comes to acquire or work out, but is rather something which occurs to a worshiper when they are drawn into the play of the liturgy.[2] Through the scriptural proclamation, worshipers are caught up in an event of truth in such a way that they belong to it. The text,

---

1. TM xxi.
2. Weinsheimer, *Gadamer's Hermeneutics*, 258.

too, belongs to the community and to the whole tradition, having emerged out of the early church community for that community.

Understanding Scripture means understanding it in relation to the present, for one has not yet understood unless it can be applied to the situation at hand.[3] Scripture's claim on the present, its claim to be applicable to people of every culture and time, is part of what it is. Understanding Scripture does not involve reasoning one's way back into the past, but having a present involvement with what is said.

A worshiper who willingly enters the play of the scriptural proclamation accepts the Lectionary's claim to validity and remains open to the fact that the text has something to say to them personally. Gadamer would argue that the aim is not to understand the Lectionary pericopes historically, but to understand the text itself and what it means in its current state of being for the present worshiper. It is of hermeneutical significance that the emergence of truth or understanding in the liturgy is regarded as an event; being an event belongs to the meaning itself, such that the meaning of the proclaimed Scripture text cannot be disentangled from the event of proclamation.

Allowing the Text to Speak

The privileged place of the liturgy as the hermeneutical home of the Scriptures is also supported by Gadamer's contention that a text remains meaningless "until it is given flesh, made concrete and real."[4] The sacred text, lying inert between the pages of the Lectionary, comes to life again when pronounced aloud by human lips. Communication is established (across centuries) and a meaningful encounter becomes possible. In the liturgy, the horizons of past and present are brought together in so total a mediation that the word is experienced and achieves full presence, although such presence requires full, conscious, active participation.[5] This leads back to Gadamer's argument that people not only belong to a tradition (*gehören*) but must also listen (*hören*) through a process of active dialogue, in order to achieve insights beyond their own horizon and experience the truth claims of the text.[6]

This can be cast in theological terms as the sacramental encounter that occurs through the proclamation in which mediation is superseded by actual presence. The aim in liturgical proclamation is a mediation in which

---

3. TM 319.
4. Weinsheimer, *Gadamer's Hermeneutics*, 222.
5. SC 14.
6. TM xv.

the medium of the Lectionary fades from view and the voice of Christ is heard speaking in the contemporary assembly. Conceptualizing the Liturgy of the Word as an event of "speaking" rather than "reading" highlights the sacramental nature of the proclamation.[7] Future printed editions of the Lectionary might be produced with editorial marks to assist the reader in transforming the written word into proclamatory speech, much like actors place scoring marks into their scripts to assist in rendering the text more effectively into speech. Ultimately, however, training for liturgical ministers should extend beyond the acquisition of skills to ensure that they are "deeply imbued with the spirit of the liturgy"[8] and should explore ways to facilitate the hermeneutical dialogue between the worshiper and the Lectionary text in the play of the scriptural proclamation so as to facilitate a fusion of horizons.

Ministers of the word have a particular role in drawing attention to the sacramental encounter taking place. They can capitalize on the dynamic social energy circulating in the liturgical space by allowing the congregation to fall silent and an air of expectation to descend. This creates a receptive atmosphere of silence into which the sacred words can resound with impact. Pausing for several moments of silence in between each reading and acclamation gives space for the community to engage in the process of inner dialogue. In times past, being a reader has required only basic literacy, yet once it is acknowledged that "the Scriptures are not modern writings but frozen speech, then the act of reading is an act of exegesis that can only be performed by one skilled in the techniques of such performance."[9] Training readers, instituted lectors, and clergy in the art of proclamation allows the horizon of the Lectionary text to enter more clearly into the hermeneutical arena.

It is worth considering the impact of giving the assembly a chance to hear the Lectionary readings proclaimed a second time after an interim period of silence, before the homilist attempts to unpack the text by adding extra words. The importance of letting the original work speak in all its indefinable complexity was illustrated admirably by composer Robert Schumann; when asked to "explain" a complicated etude, Schumann simply sat at the piano and played it a second time.[10] It is possible for readers to consult a variety of commentaries on the Lectionary in preparing to proclaim the text meaningfully. However, it is important to recognize these

7. Cullinane, "Suggestion."
8. Francis, "Address to Teachers and Students."
9. O'Loughlin, "Would You Read?," 33.
10. Steiner, *Real Presences*, 21.

commentaries as secondary discourse and to prioritize encounters with the sacred text itself. Creating space for worshipers to immerse themselves in the festival play of the scriptural proclamation so that they might experience new insights through a fusion of horizons reflects Gadamer's claim that it is possible to belong to a tradition and still experience challenge and surprise when encountering the truth claims of that tradition.

Provoking Preconceptions That Arise From Communal Tradition

In the liturgy, worshipers search for truth by entering into a dialogue with the horizon of the Bible text, with the Lectionary's arrangement of pericopes, and eventually with the perspective of the homilist. The beginning of the interpretative process is a willing response to Christ's initiatory address in the scriptural proclamation. Since the anticipation of meaning results from the commonality that binds a worshiper to the tradition, and since the homilist speaks as one within the same faith community subject to similar societal circumstances, worshipers need not look away from their own horizon, but rather aim to see more clearly within a larger perspective.

For preconceptions to be challenged in the liturgical proclamation of Scripture, they must be provoked or irritated to become conscious.[11] Worshipers must therefore be interested in and willing to acknowledge the truth claim of the Scriptures and of the homilist, while perceiving that they are being addressed directly with regards to a matter of mutual concern. Gadamer's claim that understanding a text presupposes a living relationship to what it says is particularly pertinent for the liturgical event, in which worshipers who interpret a scriptural pericope are themselves within the meaning they apprehend.[12]

Building on Gadamer's emphasis on the importance of foregrounding prejudices in the hermeneutic event, some moments of guided reflection before Mass might orient the assembly to bring their lives before God so that they enter into authentic conversation with the sacred texts, make connections to their lives, and apply these insights to their own reality. Worshipers would ideally understand themselves as participants, not only in the liturgical action, but in a continuing hermeneutical conversation.

---

11. Weinsheimer, *Gadamer's Hermeneutics*, 180.
12. TM 340.

Acknowledging the Endless Fusion of Horizons in Mediating Past and Present

The fusion of horizons that takes place in the scriptural proclamation is an infinite process that brings with it a sense of having set out but not yet arrived, a sense that accompanies worshipers throughout their lives. Gadamer proposes an ongoing interpretive dialogue, comprising memory and reflection, where an ultimate reconciliation is never achieved.[13] This endlessness has profound consequences for the conception of truth that emerges in any given liturgical proclamation of Scripture; indeed if there is any truth at all, it occurs in the ongoing process of interpretation in which worshipers are engaged throughout the liturgy (assisted by the movement of social energy and the Holy Spirit) and throughout the course of their lives. This is entirely consistent with the liturgical theological perspective which holds that the encounter with Christ in the Scriptures "is not a question of something grasped mentally but a relationship that touches all of life."[14]

A tension remains between the enduring sameness of a Lectionary text and the multiplicity of different situations to which it is applied and in which it is understood. Since a text cannot be understood independently of the particular situation to which it is applied,[15] it follows that a passage of Scripture can be understood differently in diverse situations. This diversity can be due to the liturgical rite in which a text is heard, to the personal circumstances of a worshiper, or to current societal events. For example, the same pericope may yield a distinct meaning depending on whether it is heard on a Sunday in Advent, on a feast of the Blessed Virgin Mary, or as part of a funeral liturgy. The same text may be heard differently by members of the assembly who have just welcomed a new baby, those suffering illness, or those contemplating a career change. Proclaimed texts may also resonate differently when communities are struggling to recover from natural disasters, preparing to elect a new government, or emerging from a pandemic. Each liturgical celebration is a unique event in which the horizon of the preacher has a particular role in highlighting the application of a Lectionary text in the current circumstances of the gathered assembly, conscious of the multitude of shifting horizons with which worshipers encounter the text.

Shedding further light on the polyvalence of Scripture texts proclaimed in the liturgy is the speculative structure of language in which a text multiplies itself in the infinity of its historical reflections and yet is nonetheless

---

13. TM 309, 477.
14. Francis, *Desiderio Desideravi*, 39 (hereafter DD).
15. TM 307.

one.[16] Each Lectionary pericope has a mirror relationship to itself since its historical existence as always something different, unique in each liturgical event, constitutes its way of being. Precisely because of this mirror relationship, the profuse number of historical and contemporary interpretations do not fracture into mere plenitude, for they are all reflections of the Scripture text itself.

According to the theoretical model, not only the horizons of the worshiper and the homilist, but also the horizons of the Bible and Lectionary texts, are in a constant process of evolution; "as the historical horizon is projected, it is simultaneously superseded."[17] There is an ever-present danger that the past might be unconsciously subsumed under the familiar language of the present and dominated by latent prejudices. However, abandoning contemporary linguistic and conceptual frameworks and replacing them with that of the past is equally fruitless.[18] The solution exists in the fusion of horizons that provides a mediation between past and present and allows the text to say something to modern worshipers. Participants in the liturgy ideally gather with a sense of "hermeneutic consciousness," open to experience and to the viewpoints of others, and aware that they still have something to learn.[19] The fluid nature of shifting horizons in this liturgical hermeneutic of Scripture balances the worshiper's urge for complete understanding of the scriptural proclamation with the discontent in not being able to achieve it.

Scriptural proclamation in liturgical events thus plays out the continuation of tradition in the continually expanding possibilities of significance developed by members of worshiping assemblies who participate in it. Belonging to this tradition and to the ecclesial community is an ontological way of talking about the condition achieved by the fusion of horizons. Such a fusion in the dynamic hermeneutical arena of the liturgy results in an emergence of insight into the scriptural proclamation that cannot be attributed to the worshiper, the homilist, the Bible text, or the Lectionary pericopes alone, nor to the sum of their perspectives.

---

16. Weinsheimer, *Gadamer's Hermeneutics*, 255.
17. TM 317.
18. Weinsheimer, *Gadamer's Hermeneutics*, 225.
19. Pieper, *Only the Lover Sings*, 55.

Facilitating a Fusion of Horizons in the Liturgy

Identifying Linguistic and Cultural Incongruities Between the Horizons of Lectionary and Worshiper

An element of the horizon of many worshipers in modern times is sensitivity to and concern for inclusion. The importance of removing potential dissonance between the horizon of the Lectionary and that of the worshipers stems from the Gadamerian premise that people choose to enter the play of the hermeneutical arena because they presume that the text has something of value to say to them. They engage with a commitment to reaching understanding or agreement by genuinely listening to another's insight. A key consideration for any Lectionary, therefore, is that the truths contained in the Bible texts be communicated in language which is inclusive, respectful of contemporary sensibilities, and which invites each worshiper into a hermeneutical conversation. In addition to this methodological and philosophical consideration, the theological perspective would argue that inclusive language is not simply a politically correct recognition of diversity: it is demanded by the very nature of the liturgy itself.[20] Simply adding "sisters" or "daughters" does not make a text inclusive of non-binary humans, for example. Choosing more gender-neutral terms like "friends" or "People of God" will help to ensure that the radical nature of Gospel justice and equality can be clearly heard in the assembly.

Inclusive language is relevant not only in terms of gender but also in terms of race, religion, and disability. Popular culture inevitably influences theological language, because "the meaning of words is shaped by the language system in which the words are used and the lived contexts of the communities that use them."[21] The dynamic process of tradition and its transmission to the next generation through the fusion of horizons that takes place in the liturgical proclamation therefore necessitates the continual development of a contemporary language, "a ceaseless inculturation,"[22] for "linguistic identity over time doesn't guarantee identity of meaning over time."[23] Conceiving of the liturgical proclamation as an event of play which worshipers join, get caught up in, and eventually belong to, dictates that biblical references to "the dumb," "the crippled," or "the lame," for example,

---

20. O'Loughlin, "New Books," 204–5.
21. Lynch, *Understanding Theology*, 195.
22. De Clerck, "In the Beginning," 10.
23. Tilley, "Practicing the Faith," 95.

cannot be sustained but should be replaced with modern language which does not constitute an obstacle to the horizons of contemporary worshipers.[24]

Ensuring that worshipers can enter willingly into conversation with the Lectionary text and experience insights through a fusion of horizons extends beyond matters of translation or inclusive language. It strikes to the very question of which pericopes are suitable (or unsuitable) for inclusion in the public reading of Scripture in a contemporary worship event. The criteria for judging whether a text is inclusive of women, for example, requires far more than adding "sisters" and "daughters" to those biblical passages which speak only of "brothers" and "sons." It requires an examination of pericopes chosen for the Lectionary which infer the subordinate position of women, particularly when coupled with the exclusion of verses which praise the initiative, leadership, and intellectual acuity of women.[25] When the horizons of the Bible text and the Lectionary text are brought together in these instances, a clash comes clearly into view.

The importance of attending to contemporary cultural horizons becomes particularly apparent when considering the impact of the liturgical context in ascribing divine authority to the proclaimed texts. Surrounding the texts with sacred signs, symbols, and other prayers in an ecclesial setting can suppress any tendency for worshipers to bring their horizon into an open-ended hermeneutical conversation in which they would ask questions of potentially oppressive texts.[26] Lectionary readings which advocate constant forgiveness and the acceptance of suffering need considerable contextualization in the homily so as not to enhance the suffering of those in domestic violence situations, for example.

---

24. See readings from Isaiah on Monday 2 Advent, Sunday 3 Advent (A), Sunday 23 Ordinary (B), from Leviticus on Thursday 3 Lent, from Mark's Gospel on Friday 5 Ordinary, Monday 7 Ordinary, Sunday 23 Ordinary (B), and from Matthew's Gospel on Wednesday 1 Advent, Tuesday 14 Ordinary. Contemporary horizons are also sensitive to language which has been described as "blatantly anti-Jewish." Beck, "Removing Anti-Jewish Polemic," 4–5.

25. See the description of "a perfect wife" in Proverbs 31 on Sunday 33 Ordinary (A). For a more obvious example of subordination see Eph 5:22–24 on Sunday 21 Ordinary (B). Entirely omitted from the Lectionary is the inspirational account of Hebrew midwives Shiprah and Puah who risked their lives by refusing to obey Pharoah's order that all newborn males be killed (Exod 1:15–21). Other biblical texts not heard in liturgical proclamation are the triumphant Song of Miriam, or the account of Deborah, the wise prophet and judge who orchestrated a military victory for the Israelites. Neither does the Lectionary contain references to Phoebe, Dorcas, Lydia, or the ten women publicly praised in Romans 16, thus depriving church-goers of hearing these biblical accounts of women exercising leadership in the early church.

26. Procter-Smith, "Lectionaries," 94–95.

Ultimately, for worshipers to enter the play of the scriptural proclamation and admit the truth of the scriptural proclamation, a clearing away of linguistic obstacles is required. Eliminating incongruities will encourage each worshiper to commit to the play of the proclamation, to engage with the text as a contemporary truth which concerns them personally, and to enter into dialogue with the perspectives of the Bible text, Lectionary text, and the homilist in order to experience a fusion of horizons.

Examining the Fidelity of the Lectionary to the Biblical Vision

Cultural and pastoral factors in pericope selection not only impact the horizon of the worshiper but can also distort the horizon of the biblical text as it enters the hermeneutical arena in the liturgy. Italian theologian, Luigi Sartori, suggests that a slice of humanity often seems censored and kept away from the Christian community gathered at the liturgical event, despite the fact that the Bible gives voice to situations which are serious, conflicted, and scandalous.[27] In short, he is concerned by the Lectionary's harmonizing approach which, he claims, fails to reflect the Bible's embrace of both theological pluralism and raw human experience. Sartori's position highlights the collision which occurs when the horizons of Bible and Lectionary are brought together. He laments that the texts chosen for the Lectionary are those which are more easily accommodated and which look forward to the "harmonic time" of eternity where all things are resolved, despite the fact that the biblical writers seemed to prefer the language of the "meantime" which draws upon conflicts and the realities of human existence.[28] The lack of Lectionary pericopes which express doubt, accusation, pain, and lament effectively silences part of the horizon of the Bible text and prevents it from entering into the play of hermeneutic conversation with other horizons in the liturgical event.

The practical effect of this can be to exclude those who feel marginalized: "The exclusion of the lament screens out people who find the services shallow or harmful and provides no theological and liturgical way to come to terms with disturbing human experiences."[29] In modern times, the inclusion of texts from the book of Lamentations, or those which explore the tortured experience of Job, for example, would speak to real human experiences such as the devastation of war, the desperation of unemployment or homelessness, and the suffering of those who perceive that God is either

27. Sartori, "Criteri Teologici," 271.
28. Sartori, "Criteri Teologici," 271.
29. Billman and Migliore, *Rachel's Cry*, 14.

remote or absent.[30] The ability of worshipers to encounter this aspect of the horizon of the Bible text in the liturgy would prompt them to enter into the play of interpretation and participate in the emergence of new meaning through a fusion of horizons, confident that they belong to and with the subject of the traditionary text.

The Lectionary also omits biblical texts on the grounds of theological or pastoral difficulty, such as those containing references to violence, destruction, and vengeance.[31] United States Catholic priest, Gerard Sloyan, who was pivotal in the American response to Vatican II, claims that the absence of biblical robustness in the Lectionary results in congregations "being protected from the insoluble mystery of God by a packaged providence, a packaged morality, even a packaged mystery of Christ."[32] Some have further suggested that the very passages classified as being confronting or obsolete may well be the scriptural extracts that are most vital for contemporary horizons to collide with, and have argued that difficult passages should be retained and contextualized in the expression of the homilist's horizon.[33] The act of excising challenging passages based on their supposed lack of suitability for public proclamation, leads to the argument that worshipers are being deprived of the chance to engage in the personal struggle that would ensue from the collision of their horizon with that of the Bible text, and are thus being prevented from experiencing insights that would flow from a fusion of these horizons.

American Protestant theologian and biblical scholar, Walter Brueggemann, claims that depriving a congregation of the opportunity to confront God with their frustration eliminates the chance for a "genuine covenant interaction," resulting in "psychological inauthenticity and social immobility."[34] When Psalm 88 is used in the Lectionary, for example, the congregation never hears beyond verse 34 on any liturgical day and the psalm response on the lips of the congregation is "For ever I will sing the goodness of the Lord."[35] The Lectionary's version of Psalm 88 in fact ob-

---

30. From the book of Job, only two Sunday readings and six weekday readings appear in the Lectionary across the three-year cycle, and from Lamentations only one weekday reading. See also Van Ommen, "Limping," 176.

31. Elich, "Word in Worship," 93; Fox, "Strange Omission," 13.

32. Sloyan, "Lectionary as Context," 49.

33. Conversely, some claim that good preaching cannot be assumed and that pastorally difficult passages should be omitted. Bailey, "Lectionary," 151; Boisclair, *Word of the Lord*, 97.

34. Brueggemann, *Psalms and Life of Faith*, 111.

35. Sunday 13 Ordinary (A), Sunday 4 Advent (B), 24 December, and The Nativity of the Lord Vigil as well as various weekdays in Ordinary Time and Easter, and in the Common of Pastors.

scures its true identity as a psalm of communal lament; this is something that only emerges in verses 38–49 in its biblical context. Including these verses in the Lectionary would invite worshipers to bring their own confusions, questions, and frustrations into the hermeneutical context, prompting an authentic dialogue with the horizon of the Bible text and the perception of new insights through an honest experience of lament.

There is clearly a balance to be struck. The inclusion of challenging texts is important for preserving fidelity to the biblical horizon and for providing worshipers with an opportunity to hear their own struggles and disappointments in the texts of Scripture. However, this does not extend to violent or disturbing texts which would clearly cause offense in the current cultural and pastoral context, especially when following such texts with the declaration "This is the word of the Lord." Including the final verses of Psalm 136 when it is used in the Lectionary on the Fourth Sunday of Lent (B), for example, and proclaiming "Blessed whoever grasps and shatters your children on the rock" could not be justified.[36] Any pericopes which have the potential to create division, offense, or disunity in the contemporary worshiping assembly must be judged as unsuitable for public proclamation since they distort rather than support Christian identity. Furthermore, such texts reduce the likelihood that worshipers might willingly bring their own horizon into dynamic conversation with the other horizons operating in the festival event of liturgy while remaining open to the emergence of new insights.

Preserving the Unique Contribution of the Homilist

The homilist contributes the perspective of their own horizon as a member of the local ecclesial community, alert to the existing struggles, frustrations, joys, and triumphs of that community. They also offer insights in the liturgical event as a member of the broader socio-cultural context; in this way, the homilist is pivotal in promoting cultural and pastoral inclusivity even where the horizon of the Lectionary text can seem jarring to modern sensibilities. Where offensive terminology appears in the Lectionary text, homilists have a role, acting as mediator between the worshiper and the sacred text, to offer alternative language and to contextualize the Scripture passage through an inclusion-centered homily. Further, in situating a Lectionary pericope within its broader biblical context, the homilist is the vehicle through which the horizon of the Bible text is brought into play in the liturgy and through which it can enter the hermeneutical conversation taking place in the minds

36. The Benedictine Monks, *Revised Grail Psalms*, 304.

of the worshipers. The homilist must be open to being addressed by the pericopes assigned to that liturgical day and to experiencing a shift in their own horizon, aware of the tradition in which they and other worshipers stand.[37]

In line with Gadamer's concepts of play and festival, the homilist joins the dialogue that is already open, as one voice among others, and as one of many participants in the liturgical celebration. The homilist has time during their homily preparation to grapple with the juxtapositions between Lectionary readings and to observe how the texts rub together to create new meanings. It is the role of the homilist to illuminate these contemporary truths for the assembly, drawing out the connective threads between readings, and noting the hermeneutical impact of assigning such readings to the particular liturgical feast or season. It is not sufficient for the homily to be simply informative; much more importantly, it must be communicative, intertwined with the lived reality of the faith community, and relevant to their social and cultural situation. The homilist should preach from their personal faith experience, suggesting what the sacred text may be saying to the diverse members of the assembly within a contemporary frame of reference, while acknowledging the potential for ambiguity and polyvalence. Homilists have a key role in prompting an open-ended conversation which incorporates the horizon of worshiper, homilist, Bible text, and Lectionary text, resulting in a fusion of horizons and a subsequent response by each person present at the liturgy in applying this new insight in their life. American writer, novelist, and theologian, Frederick Buechner, encourages a style of preaching which assists in creating this hermeneutical context:

> Let [the preacher] use words, but in addition to using them to explain, expound, exhort, let him use them to evoke, to set us dreaming as well as thinking... Let him use words which do not only try to give answers to the questions that we ask or ought to ask but which help us to hear the questions that we do not have words for asking.[38]

The homilist thus contributes their own particular horizon, acting as an agent of interruption in the minds of the worshipers, but also surrenders to the dynamic event of play taking place in which meanings will emerge in unpredictable ways.

---

37. Those who prepare homilies or write commentaries on the Lectionary should maintain an educated familiarity with literary critics, artists, historians, and philosophers to ensure that their reflections are meaningful to contemporary Catholics who belong to the broader culture. See Kaufman, "Theology as Imaginative," 79.

38. Buechner, *Telling the Truth*, 23–24.

II. SCRIPTURE PROCLAMATION AS SOCIAL EVENT AND PERSONAL ENCOUNTER

Encouraging Worshipers to Enter the Play of the Scriptural Proclamation

The continuing event of truth that takes place in the scriptural proclamation is something which happens to worshipers as they participate actively in the play and festival of liturgy. As distinct from an exegetical approach, the truth of tradition "occurs" to worshipers in the liturgy. Gadamer would describe this as the "primacy of play" over the consciousness of the individual worshipers.[39]

It is not possible to avoid being played; indeed, Gadamer would suggest it is not desirable to avoid it.[40] In the play of the liturgy, participants ideally take leave of themselves and the play of the liturgy takes over. The repeated circular motion of excursion and return is not under the control of the worshiper but belongs to the playing of the game. While the game plays itself, the worshipers present themselves in it, participating actively, such that they too belong to the meaning of the scriptural proclamation.

Through a theological lens, the transformative power of the play of the liturgy emerges when participants in the liturgy surrender humbly to the action of the Holy Spirit who operates in the liturgical celebration to conform worshipers more fully to Christ and to unify those gathered as the Body of Christ.[41] Individual members of the assembly are transformed into a communion; they do not remain as they were. This communion as the Body of Christ occurs, not because the assembly has mentally assimilated knowledge or ideas, but through "real existential engagement" with the person of Christ present among them.[42] For any participant in the liturgy, it is never the same self that understands from one liturgical event to the next; the self is a product as well as a condition of understanding in a hermeneutic spiral.

A liturgical hermeneutic is not concerned with abstract cognitive processes in textual exegesis, therefore, but with interpretation of Scripture in the liturgy as an event of being. The mediation that occurs between the four horizons operating in the liturgy has the result that neither remains what it was. Understanding is the fusion of these horizons within a particular

---

39. TM 107.
40. TM 111.
41. VD 16.
42. DD 41.

liturgical event in the context of the ecclesial community and situated within the broader cultural context; understanding always transmits the synthesis of a shared truth which is entirely contemporary with each age and culture in which it is understood.

Facilitating Bodily Engagement of the Senses in a Communal Setting

The hermeneutic importance of engaging the senses has been well established in earlier chapters and has serious implications for the place of music and singing during the Liturgy of the Word. Purposefully producing rhythmic and melodic sounds to sing the responsorial psalm and Gospel acclamation engages the participatory and interpretive capacities of the worshipers in a way which is quite distinct from speech. By singing the words of Scripture in the liturgy,

> the images, themes, and claims of the text are realized not as text but as a "writing on the body" in performance. To the extent that the hymn is sung by a corporate body, it not only requires our engagement in mind and body, but requires a bodily engagement that is simultaneously individual and communal . . . if we are to sing, we must sing and breathe together. What is registered integrally is registered communally.[43]

The transformative impact of the "sounding of bodies" is therefore relevant, not only due to the established Catholic ritual tradition, but also due to the physiological and hermeneutical implications of producing and receiving sound in a communal setting.[44] This sounding of bodies is also indicative of Gadamer's notion of festival in which people gather together because they want to be with one another and to communicate in ways that surpass the spoken word. For Gadamer, voluntary participation in a communal event and the willingness to let oneself be immersed in the festive occasion are precursors to the emergence of meaning for each worshiper.

A crucial issue in the renovation or redesign of churches is the ability of each person to hear their own voice and the voices of others, as well as the instruments and voices of the liturgical ministers. Great emphasis has been placed on the visual aspects of church architecture and design so that worshipers might perceive themselves as members of the Body of Christ and be able to participate fully as members of the baptized priesthood. Contrary to

---

43. Anderson, "O for a Heart," 120.
44. Morrill, "Liturgical Music," 26.

the lofty positioning of the ambo prior to Vatican II, which carried implications that God's word was coming down from heaven, contemporary church design situates the ambo on a similar level to the seating of the assembly, to emphasize that Christ is speaking in the midst of those gathered.[45] Modern church renovation projects have tended towards a circular or "sociopetal" layout of the liturgical space with the altar and ambo in the center and the pews situated around in circular, semi-circular, or antiphonal arrangement. This physical space draws worshipers into the play of the ritual action as celebrants of the liturgy and promotes the dynamic circulation of social energy amidst the gathered ecclesial community.[46]

In order for the sacred texts to be heard clearly and a hermeneutical dialogue facilitated, there is need for an equal focus on the auditory qualities of church buildings, with considerations of the shape and material of the roof, ceiling, and walls, as well as coverings for floors and seating.[47] Adequate sound equipment will ensure that the voice of the reader resounds in all areas of the liturgical space. Where elements of the visual or auditory space are inadequate or extreme, both the senses and the intellect are inhibited in the hermeneutical process, making a worshiper reluctant to enter the play of the scriptural proclamation or to remain open to encountering other horizons. For example, a microphone volume which is too soft or excessively loud is not suitable for active listening. A liturgical space which is too dark or too brightly lit does not optimally engage the visual sense.[48] Careful preparation of the liturgical space, in terms of sound amplification, lighting, environment, and symbol, enhances the quality of the communicative event and produces a context in which those gathered can attend actively to the proclamation, engage in a hermeneutical conversation, and experience a fusion of horizons.[49]

When the assembly performs the same gesture, or speaks together in one voice, the energy of the entire social group is transmitted to each person such that individual worshipers discover the uniqueness of their own

---

45. Burns, "Processions of the Ordo," 169.

46. Vosko, *Art and Architecture*, 133.

47. The Australian Catholic Bishops Conference publication, *And When Churches*, emphasizes visual aspects of architectural design. Building materials are referred to only with regard to their symbolic significance and the preference that these materials be "natural." Nowhere in the discussion of building materials, or the specific elements of ceiling, roof, floor, or walls, is reference made to resonance or clarity of sound (96–101). However, mention is made of sound systems for both vocal and instrumental amplification (116, 124).

48. Hughes, "Ease of Beauty," 101.

49. GIL 32–34.

horizon and the meaning they derive from Scriptures in the awareness of being a member of one body. As referred to in chapter 8, the hermeneutical importance of gathering physically, rather than virtually, to celebrate the liturgy and listen to the Scriptures proclaimed, cannot be overstated in this theoretical model.

Creating Spaces for Corporate Silence

To create a hermeneutical context of "play" within which understanding can emerge in the Catholic liturgy, moments for silence and reflection are essential structural elements. Flowing from an acknowledgment of the scriptural proclamation as a dialogical encounter is the implication that sufficient time be set aside for liturgical conversation. Without intentional moments of silence, almost everything is spoken or sung aloud in the Catholic Mass from beginning to end, resulting in something of a verbal imperialism and leaving no "time or space or bodily inclination to meander in the spirit."[50]

Providing time for the frenetic pace of the outside world to subside allows worshipers to enter the play of the liturgy and prepare their hearts and minds to receive the sacred texts. Moments of communal, festive silence after each Lectionary reading and after the homily, provide necessary space for worshipers to enter into an internal dialogue with the sacred texts and the perspective of the homilist in the midst of the ecclesial community, prompting a fusion of horizons and the emergence of new insights.[51] Silence in this context is different from being quiet. It is "not an inner haven in which to hide oneself in some sort of intimate isolation, as if leaving the ritual form behind as a distraction. That kind of silence would contradict the essence itself of the celebration."[52] Instead, the assembly falls quiet together, with an awareness of the dynamic social energy that is circulating, such that the liturgical silence signals "the presence and action of the Holy Spirit who animates the entire action of the celebration."[53]

---

50. Grimes, "Liturgical Renewal," 24.

51. When periods of silence are being introduced for the first time, it is important to inform the assembly before Mass begins, and to invite people to use this silence to enter into quiet reflection. Unusual silences can otherwise be a distraction, as the assembly wonders which of the liturgical ministers has forgotten to come forward or presumes that the liturgical musicians have missed their cue.

52. DD 52.

53. DD 52.

III. LITURGY AS EVENT OF TRADITION

Preserving Tradition: Facilitating Play

The art of liturgical celebration requires a continual process of education lest the language and the ritual action lose their meaning over time. Jan Assmann's work on cultural memory, outlined in chapter 7, supports the notion that the Catholic cultural memory is preserved, stabilized, and communicated through the use of sacred texts, liturgical books, and ritual practices. Yet this must be considered in light of Gadamer's concept of *Bildung* (education or formation) in which the tradition needs to be affirmed, embraced, and cultivated since understanding begins with the provisional meaning projected from one's relationship with the tradition.[54] In articulating its call for the reform of the liturgy, *Sacrosanctum Concilium* specifically addressed the need for the "promotion of liturgical instruction."[55] It has been argued that the Council's vision for adequate liturgical catechesis and formation has never been realized,[56] and this has only been amplified following the cultural and societal shifts of recent decades. The current challenge is to ensure that the scriptural proclamation addresses worshipers of the postmodern world and that the Lectionary texts are actualized in a societal context that could not have been foreseen at the Second Vatican Council.

Pope Francis, in his apostolic letter, *Desiderio Desideravi*, noted the need for serious and dynamic liturgical formation of "all the faithful." He observed that active participation in the liturgical action has become exceedingly difficult in modern cultures where the capacity to engage with symbolic action has been largely lost, and where individualism and subjectivism have quashed the sense of contributing to a corporate action.[57] This is not to suggest that liturgical formation has not been attempted with great energy in the years following Vatican II, nor that education in the theological underpinnings of the liturgy would necessarily prompt a worshiper to enter fully into the hermeneutical play so as to experience a fusion of horizons in the scriptural proclamation. However, the need for greater work in this area has been identified. Ultimately, while knowledge and education may inform the preconceptions of worshipers, facilitate their ability to enter into the play of the scriptural proclamation more deeply, promote a fruitful dialogical encounter with the other horizons present in the liturgy, and thereby lead to new insights through a fusion of horizons, a key component

54. TM 293.
55. SC 14–20.
56. Irwin, *What We Have Done*, 135.
57. DD 27–28.

of effective formation, or *Bildung*, is participation in the liturgy celebrated well. Consequently, adequate and ongoing formation of liturgical ministers in the art of liturgical celebration is also vital. Two avenues of formation might now be considered: formation *for* the liturgy and *by* the liturgy.[58]

For the Liturgy

Scripture

While the Lectionary is a distinct entity and itself a particular interpretation of the Scriptures, nonetheless "the Lectionary presupposes an adequate acquaintance with the Bible. It serves an anamnetic purpose, to recall and evoke the key moments and reflections of the history of salvation centered in the paschal mystery."[59] In addition to external opportunities to become familiar with Scripture texts in their broader biblical context, there may be some scope within the liturgy itself to enhance the biblical literacy of those present. It has been noted that the horizon of the homilist serves a key function in allowing the horizon of the biblical text to enter the hermeneutical arena. Two further suggestions are given in the General Introduction to the Lectionary, whereby concise introductions may be given before the readings, as well as brief comments about the selection of the psalm and its correspondence to the readings.[60]

A Corporate Mindset as a Precursor to Play

It is unclear to what extent Catholics in the modern age appreciate the profoundly communal nature of the liturgical action in which they participate. Some may attend Mass to fulfil a sense of personal obligation, while others come in search of answers for their own life circumstances; both of these perspectives may prompt a worshiper to sit in silent prayer. Yet a fundamental element of a liturgical hermeneutic of Scripture is that interpretation takes place within the ecclesial assembly gathered for worship, where each person participates in the festive play of the liturgical action surrounded by the symbols and rituals which have carried the Scriptures in communal memory. Insight is not controlled or produced at will by the members of the assembly; rather, through their active participation in the play of the liturgy, something occurs to them. As discussed in chapter 8, worshipers may

---

58. DD 34.
59. Bonneau, *Sunday Lectionary*, 49.
60. GIL 15.

experience a personal encounter, yet the experience is not an individual one. Indeed, Gadamer would argue that a knowledge-generating individual "is never simply an individual because he is always in understanding with others," and that knowledge cannot be developed through solitary self-contemplation.[61] It is an ongoing challenge for contemporary worshipers to become aware that the scriptural proclamation, and indeed the liturgy as a whole, contains a series of communal interconnections between information and celebration, memory and encounter, invitation and response.[62]

The corporate dimension of the liturgy immediately sets it apart as a hermeneutical context in the realm of biblical scholarship. Pope Francis explains the interpretive influence of the liturgy in this way:

> The Liturgy does not leave us alone to search out an individual supposed knowledge of the mystery of God. Rather, it takes us by the hand, together, as an assembly, to lead us deep within the mystery that the Word and the sacramental signs reveal to us. And it does this, consistent with all action of God, following the way of the Incarnation, that is, by means of the symbolic language of the body, which extends to things in space and time.[63]

Authentic participation in the scriptural proclamation must therefore be understood as the dynamic equilibrium between personal interiorization and external communal expression. In other words, the full, conscious, active participation that the liturgy requires depends on a worshiper's ability to enter into the play of the liturgy, and participate in a common, festive expression, rather than retreating into a personal meditation.

If a sufficient number of worshipers approach the liturgy with this mindset, a context will be created for the movement of social energy and the emergence of new insights through a fusion of horizons. This demands not only liturgical formation, but also lived experience of transformative participation in the festival event of play.

By the Liturgy

Corporate Silence

In an age and culture where people are frequently immersed in highly stimulating audio-visual content from a variety of electronic devices, the liturgy

---

61. TM 315.
62. O'Loughlin, "Bible in Context," 49.
63. DD 19.

provides a unique opportunity to cultivate the art of attentive listening and mental silence. This emphasis finds expression in the Introduction to the Lectionary which names attentive listening as a key skill to be acquired.[64] It is not a superficial listening but a sense of active engagement which is necessary for meaning and relevance to emerge.

It was accepted in the Middle Ages that "mental silence," or "mental solitude," was a prerequisite for internalizing and memorizing words that were heard. It was also widely accepted in medieval times that the skill of active concentration could be learned, so strategies were taught and practiced to improve this ability.[65] The importance of internalizing and remembering the Scriptures finds echoes in the GIRM which indicates that the Liturgy of the Word is to be celebrated "in such a way as to favor meditation . . . any kind of haste such as hinders recollection is clearly to be avoided."[66] The GIRM also advocates silence before and after the readings so that "the Word of God may be grasped by the heart."[67] This aligns with Gadamer's notion of a "festive silence" in which the community falls quiet together, aware of being gathered before the thing being encountered—meaning is not only communicated through the words of the scriptural proclamation, but also through the silence which unifies the community. This corporate silence also provides a space for the hermeneutical dialogue to unfold in the minds of each worshiper, as they engage with the horizons of the Bible text, Lectionary text, and homilist. There are clear implications for formation in the art of mental silence and attentive concentration so that modern worshipers can engage deeply with the Lectionary pericopes by entering the play of the scriptural proclamation, remaining open to the transcendent, and entering into an experience of transformative dialogue that results in the emergence of new meaning in a fusion of horizons.

Revitalizing Understanding of Catholic Liturgical Symbols

Pope Francis is not the first to lament that modern people have, to a greater or lesser degree, "lost the capacity to engage with symbolic action."[68] More than forty years ago, French philosopher, Paul Ricoeur, claimed that humanity was living in an age of forgetfulness of the signs of the sacred. His suggested course of action was not to abandon old symbols in search of new

---

64. GIL 6.
65. Carruthers, *Book of Memory*, 274, 324.
66. GIRM 56.
67. GIRM 56.
68. DD 27.

ones, but rather to work towards a "second naïveté."[69] The same challenge remains for Catholics in contemporary times so that traditional symbols might become newly accessible without sacrificing the symbol's integrity or the worshiper's modernity.

The loss of experience with primary liturgical symbols in daily life constitutes a serious obstacle for the active participation that might enable modern worshipers to make connections between the symbolic language of the Scriptures and the patterns of their life experience. For Gadamer, the event of understanding begins with the awakening of predispositions based on prior experience,[70] and the emergence of new insights in the play event requires that the player understand the "rules" of the game in order to participate fully.[71] The process of awakening the assembly's capacity to engage with the symbols of water, fire, oil, bread, light, silence, and gestures embedded in the liturgical action would ideally be "evocative, imaginative, and experiential—but constantly grounded in the biblical witness to a living tradition."[72] Building the social capacity to respond to symbols is both a catechetical and mystagogical undertaking, and requires "bringing our cultural experience and pattern of life into contact with the otherness of the symbol-embedded word, and the word-permeated sign-action."[73]

The insight of Saint Augustine in relation to the sacramental and symbolic centrality of the scriptural proclamation is fundamental: sacraments are both visible words and audible symbols.[74] It is probable that many Catholics participating in the Liturgy of the Word at Mass simply hear the voice of the reader proclaiming the words of the ancient text, rather than perceiving the voice of Christ, present in the scriptural proclamation and addressing them directly in the here-and-now. A deeper appreciation of sacramental encounter would prevent a focus on the proclamation style or personality of the reader, and instead facilitate a hermeneutical dialogue with the horizon of the Lectionary text.

While language has primacy in Gadamer's philosophical hermeneutics, the non-verbal elements of liturgy call into question the adequacy of language alone to convey understanding. The principle of ineffability, captured by phrases such as "words cannot express . . ." is brought into play through the hermeneutical impact of sacred music, symbols, space, processions, and

69. Ricoeur, *Symbolism of Evil*, 351.
70. TM 309–10.
71. TM 107–12.
72. Saliers, "Symbol in Liturgy," 76.
73. Saliers, "Symbol in Liturgy," 76.
74. Augustine, "Tractates," 117–18; Irwin, *Models of Eucharist*, 117.

singing. Indeed, the profound insights experienced by worshipers in the Liturgy of the Word may exceed the expressive capacity of common language usage to capture what they have understood.[75] This could be conceptualized as an instance of the play of the liturgical event having primacy over the consciousness of a worshiper, and an example of the ways in which meaning can emerge when worshipers commit to the festival play of the scriptural proclamation. Such an explanation can be held in harmonious tension with the theological position which would attribute such effects to an encounter with Christ in the word, or the movement of the Holy Spirit.

In 2010, following the Synod of Bishops on the Word of God, it was proposed that churches "give a place of honor to the Scriptures, even outside of liturgical celebrations,"[76] and that the Gospel book be designed with particular beauty and carried in procession. The ritual prominence given to the Book of the Gospels as provided for in the GIRM, with procession and incense, is an ongoing reminder that reverence is due to this symbol of Christ's presence.[77] However, worshipers should realize that while a book is a significant visible sign, the primary symbol is "the voice of the minister who proclaims the text from faith to faith, and its reception by the faithful from heart to heart."[78] This important distinction reflects the Gadamerian premise that a festival, as a particular example of play, only reaches its accomplishment when it is celebrated by a community gathered for that specific purpose and that, despite its historical origins, the primary focus is on the current celebration.[79]

Despite the challenges associated with perceiving meaning in liturgical symbols in modern times, Pope Francis argues that an openness to the transcendent is constitutive of the human condition, and that the recovery of an ability to engage with the symbols of the liturgy is eminently possible.[80] While worshipers will only become fully engaged in the play of the liturgical event if these symbols form part of their lived experience, such an existential engagement occurs within the liturgy in a sacramental way, using "things that are the exact opposite of spiritual abstractions: bread, wine, oil, water, fragrances, fire, ashes, rock, fabrics, colors, body, words, sounds, silences,

---

75. Weinsheimer, *Gadamer's Hermeneutics*, 226.

76. VD 68.

77. Establishing a reverence for the symbols relating to the Liturgy of the Word weighs heavily against the practice of using an iPad or other digital device in place of the Lectionary or Missal. The fact that there may be other things on an electronic device, apart from the liturgical texts, makes it an unsuitable symbol for worship.

78. Australian Catholic Bishops Conference, *And When Churches*, 319.

79. TM 126–27.

80. DD 44.

gestures, space, movement, action."[81] A deeper appreciation of liturgical symbol is made possible by entering into the festive play of the liturgy itself, engaging in a hermeneutical dialogue with the words, music, and multisensory ritual actions that accompany the symbols, putting preconceptions at risk, and remaining open to encountering the truths contained in symbolic action and language.[82] The power of each liturgical symbol, therefore, is not in referencing an abstract ethereal concept, but rather in expressing concretely that which it signifies. Illuminating the interpretive role of symbol in contributing to the meaning which results from a fusion of horizons in the context of the liturgical event, further extrapolates Gadamer's original concept.

Engaging the Missionary Dimension of Scripture and Tradition

A liturgical hermeneutic of Scripture cannot be conceived without reference to the world which lies beyond the bounds of the parish assembly since a Scripture text that is proclaimed in the liturgy becomes real and actual "in the measure that it becomes actualized in the concrete living of the values of the Gospel outside of the liturgy, or, within the liturgy of the world."[83] Indeed, for Gadamer, understanding, interpretation, and application constitute a single integrated process; understanding a text necessarily involves applying the text in every moment and in every situation.[84] The texts proclaimed from the Lectionary are not intended to be understood historically from within the confines of a church building, but rather in a way that exercises their saving effect in the modern world.

Since the liturgical celebration is the summit and source of the Christian life,[85] hearing the Scriptures proclaimed in the communal, festive play of the liturgical proclamation highlights the missionary dimension of Scripture, in addition to its individual and communal dimensions. Active participation in the festival event of liturgy which leads to a fusion of horizons, or a conversion of mind and heart, presumes active participation in the mission of Christ which ultimately consummates the liturgical action.[86] This is because liturgy and the sacraments do not beckon worshipers

81. DD 42.
82. TM 280.
83. Haight, "Liturgy as Community Consciousness," 37.
84. TM 318–22.
85. SC 10.
86. Archbishop Mark Coleridge, "World, Word, Worship."

"to withdraw from the world, but . . . point back to the world itself as the place where God loves to dwell."[87] Ultimately, therefore, ecclesial activity should operate as an extension of and a precursor to the liturgical celebration of the community. Once it is acknowledged that mission is the task of all the baptized, the scriptural proclamation in the liturgy becomes not only inspiration, consolation, or encouragement, but rather a continual and fundamental formation of the Christian identity.[88] Gadamer would assert that such formation in the Christian identity (*Bildung*) prompts a turning of the gaze from oneself towards something universal, and that the play of the liturgical event, like all instances of play, points beyond itself to a wider reality.[89] The dynamic play of the scriptural proclamation which leads worshipers to experience the emergence of truth or insight (*aletheia*) through a fusion of horizons, thereby has an outward motion for the transformation of the world. This resonates strongly with the axiom of liturgical theology which expresses the intrinsic connection between worship, belief, and lived response: *lex orandi, lex credendi, lex vivendi*.[90]

SUMMARY

The theoretical model developed throughout this investigation accounts for the way a tradition changes and further determines itself from within. In the hermeneutic conversation that takes place in the liturgy during the scriptural proclamation, an event occurs in which tradition is furthered and produced. The word event, not the Scripture text, is the bearer of tradition. The scriptural tradition is carried on not through the book but through the continuity of memory in the ecclesial community, where Lectionary pericopes have been heard in association with particular feasts and seasons, as part of a eucharistic event, and juxtaposed with other pericopes such that particular emphases emerge.

Throughout history, the interpretation of Scripture as proclaimed from the Lectionary in the liturgical event has both contributed to and become part of Catholic tradition. In each liturgical proclamation of Scripture, tradition itself has occurred, and with each new liturgical event, the tradition continues to evolve. Thus, the meaning of each scriptural pericope is to some extent a product of its liturgical use.

---

87. Mitchell, "Spirituality of Christian Worship," 10.
88. Hellwig, "Twenty-Five Years," 62.
89. TM 11–15, 113.
90. Irwin, *Context and Text*, 95, 438.

Gadamer argues that whatever can be understood does not exist in itself, but in the unity of its understandings.[91] The Scriptures exist not as a closed text but rather as understood, and what the Bible text *is* therefore cannot be separated from the way it presents itself in liturgical events. When interpreting pericopes proclaimed from the Lectionary in the liturgy, worshipers themselves are being interpreted and thus belong to the continuing life of Scripture that embodies its own possibilities in the variety of its interpretations. Scripture *is* differently as it is interpreted differently.

It is therefore proposed that the arrangement of Scripture texts in the Lectionary for the purpose of liturgical proclamation be considered in the field of biblical hermeneutics alongside other hermeneutical approaches used by biblical scholars. The Lectionary constitutes a particular application of Scripture and its use in the corporate celebration of liturgy has set a precedent that now unavoidably belongs to the meaning of the Scripture texts. In the case of a biblical scholar writing a commentary on the Gospel of Luke, for example, the tradition which has been established in associating pericopes from Luke's Gospel with particular liturgical feasts, seasons, or rites cannot be ignored. Since the trajectory of interpretation is the dialectical progression of the tradition itself as it is understood in new scenarios and new situations by different interpreters, the use of Scripture texts in the Lectionary and in the liturgy has altered the tradition precisely by belonging to it. The arrangement of scriptural pericopes in the Lectionary and the proclamation of these texts in worshiping communities according to the framework of the liturgical year has directly influenced the meaning of these Scripture texts over time such that their liturgical use has become part of what they are.

---

91. TM 305.

CHAPTER 10

Conclusion

I. REVIEW OF AIMS AND INTENTIONS

This investigation has placed biblical and liturgical theology into a critical dialogue with Gadamer's philosophical hermeneutics to arrive at a hermeneutical model for interpreting Scripture texts proclaimed from the Lectionary within the Catholic liturgical event. The theoretical model which underpins this liturgical hermeneutic of Scripture extrapolates Gadamer's fusion of horizons to depict the emergence of meaning in the liturgical proclamation in a four-way collision between the horizons of the Bible text, the Lectionary text, the homilist, and the worshiper. The meaning which emerges for worshipers as they engage with the Scripture texts is inevitably influenced by two contextual factors, namely the ecclesial community which they identify as belonging to, and the liturgical event which they actively participate in. The use of Gadamer's hermeneutical theory lends a philosophical ecumenical dimension to this project which, it is hoped, will give this work a broader applicability beyond Catholic liturgy and theology.

The significance of developing a liturgical hermeneutic of Scripture has stemmed from the cultural reality that the majority of contemporary Catholics only encounter the texts of Scripture during Sunday Mass, in which short, often unrelated pericopes are proclaimed from the Lectionary within the richly symbolic, multisensory context of the corporate worship event. Conceiving of the scriptural proclamation as an event of meaning, an event of tradition, an event which is both a social event and a personal encounter, carries implications for praxis so that worshipers might be drawn into the play of the liturgical event, aware that the text has something to say to them in the present, and thereby experience new insights through a fusion of horizons.

In response, this investigation has been conducted within the discipline of practical theology and has utilized a critical correlational approach in bringing theology into a dynamic conversation with philosophy and contemporary culture. Within the overarching methodological framework of mutually critical correlation, the four dimensions of fundamental practical theology expounded by Don Browning have provided the structure for the investigation. It is illustrative now to retrace the cumulative steps in the argument in order to support the contention that a liturgical hermeneutic of Scripture is a necessary addition to the field of biblical hermeneutics.

II. RETRACING THE ARGUMENT

In the descriptive theology phase, the unique structure of the Lectionary, with its assignment of pericopes to a particular liturgical feast or season, and its juxtaposition of previously unrelated texts, was seen to produce new and unforeseen meanings independent of a pericope's native biblical context. The Lectionary thus emerged as a distinct entity from the Bible in need of its own hermeneutic (chapter 3). A study of the purpose and aims of the Lectionary as a liturgical book highlighted the inextricable link between the pericopes and the dynamics of the ritual in which the texts are proclaimed. It became clear that the primary commitment of the Lectionary is not to historical or exegetical interpretation, but rather to the contemporary worshiping assembly and the proclamation of meaning in the present. The presumption that pericopes are proclaimed in a public worship event, rather than being read privately, indicated a hermeneutical role for the Catholic liturgical context and the ecclesial community.

The features of the Catholic liturgical paradigm emerged as key influences in interpreting the Lectionary readings (chapter 4). The complex interplay of multisensory elements was seen as not only supporting the proclaimed text, but as a significant part of the message being transmitted. The interweaving of text, symbol, and action in the ritualization of the proclamation of Scripture was shown to facilitate the movement of the texts from potentiality to actuality in the word event which is always unique and unrepeatable by virtue of the ever-changing shifts in time, culture, personal circumstances, and social situations. It became apparent that the proclamation could be viewed as a complex social and ecclesial event in which the assembly's reception of the Lectionary texts through a bodily, incarnational, and communal speech act, is inescapably influenced by a variety of social exchanges, both modern and historical. The sacramental encounter with Christ, facilitated by the Holy Spirit, was seen to occur not by virtue of the printed text alone but in the living proclamation event in which worshipers participate fully, consciously, and actively. While the dynamic energy flowing from the interactions between text, ritual context, and worshipers can prompt rich and diverse meanings being attributed to the Lectionary texts, it was observed that the *sensus fidelium* of the ecclesial community functions as an important reference point for testing individual interpretations.

In the historical theology phase (chapter 5), the study of the origin and evolution of liturgical texts and practices was expressly directed towards understanding the present worship context of liturgical communities. The reading event emerged as a complex sociocultural system from earliest times, comprising the ecclesial community, the ritual action of Christian worship, the proclamation of scriptural pericopes, the ceremonials surrounding the proclamation, and the homily, all of which unfold in a particular cultural milieu. The biblical texts, and later the liturgical books of Scripture, were noted as manuscripts of living literature, which were adapted over the centuries in response to changing socio-cultural and liturgical practice. The implication for the contemporary worship event is that the Lectionary must continue to be viewed as a living text, subject to revision in light of current social, cultural, and ecclesial circumstances.

The systematic theology phase began with an examination of Gadamer's theory of philosophical hermeneutics (chapter 6). This analysis revealed Gadamer's framework to be entirely consistent with the theological position canvassed in the descriptive phase, holding that meaning exists only as potential, moving into actuality in the concrete event of interpretation. Gadamer's recognition of tradition as an active dialogue partner in the task of interpretation was important for preserving the historicity of both worshiper and Lectionary text in the dynamic process of understanding that takes place in the liturgy. Acknowledging pre-existing assumptions and prejudices as the productive basis for understanding, rather than seeking to remove subjectivity from the interpretive process, was consistent with the reality of a heterogeneous assembly. It was argued that the disclosure of meaning, or truth, arises from a fusion of horizons in which a person requires a conscious openness to the impact of history in forming their current horizon, and a willingness to allow their existing horizon to collide with other perspectives and thereby be challenged. This fusion of horizons was identified as occurring within the rich philosophical construct of play and, more specifically, festival, which corresponded with remarkable similarity to the liturgical event. From a Gadamerian perspective, it was established that the play of the liturgical event has primacy over the consciousness of a worshiper, and the meaning that emerges from the proclamation of the Scriptures is less the result of what a person does, and more a matter of the liturgy acting upon the gathered celebrating assembly. This was held in harmonious balance with the theological position which would attribute such effects to the presence of Christ in the scriptural proclamation, the movement of the Holy Spirit, or the initiative of God's communication in the liturgy.

Considering the liturgical event through the lens of Gadamer's concept of festival emphasized the corporate nature of interpretation and highlighted the liturgy's role in creating a dynamic tradition and preserving corporate memory (chapter 7). By virtue of its unique capacity to actualize the living memory through ritual and narrative, each liturgical proclamation of Scripture was viewed as an event of living tradition in which past and present are mediated and in which the corporate memory has a contemporary frame of reference. It was demonstrated that the interpretation of Lectionary pericopes proclaimed in the liturgical event has both contributed to and become part of the scriptural tradition. In other words, the contemporary meaning of scriptural pericopes is, to some extent, a product of their liturgical use in the ecclesial community.

Although the liturgy is a communal, social event, it became evident that a deeply personal encounter may also be experienced by each worshiper (chapter 8). A sense of interconnectedness between worshipers was identified along with their social embeddedness in the corporate ritual structure which leads them to experience the scriptural proclamation within the social context of the ecclesial community. It was recognized that each individual arrives at a meaning of their own, but that this construction of meaning is unavoidably influenced by the socio-cultural elements of the liturgical event. There emerged an indisputable need to preserve the dynamic equilibrium between personal interiorization and external corporate expression in the liturgy.

The social energy circulating in the liturgical event, conceived theologically as the dynamism of grace, illuminated the hermeneutical interplay between Christ, the Lectionary pericopes, the personal and shared history of gathered worshipers, the Scripture text, the words of the homilist, the multisensory and physically embodied liturgical ritual, and the movement of the Holy Spirit. It became apparent that the hermeneutical focus of the scriptural proclamation is not the text alone, but rather the complex network of interrelationships that draw together worshipers, liturgical symbols and texts, ritual action, and sensory stimuli.

The celebratory dynamic of the liturgical proclamation found expression in Gadamer's concept of the "festival" where a common intention and a commitment to participate unites those gathered and prevents them withdrawing into subjective experiences. Yet, unity is not the same as uniformity. A critical tension was recognized as being always at play, simultaneously upholding the integrity of the sacred text, the position of the individual worshiper, and the community to which that person belongs and draws their identity. The interpretation arrived at by each worshiper was viewed not as a process of submission to the text, but rather as the result of deep engagement with the text in the contemporary community.

Drawing the elements of this complex network together to arrive at the key elements of a liturgical hermeneutic of Scripture was the work of the strategic practical theology phase (chapter 9). The scriptural proclamation was identified as an event of meaning in which truth emerges for participants by virtue of their voluntary and active participation in the play of the liturgy. It became clear that people would choose to enter into dynamic conversation with the other horizons operating in the liturgical event and remain open to the emergence of new insights on the basis that the text had something of value to say to them in their present situation. Thus, the importance of removing obstacles, such as non-inclusive language, that would prevent contemporary worshipers from entering the play of the interpretive event and experiencing new insights through a fusion of horizons, was identified as a pressing consideration.

The strategic practical theology phase also uncovered a need to respect the tension which exists between the unceasing sameness of a Scripture text and the variety of different situations to which it is applied. It was discovered that the proposed hermeneutical model, which has its basis in the fusion of fluid horizons, could account for the possibility of multiple interpretations of a Scripture passage that can all be true without disintegrating into fragments. Such a fusion of horizons in the dynamic liturgical context thereby led to insights into the scriptural proclamation that could not be ascribed to the worshiper, the homilist, the Bible text, or the Lectionary pericopes, nor even to the sum of their contributions.

Another element which emerged as fundamental in a liturgical hermeneutic of Scripture was the nature of the scriptural proclamation as both a social event and personal encounter, highlighting the importance of gathering physically, rather than virtually, to celebrate the liturgy and listen to the Scriptures proclaimed. The impact of lifting one's voice in prayer, response, or song, together with others who are physically present, was seen to be imperative not only due to the Catholic ritual tradition, but also due to the physiological and hermeneutical effects of producing and receiving sound in a corporate context. It was shown that the corporate discipline, which engages the body as well as the mind, allows worshipers to not only listen to ideals that inspire them, but to be actively formed in the attitudes and behaviors proclaimed from the Scriptures in the context of the ecclesial community.

Formation both *for* the liturgy and *by* the liturgy was identified as a necessary precursor in facilitating the capacity of modern worshipers to enter into the play of the scriptural proclamation, so that they might engage in a fruitful hermeneutical dialogue and experience a fusion of horizons. The purpose of formation is not to promote a "correct" interpretation but is rather to enable worshipers to understand the "rules of the game" and participate more actively in the festive play of the liturgical event.

Finally, it was evident that a liturgical hermeneutic of Scripture cannot be conceived without a missionary dimension which considers the world beyond the bounds of the worshiping assembly. In line with the Gadamerian perspective that conceives of understanding, interpretation, and application as one unified process, so too the liturgical proclamation of Scripture, and the sacramental encounter that ideally ensues, were not viewed as occurring in a vacuum but rather as pointing back to the world and the continuation of Christ's work in it. For an adequate understanding of the sacred text, therefore, it was concluded that the world of the Scriptures cannot remain foreign to the world of the worshiper; rather a person learns to understand themselves *in it*. Any new insight or conversion experienced through a fusion of horizons in the liturgy was seen to have an outward focus with its ultimate expression in lived response. A worshiper's transformed horizon is carried out from the liturgy for the transformation of the world.

III. LIMITATIONS AND DIRECTIONS FOR FUTURE RESEARCH

The theoretical model proposed in this book is as yet untested and is open to ongoing refinements in response to future research. It must be acknowledged that the model presumes an ideal scenario in which worshipers are actively participating in the play of the liturgical proclamation, are open to encountering other perspectives, and have an appreciation of the sacramental encounter taking place. It presumes that the homilist has a connection with the community and that worshipers are willing to allow the horizon of the homilist to collide with their own. It operates on the premise that worshipers identify as members of the ecclesial community, participate with a corporate mindset, are aware of their situatedness within a living tradition, and possess an appreciation of the Catholic liturgical paradigm in all its richness. Future research could therefore explore the kinds of formation required *for* the liturgy so that people can be formed more effectively *by* the liturgy. Instances of formation *for* the liturgy might foster an appreciation of liturgical symbol and its hermeneutical role in making meaning of Scripture texts in the context of the liturgical event. Formation *for* the liturgy might also illuminate the corporate mindset, corporate silence, internal and external participation, an understanding of the Lectionary cursus, and a greater familiarity with the Bible.

Further research into how people are formed *by* the liturgy could examine creative ways to draw people into the play of the scriptural proclamation and into the powerful moments of participatory, corporate silence so that, "after hearing the mystery of Christ proclaimed, [they] consciously and freely seek the living God and enter the way of faith and conversion as the Holy Spirit opens their hearts."[1] Possibilities might include the impact of visual images projected onto a screen as part of the hermeneutical dialogue, or opportunities to discuss an element of the readings with other members of the assembly. It may also be beneficial to set aside time after the Liturgy of the Word for contemplation, perhaps with the use of appropriate instrumental music, to lead worshipers into nonverbal realms of meaning-making which elicit new insights.[2] A range of strategies might be devised to ensure that each member of a liturgical congregation, with their particular effective history and engagement style, is able to participate fully, actively, and consciously in the liturgy and perceive new insights in the Scripture texts.

Despite the acknowledged limitations to the Lectionary, it is beyond the scope of this book to propose suggestions for drafting an update to the Lectionary. Further research could propose modifications to the Lectionary that would ensure inclusivity and improve fidelity to the Bible text by incorporating verses and passages notably missing from the current Lectionary and by removing passages assessed as likely to offend modern sensibilities. Another valuable topic for further exploration would be the place of the Pauline letters in the Lectionary, which are currently not thematically connected to the first reading or Gospel, yet which offer profound, and often overlooked, opportunities for preaching.[3]

The question of ecclesial identity is also ripe for further research. How, in an increasingly secular culture, can a sense of Catholic identity be nurtured such that believers might identify as members of an ecclesial community and thus be able to participate in the liturgy with a corporate mindset? Beyond a cursory understanding of the liturgy as the action of the whole church community (the *Christus totus*), there is a need to appreciate that

---

1. Catholic Church, *Rite of Christian Initiation*, 1.
2. Wakeling, "Divine Resonance," xv.
3. Bonneau, "Second Readings," 254–55.

the ecclesial community includes not only the gathered liturgical assembly but baptized Christians of all times and places. This imports a profound sense of solidarity and unity with Christian communities from every corner of the globe, including those in the grips of war or extreme poverty, which may color the meaning that emerges from the liturgical proclamation of Scripture.

The corporate dimension of the liturgy sets it apart as a hermeneutical context in the realm of biblical scholarship, yet this need not be confined to a parish context. While the number of people attending parish Masses may have sharply declined, school liturgies which celebrate significant educational milestones attract hundreds of parents and students who enter the play of the scriptural proclamation. An investigation of the potential for the scriptural proclamation to provoke new insights for those who gather to celebrate the liturgy in "faith communities," as distinct from traditional parish settings, therefore emerges as an important practical theology project for the future.

Furthermore, the question of revelation in contemporary times would be a fascinating topic for future research. The current investigation has suggested that revelation is mediated in the festive play of the liturgy through Scripture texts as proclaimed from the Lectionary through the symbols, music, prayers, and actions of the liturgical event, through the Holy Spirit moving amongst the assembly, and ultimately through the fusion of horizons in which worshipers derive meaning from the scriptural proclamation. While the liturgical proclamation of Scripture is a pivotal event whereby God communicates with human beings, it is by no means the only medium. Further work could adopt a broader lens of sacramentality to investigate the ways in which people make meaning as God communicates through creation, the arts, and through other people.

In addition to prompting further research, it is hoped that this investigation might also suggest a particular focus for the ongoing quest to reinvigorate attendance at communal worship. The search for contemporary meaning in the Scripture texts finds a parallel in the human search for meaning operating powerfully in the broader culture. While church attendance may seem to be counter-cultural, and the existence of a Catholic corporate memory amongst younger members of the community may be a tenuous claim at best, the human quest for a significant existence continues to find expression in music, theater, and the visual arts. An exploration of the links between the religious enterprise and the broader cultural search for meaning in secular contexts would likely uncover some interesting implications for liturgical praxis. Future research opportunities could include an extrapolation of the theoretical model proposed here, situating the horizons operating in the liturgy, and the key contexts of liturgical event and ecclesial community, within a broader circle of contemporary culture. Cultural influences could be examined for their influence on the prejudices of worshipers, and for their capacity to either promote or hinder the ability and willingness of worshipers to enter the play of the liturgical event.

As mentioned at the outset of this book, the liturgical hermeneutic of Scripture proposed here does not attempt to supersede or contradict existing approaches to biblical interpretation. Biblical hermeneutical approaches which draw on the skill of historical experts and literary critics form a vital piece of the puzzle in understanding the complexities of the biblical texts and their origins. However, a liturgical hermeneutic contributes an additional tier to the interpretive enterprise by addressing the primary context in which modern Catholics encounter the Scriptures. While the norms of biblical interpretation or the establishment of a liturgical hermeneutic are, to some extent, human constructs, they are ultimately directed towards something far greater, namely an encounter with Christ through the words of Scripture. A liturgical hermeneutic of Scripture accounts for the event of understanding which emerges when contemporary Catholics, with their vastly diverse personal histories and circumstances, hear the Scriptures proclaimed in the liturgy according to the Lectionary's unique structure while participating actively in the play of the liturgy as members of the ecclesial community. Recognizing the significance of such a hermeneutic is reflective of the conviction that Scripture "cannot be just the heritage of some, much less a collection of books for the benefit of a privileged few. It belongs above all to those called to hear its message and to recognize themselves in its words."[4]

---

4. Francis, *Aperuit Illis*, 4.

Bibliography

Abrams, M. H. *A Glossary of Literary Terms*. New York: Holt, Rinehart & Winston, 1981.
Achtemeier, Paul J. "Omne Verbum Sonat: The New Testament and the Oral Environment of Late Western Antiquity." *Journal of Biblical Literature* 109 (1990) 3–27.
Aichele, George. "Canon, Ideology, and the Emergence of an Imperial Church." In *Canon and Canonicity: The Formation and Use of Scripture*, edited by Einar Thomassen, 45–65. Copenhagen: Museum Tusculanum, 2010.
Alan, Kirk. "Memory." In *Jesus in Memory: Traditions in Oral and Scribal Perspectives*, edited by Werner H. and Samuel Byrskog Kelber, 155–72. Waco, TX: Baylor University Press, 2009.
Alcuin. "Carmen 69." In *Poetae Latini Aevi Carolini*, edited by Ernst Dümmler, 1:160–351. Berlin: Weidmann, 1881.
Alikin, Valeriy A. *The Earliest History of the Christian Gathering—Origin, Development and Content of the Christian Gathering in the First to Third Centuries*. Boston: Brill, 2010.
Allen, Horace. "Common Lectionary: Origins, Assumptions, and Issues." *Studia Liturgica* 21 (1991) 14–30.
Allen, P. L. *Theological Method: A Guide for the Perplexed*. London: T. & T. Clark, 2012.
Anderson, E. Byron. "Liturgical Reform: For Participation and/or Mission." *Liturgy (Washington)* 31 (2016) 11–18.
———. "'O for a Heart to Praise My God': Hymning the Self before God." In *Liturgy and the Moral Self: Humanity at Full Stretch before God*, edited by D. E. Saliers et al., 111–25. Collegeville, MN: Liturgical, 1998.
———. "Practicing Scripture, Unsealing the Book." *Wesleyan Theological Journal* 46 (2011) 86–104.
———. "Scripture and Liturgy: Offering Christ." *Studia Liturgica* 39 (2009) 185–201.
Archbishop's Diocesan and Cathedral Library (Digital). "Gospels." Cod. 56 (Dom Hs. 56). Cologne, Germany. https://nbn-resolving.org/urn:nbn:de:hbz:kn28-3-1791-p0029-4.
Aristotle. "De Anima (on the Soul)." Translated by J. A. Smith. Classics in the History of Psychology, Book III, York University. https://psychclassics.yorku.ca/Aristotle/De-anima/de-anima3.htm.
———. *De Sensu and De Memoria*. Translated by G. R. T. Ross. Cambridge: Cambridge University Press, 1906.

Assmann, Jan. "Collective Memory and Cultural Identity." Translated by John Czaplicka. *New German Critique* no. 65 (1995) 125–33.

———. *Das Kulturelle Gedächtnis: Schrift, Erinnerung und Politische Identität in Frühen Hochkulturen*. München: Beck, 2007.

Augustine. *Confessions*. Translated and edited by Carolyn J. B. Hammond. Loeb Classical Library. Cambridge, MA: Harvard University Press, 2014. https://www.loebclassics.com/view/augustine-confessions_2014/2014/pb_LCL026.243.xml.

———. "Confessions, Book XI." In *Augustine: Confessions and Enchiridion*, edited by Albert Cook Outler, 244–69. Louisville, KY: Westminster John Knox, 2006.

———. "Tractates on the Gospel of John." In *Tractates on the Gospel of John 55–111 (The Fathers of the Church, Vol 90)*, translated by John W. Rettig. Washington: The Catholic University of America Press, 1994.

———. *The Works of Saint Augustine: A Translation for the 21st Century*. Edited by E. Hill and J. E. Rotelle. New York: New City, 1990.

Australian Catholic Bishops Conference. *And When Churches Are to Be Built: Preparation, Planning and Construction of Places of Worship*. Brisbane: Liturgy Brisbane, 2014.

Australian Episcopal Conference of the Roman Catholic Church. "Music in the Order of Mass." In *Catholic Worship Book II Full Music Edition Part I*, xiii–xvii. Northcote: Morning Star, 2015.

Averroës. *Epitome of Parva Naturalia*. Translated by H. Blumberg and edited by A. L. Shields and H. Blumberg. Cambridge, MA: Medieval Academy of America, 1961.

Aždajić, Dejan. "Externalizing Faith: Countering Individualism through an Embodied Emphasis." *Studia Liturgica* 51 (2021) 86–102.

Bailey, Lloyd R. "The Lectionary in Critical Perspective." *Interpretation* 31 (1977) 139–53.

Bakhtin, M. M. *The Dialogic Imagination Four Essays*. Translated by Caryl Emerson and Michael Holquist and edited by Michael Holquist. Austin: University of Texas Press, 1981.

Baldovin, John. "The Bible and Liturgy Part Two: Their Interrelation." *Catechumenate* 11 (November 1989) 2–10.

———. "Biblical Preaching in the Liturgy." *Studia Liturgia* 22 (1992) 100–118.

———. "How Are They to Hear without Someone to Proclaim Him?" In *Lively Oracles of God: Perspectives on the Bible and Liturgy*, edited by G. Jeanes et al., 15–32. Collegeville, MN: Liturgical, 2022.

———. "Pastoral Liturgical Reflections on the Study." In *The Awakening Church: 25 Years of Liturgical Renewal*, edited by Lawrence J. Madden SJ, 98–114. Collegeville, MN: Liturgical, 1992.

Bardot, Jules. *The Lectionary: Its Sources and History*. Translated by Ambrose Cator. London: Catholic Truth Society, 1910.

Barth, Karl. *Church Dogmatics*. Volume 3.2. Edinburgh: T. & T. Clark, 1936.

———. *The Word of God and the Word of Man*. London: Hodder and Stoughton, 1928.

Barth, K., and A. Marga. *The Word of God and Theology*. London: Bloomsbury Academic, 2011.

Bartholomew, Craig G. "Three Horizons: Hermeneutics from the Other End—An Evaluation of Anthony Thiselton's Hermeneutic Proposals." *European Journal of Theology* 5 (1996) 121–36.

Baumann, Holger. "Reconsidering Relational Autonomy: Personal Autonomy for Socially Embedded and Temporally Extended Selves." *Analyse and Kritik* 30 (2008) 445–68.

Baumeister, Roy F., and Mark R. Leary. "The Need to Belong: Desire for Interpersonal Attachments as a Fundamental Human Motivation." *Psychological Bulletin* 117 (1995) 497–529.

Bechard, D. P., and J. A. Fitzmyer. *The Scripture Documents: An Anthology of Official Catholic Teachings*. Collegeville, MN: Liturgical, 2002.

Beck, Norman. "Removing Anti-Jewish Polemic from Our Christian Lectionaries: A Proposal." *Jewish-Christian Relations: Insights and Issues in the Ongoing Jewish-Christian Dialogue*, 1–15. https://www.jcrelations.net/article/removing-anti-jewish-polemic-from-our-christian-lectionaries-a-proposal.pdf.

Bell, Catherine. *Ritual: Perspectives and Dimensions*. Oxford: Oxford University Press, 1997.

Benedict. *The Rule of Benedict: An Invitation to the Christian Life*. Translated by Georg Holzherr and Mark Thamert. Collegeville, MN: Liturgical, 2016.

Benedict XVI. "Sacramentum Caritatis: Post-Synodal Apostolic Exhortation on the Eucharist as the Source and Summit of the Church's Life and Mission." February 22, 2007. http://w2.vatican.va/content/benedict-xvi/en/apost_exhortations/documents/hf_ben-xvi_exh_20070222_sacramentum-caritatis.html.

———. *Verbum Domini: The Word of God in the Life and Mission of the Church*. Post-Synodal Apostolic Exhortation. Strathfield, NSW: St Paul's Publications, 2010.

Bennett, Zoë, et al. *Invitation to Research in Practical Theology*. 1st ed. Abingdon: Routledge, 2018.

Benofy, Susan. "The Day the Mass Changed, How It Happened and Why—Part I." Adoremus Bulletin, February 2010. https://www.catholicculture.org/culture/library/view.cfm?recnum=9377.

Bernstein, Richard J. *Beyond Objectivism and Relativism: Science, Hermeneutics, and Praxis*. Philadelphia: University of Pennsylvania Press, 2011.

———. "From Hermeneutics to Praxis." In *Hermeneutics and Modern Philosophy*, edited by Brice R. Wachterhauser, 87–110. Albany: State University of New York, 1986.

———. "Reviews: Gadamer, Hans-Georg. The Relevance of The Beautiful and Other Essays." *The Journal of Aesthetics and Art Criticism* 46 (1988) 421–23.

Best, Thomas. "Memory and Meaning. Liturgy as Transformation: To Heal a Broken World—The Ecumenical Dimension." *Studia Liturgica* 36 (2006) 60–73.

Billings, J. Todd. *The Word of God for the People of God: An Entryway to the Theological Interpretation of Scripture*. Grand Rapids, MI: Eerdmans, 2010.

Billman, Kathleen D., and Daniel L. Migliore. *Rachel's Cry: Prayer of Lament and Rebirth of Hope*. Eugene, OR: Wipf & Stock, 1999.

Black, C. Clifton. "Journeying through Scripture with the Lectionary's Map." *Interpretation (Richmond)* 56 (2002) 59–72.

Blowers, Paul. "Interpreting Scripture." In *The Cambridge History of Christianity: Constantine to C.600*, edited by Augustine Casiday and Frederick W. Norris, 618–36. Cambridge: Cambridge University Press, 2007.

Bockmuehl, Markus. "A Commentator's Approach to the 'Effective History' of Philippians." *Journal for the Study of the New Testament* 18 (1996) 57–88.

Boeve, Lieven. "Revelation, Scripture and Tradition: Lessons from Vatican II's Constitution Dei Verbum for Contemporary Theology: Revelation, Scripture and Tradition." *International Journal of Systematic Theology* 13 (2011) 416–33.
Bohren, Rudolf. *Predigtlehre*. Munich: Christian Kaiser Gütersloher Verlagshaus, 1986.
Boisclair, R. A. *The Word of the Lord at Mass: Understanding the Lectionary*. Chicago: Liturgy Training, 2016.
Bonneau, Normand. "The Second Readings of the Sunday Lectionary: An Appreciation." *Worship* 96 (2022) 240–56.
———. *The Sunday Lectionary: Ritual Word, Paschal Shape*. Collegeville, MN: Liturgical, 1998.
Boselli, Goffredo. *The Spiritual Meaning of the Liturgy: School of Prayer, Source of Life*. Collegeville, MN: Liturgical, 2014.
Botha, P. *Orality and Literacy in Early Christianity*. Eugene, OR: Wipf & Stock, 2012.
Botham, Pieter J. J. "Authorship in Historical Perspective and Its Bearing on New Testament and Early Christian Texts and Contexts." *Scriptura* 102 (2009) 495–510.
Boyarin, Daniel. "Placing Reading: Ancient Israel and Medieval Europe." In *Summoning: Ideas of the Covenant and Interpretive Theory*, edited by Ellen Spolsky, 155–86. New York: State University of New York Press, 2012.
Brackett, Tom. "Let's Do Theology." *Anglican and Episcopal History* 80 (2011) 222–24.
Bradshaw, Paul F. "Foreword." In *Lively Oracles of God: Perspectives on the Bible and Liturgy*, edited by G. Jeanes et al., ix–x. Collegeville, MN: Liturgical, 2022.
———. "Liturgy and Living Literature." In *Liturgy in Dialogue: Essays in Memory of Ronald Jasper*, edited by Paul Bradshaw and Bryan Spinks, 138–53. London: SPCK, 1993.
———. "The Reshaping of Liturgical Studies." *Anglican Theological Review* 72 (1990) 481–87.
———. *The Search for the Origins of Christian Worship: Sources and Methods for the Study of Early Liturgy*. New York: Oxford University Press, 1992.
———. "The Use of the Bible in Liturgy: Some Historical Perspectives." *Studia Liturgica* 22 (1992) 35–52.
Brakke, David. *Athanasius and the Politics of Asceticism*. Oxford Early Christian Studies. Oxford: Clarendon, 1995.
———. "Canon Formation and Social Conflict in Fourth-Century Egypt: Athanasius of Alexandria's Thirty-Ninth Festal Letter." *Harvard Theological Review* 87 (1994) 395–419.
Brinkworth, Jenny. "Church Must Adapt to Changing Times: Coleridge." *The Southern Cross*, April 7, 2022. https://thesoutherncross.org.au/news/2022/04/07/church-must-adapt-to-changing-times-coleridge/.
Brodie, Louis. "The Two Horizons. New Testament Hermeneutics and Philosophical Description with Special Reference to Heidegger, Bultmann, Gadamer, and Wittgenstein by Anthony C. Thiselton." *The Thomist: A Speculative Quarterly Review* 45 (1981) 480–86.
Brooke, George J. *Reading the Dead Sea Scrolls: Essays in Method*. Atlanta: SBL, 2013.
Brown, Dennis. "Jerome and the Vulgate." In *A History of Biblical Interpretation*, edited by Alan J. Hauser and Duane F. Watson, 355–79. Grand Rapids: Eerdmans, 2003.
Brown, R. E., et al. *The New Jerome Biblical Commentary*. Englewood Cliffs, NJ: Prentice-Hall, 1990.

Brown, Sally. "Hermeneutical Theory." In *The Wiley-Blackwell Companion to Practical Theology*, edited by Bonnie J. Miller-McLemore, 112–22. Chichester: Wiley-Blackwell, 2012.

Browning, Don S. *A Fundamental Practical Theology: Descriptive and Strategic Proposals*. Minneapolis: Fortress, 1995.

———. "Integrating Approaches: A Practical Theology". In *Building Effective Ministry: Theory and Practice in the Local Church*, edited by Carl S. Dudley, 220–37. San Francisco: Harper & Row, 1983.

———. "Mapping the Terrain of Pastoral Theology: Toward a Practical Theology of Care." *Pastoral Psychology* 36 (1987) 10–28.

Brueggemann, Walter. *Disruptive Grace: Reflections on God, Scripture, and the Church*, edited by Carolyn J. Sharp. London: SCM, 2011.

———. "Preaching as Reimagination." *Theology Today* 52 (1995) 313–29.

———. *The Psalms and the Life of Faith*, Minneapolis: Fortress, 1995.

Brunk, Timothy. "Consumerism and the Liturgical Act of Worship." *Horizons* 38 (2011) 54–74.

Büchler, A. "The Reading of the Law and Prophets in a Triennial Cycle." In *Contributions to the Scientific Study of Jewish Liturgy*, edited by J. J. Petuchowski, 181–229. New York: Ktav, 1970.

Buechner, Frederick. *Telling the Truth: The Gospel as Tragedy, Comedy, and Fairy Tale*. San Francisco: Harper and Row, 1977.

Bugnini, Annibale. *The Reform of the Liturgy, 1948–1975*. Collegeville, MN: Liturgical, 1990.

Bujo, Bénézet. *Foundations of an African Ethic: Beyond the Universal Claims of Western Morality*. Nairobi: Paulines Publications Africa, 2003.

Burns, John Mary. "The Processions of the Ordo Missae: Liturgical Structure and Theological Meaning." *Antiphon: A Journal for Liturgical Renewal* 13 (2009) 159–74.

Butler, Christopher, OSB. "The Aggiornamento of Vatican II." Vatican II—Voice of the Church. https://vatican2voice.org/3butlerwrites/aggiorna.htm.

Cabié, Robert. *The Church at Prayer: An Introduction to the Liturgy*. Volume 2. Translated by Matthew O'Connell, edited by Aimé-Georges Martimort. Collegeville, MN: Liturgical, 1986.

Cahalan, Kathleen A. "Locating Practical Theology in Catholic Theological Discourse and Practice." *International Journal of Practical Theology* 15 (2011) 1–21.

———. "Three Approaches to Practical Theology, Theological Education, and the Church's Ministry." *International Journal of Practical Theology* 9 (2005) 63–94.

Cahalan, Kathleen A., and Bryan Froehle. "A Developing Discipline: The Catholic Voice in Practical Theology." In *Invitation to Practical Theology: Catholic Voices and Visions*, edited by Claire E. Wolfteich, 27–51. New York: Paulist, 2014.

Cahalan, Kathleen A., and Gordon S. Mikoski. *Opening the Field of Practical Theology: An Introduction*. Lanham, MD: Rowman and Littlefield, 2014.

Carr, Ephrem. "Sacrosanctum Concilium and Its Consequences: The Reform of the Liturgy." *Questions Liturgiques: Studies in Liturgy* 92 (2011) 183–94.

Carruthers, Mary. *The Book of Memory: A Study of Memory in Medieval Culture*. Cambridge: Cambridge University Press, 2008.

———. *The Craft of Thought: Meditation, Rhetoric, and the Making of Images, 400–1200*. Cambridge: Cambridge University Press, 2000.

Carvalhaes, Cláudio. "And the Word Became Connection: Liturgical Theologies in the Real/Virtual World." *Liturgy* 30 (2015) 26–35.
Casey, Damien. "Liturgy Matters: Liturgy and Scripture as the Mirrors of Catholicity." *Australian eJournal of Theology* no. 4 (2005) 1–11.
Cassian, John. *John Cassian: The Conferences*. Translated and edited by Boniface Ramsey. Mahwah, NJ: Paulist, 1997.
Catholic Church. *Catechism of the Catholic Church*. 2nd ed. Vatican City: Vatican, 1997.
———. *The Code of Canon Law*. Sydney: Collins Liturgical, 1983.
———. *The General Instruction of the Roman Missal*. Strathfield: St Paul's, 2012.
———. "General Introduction." In *Lectionary I: Proper of Seasons, Sundays in Ordinary Time. Revised Edition Approved for Use in the Diocese of Australia*. London: Collins Liturgical, 1981.
———. *Lectionary for Mass*. Edited by International Commission on the Liturgy. London: Collins Liturgical, 1981.
———. *Lectionary: Sundays and Solemnities*. Ottawa: Canadian Conference of Catholic Bishops, 1993.
———. *Ordo Lectionum Missae (Editio Typica)*. Edited by Congregatio pro Cultu Divino. Vatican City: Libreria Editrice Vaticana, 1969.
———. *Rite of Christian Initiation of Adults*. Strathfield: St Paul's, 2003.
———. *The Rites*. Volume 2. Collegeville, MN: Liturgical, 1991.
———. *The Roman Missal—English Translation According to the Third Typical Edition*. London: Catholic Truth Society, 2010.
———. *The Rubrics of the 1962 Missale Romanum: Ritus Servandus*. Chicago: Biretta, 2007.
———. *Sunday Celebration of the Word and Hours*. Ottawa: Canadian Conference of Catholic Bishops, 1995.
———. "Universal Norms for the Liturgical Year and the General Roman Calendar." In *The Roman Missal*, 123–42. London: Catholic Truth Society, 2010.
Celiński, Łukasz. "Per una Rilettura della Storia della Formazione e Dello Sviluppo del Messale Romano. Il Caso del Messale di Clemente V." *Ecclesia Orans* 33 (2020) 383–404.
Chauvet, Louis-Marie. *Symbol and Sacrament: A Sacramental Reinterpretation of Christian Existence*. Collegeville, MN: Liturgical, 1995.
———. "What Makes the Liturgy Biblical?—Texts." *Studia Liturgica* 22 (1992) 121–33.
Chavasse, Antoine. "Aménagements Liturgiques, à Rome, au VIIe et au VIIIe Siècle." *Revue Bénédictine* 99 (1989) 75–102.
Christman, John. "Relational Autonomy, Liberal Individualism, and the Social Constitution of Selves." *Philosophical Studies* 117 (2004) 143–64.
Cilliers, Johan. *The Living Voice of the Gospel: Revisiting the Basic Principles of Preaching*. Stellenbosch: Sun Press, 2004.
Clark, Rolo. "The Lenten Celebration." And Words Became Books, March 17, 2014. Review of Alexander Schmemann, *Great Lent*. New York: St. Vladimir's Seminary Press, 1974. https://wordsbecamebooks.com/2014/03/17/the-lenten-celebration/.
Cockayne, Joshua, and Gideon Salter. "Feasts of Memory: Collective Remembering, Liturgical Time Travel and the Actualisation of the Past." *Modern Theology* 37 (2021) 275–95.
Colapietro, Vincent. "The Dissenting Voice of Charles Peirce: Individuality, Community, and Transfiguration." In *The Varieties of Transcendence: Pragmatism*

and the Theory of Religion, edited by Hermann Deuser et al., 185–218. New York: Fordham University Press, 2016.

Colburn, William C., and Sanford B. Weinberg. *An Orientation to Listening and Audience Analysis*. Chicago: Science Research Association, 1976.

Coleridge, Mark. "World, Word, Worship. The Liturgy in Context According to Vatican II." Lecture at the Lift Up Your Hearts National Liturgy Conference, Wollongong, January 15, 2014. https://brisbanecatholic.org.au/articles/world-word-worship-liturgy-context-according-vatican-ii/.

Confraternity of Christian Doctrine. "Introduction." In *Lectionary for Masses with Children*, edited by United States National Conference of Catholic Bishops, 13–23. New York: Catholic Book Publishing, 1993.

Congar, Yves. *Tradition and the Life of the Church*. Translated by A. N. Woodrow. London: Burns & Oates, 1964.

———. *Tradition and Traditions*. New York: Macmillan, 1967.

Congregation for Divine Worship and the Discipline of the Sacraments. "Homiletic Directory." 2015. https://www.vatican.va/roman_curia/congregations/ccdds/documents/rc_con_ccdds_doc_20140629_direttorio-omiletico_en.html.

Connell, Martin. *Hear the Word of the Lord: The Lectionary in Catholic Ritual*. Chicago: Liturgy Training, 2015.

———. "On Liturgy and Lectionary: The Word of Life in the Body of Christ." *Liturgy* 29 (2014) 33–37.

Connerton, Paul. *How Societies Remember*. Cambridge: Cambridge University Press, 1989.

Cooper, T. D. *Don Browning and Psychology: Interpreting the Horizons of Our Lives*. Macon: Mercer University Press, 2011.

Copeland, M. Shawn. "Weaving Memory, Structuring Ritual, Evoking Mythos: Commemoration of the Ancestors." In *Invitation to Practical Theology: Catholic Voices and Visions*, edited by Claire E. Wolfteich, 125–48. New York: Paulist, 2014.

Corrington, R. S. *The Community of Interpreters: On the Hermeneutics of Nature and the Bible in the American Philosophical Tradition*. Macon, GA: Mercer University Press, 1987.

Cullinane, Peter. "A Suggestion for the Liturgy of the Word." *La Croix International*, June 20, 2022. https://international.la-croix.com/news/religion/a-suggestion-for-the-liturgy-of-the-word/16271.

Culpepper, James Edward. "The Value of Hans-Georg Gadamer's Hermeneutic Philosophy for Christian Thought." PhD diss., Southern Baptist Theological Seminary, 1987.

Cyprian. *St Cyprian Letters (1–81)*. Translated by Sister Rose Bernard Donna CSJ. The Fathers of the Church: A New Translation 51. Washington, DC: Catholic University of America Press, 1964.

Dalmais, Irénée Henri. "The Liturgy as Celebration." In *The Church at Prayer*, translated by Matthew O'Connell and edited by A.G. Martimort, 233–43. Collegeville, MN: Liturgical, 1987.

Daniel, David B., and William Douglas Woody. "They Hear, but Do Not Listen: Retention for Podcasted Material in a Classroom Context." *Teaching of Psychology* 37 (2010) 199–203.

Danielou, Jean. *The Bible and the Liturgy*. Notre Dame, IN: University of Notre Dame Press, 1956.

Danneels, Godfried "Comment Entrons-Nous dans la Liturgie?" *La Documentation Catholique* 2132 (1996) 172–75.
Darragh, Neil. "The Practice of Practical Theology: Key Decisions and Abiding Hazards in Doing Practical Theology." *Australian ejournal of Theology* 9 (2007).
Day, Juliette J. *Reading the Liturgy: An Exploration of Texts in Christian Worship.* London: Bloomsbury, 2014.
De Clerck, Paul. "In the Beginning Was the Word." *Studia Liturgica* 22 (1992) 1–16.
Dean, William. "The Challenge of the New Historicism." *Journal of Religion* 66 (1986) 261–81.
Dillen, Annemie, and Robert Mager. "Research in Practical Theology—Methods, Methodology and Normativity." In *Invitation to Practical Theology: Catholic Voices and Visions*, edited by Claire E. Wolfteich, 301–28. New York: Paulist, 2014.
Dingemans, G. D. J. *Als Hoorder Onder de Hoorders: Een Hermeneutische Homiletie.* Kampen: Kok, 1991.
Dix, Gregory. *The Shape of the Liturgy.* 3rd ed. London: Bloomsbury Academic, 2005.
Donaldson, James D. D., ed. *Constitutions of the Holy Apostles.* Ashford, CT: Codex Spiritualis, 2013.
Dorman, Ted M. "Holy Spirit, History, Hermeneutics and Theology: Toward an Evangelical/Catholic Consensus." *Journal—Evangelical Theological Society* 41 (1998) 427–38.
Dosse, François. *Paul Ricoeur: Les Sens d'une Vie (1913–2005).* Rev. ed. Paris: La Découverte, 2008.
Dostal, Robert J. "The Experience of Truth for Gadamer and Heidegger: Taking Time and Sudden Lightening." In *Hermeneutics and Truth*, edited by B. Wachterhause, 47–67. Evanston, IL: Northwestern University Press, 1994.
Douglas, Brian. "Anglican-Roman Catholic International Commission (ARCIC) and the Eucharist: Review and Prospects." *Journal of Religious History* 36 (2012) 351–67.
Dulles, Avery. "The Symbolic Structure of Revelation." *Theological Studies* 41 (1980) 51–73.
Dunn, James D. G. "Criteria for a Wise Reading of a Biblical Text." In *Reading Texts, Seeking Wisdom: Scripture and Theology*, edited by David F. Ford and Graham Stanton, 38–52. Grand Rapids: Eerdmans, 2003.
———. "The Role of the Spirit in Biblical Hermeneutics." In *Spirit and Scripture: Exploring a Pneumatic Hermeneutic*, edited by Kevin L. Spawn and Archie T. Wright, 154–59. London: T. & T. Clark, 2012.
Ebeling, Gerhard. "Word of God and Hermeneutics." *Journal for Theology and Church* 56 (1959) 224–51.
Eco-Justice Ministries. "Is the Lectionary Serving Us Well? An Invitation to an Ecumenical Conversation About Faithful and Relevant Worship." http://www.eco-justice.org/Is_Lectionary_Serving_Well.asp.
Edwards, James R. "The Hermeneutical Significance of Chapter Divisions in Ancient Gospel Manuscripts." *New Testament Studies* 56 (2010) 413–26.
Elbogen, Ismar. *Jewish Liturgy: A Comprehensive History.* Translated by Raymond P. Scheindlin. Philadelphia: Jewish Publication Society, 1993.
Elich, Tom. "Bible and Liturgy." *Liturgy News* 21 (1991) 1–3.
———. "Discussing Eucharist." *Liturgy News* 50 (2020) 2–5.

———. "Full, Conscious and Active Participation." In *Vatican Council II: Reforming Liturgy*, edited by David Orr et al., 25–42. Adelaide: ATF, 2013.
———. "The Word in Worship." *Australian Journal of Liturgy* 14 (2015) 92–101.
Eliot, T. S. "Tradition and the Individual Talent." *Perspecta* 19 (1982) 36–42.
Ellingsen, Mark. *The Integrity of Biblical Narrative: Story in Theology and Proclamation*. Eugene, OR: Wipf & Stock, 1990.
Evans, Robert. *Reception History, Tradition and Biblical Interpretation: Gadamer and Jauss in Current Practice*. London: T. & T. Clark, 2014.
Faggioli, Massimo. "The Liturgical Reform from 1963 until Today . . . And Beyond." *Toronto Journal of Theology* 32 (2016) 201–17.
———. *True Reform: Liturgy and Ecclesiology in Sacrosanctum Concilium*. Collegeville, MN: Liturgical, 2012.
Federici, Tommaso. "La Bibbia Diventa Lezionario: Storia e Criteri Attuali." In *Dall'Esegi all'Ermeneutica Attraverso la Celebrazione*, Bibbia e Liturgia I, edited by R. Cecolin, 192–222. Padua: Edizioni Messagero Padova, 1991.
Feezell, Randolph M. "Thinking About the Aesthetic Attitude." *Philosophical Topics* 13 (1985) 19–32.
Fentress, James, and Chris Wickham. *Social Memory*. Oxford: Blackwell, 1992.
Fish, Stanley. *Doing What Comes Naturally: Change, Rhetoric and the Practice of Theory in Literary and Legal Studies*. Oxford: Clarendon, 1989.
Flanagan, Kieran. "Liturgy as Play: A Hermeneutics of Ritual Re-Presentation." *Modern Theology* 4 (1988) 345–72.
Fodor, Jim. "Reading the Scriptures: Rehearsing Identity, Practicing Character." In *The Blackwell Companion to Christian Ethics*, edited by Stanley Hauerwas and Samuel Wells, 155–69. Oxford: Blackwell, 2011.
Foley, Edward. "Toward a Sound Theology." *Studia Liturgica* 23 (1993) 121–39.
Fortin, Jean-Pierre. "Christian Rationality: Embracing the Divine Mystery." *Toronto Journal of Theology* 29 (2013) 337–50.
Fowler, Robert M. "Who Is 'The Reader' in Reader Response Criticism?" *Semeia* 31 (1985) 5–21.
Fox, Ruth. "Strange Omission of Key Women in the Lectionary." *National Catholic Reporter* 30 (1994) 13–14.
Francis. "Address of His Holiness Pope Francis to Teachers and Students of the Pontifical Liturgical Institute." Sant'Anselmo, Consistory Hall, May 7, 2022. https://www.vatican.va/content/francesco/en/speeches/2022/may/documents/20220507-pont-istituto-liturgico.html.
———. *Aperuit Illis: Instituting the Sunday of the Word of God*. Apostolic Letter. September 30, 2019. https://www.vatican.va/content/francesco/en/motu_proprio/documents/papa-francesco-motu-proprio-20190930_aperuit-illis.html.
———. *Desiderio Desideravi: On the Liturgical Formation of the People of God*. Apostolic Letter. June 29, 2022. https://www.vatican.va/content/francesco/en/apost_letters/documents/20220629-lettera-ap-desiderio-desideravi.html.
———. *Evangelii Gaudium: The Joy of the Gospel*. Post-Synodal Apostolic Exhortation. November 24, 2013. https://www.vatican.va/content/francesco/en/apost_exhortations/documents/papa-francesco_esortazione-ap_20131124_evangelii-gaudium.html.
———. "On the Liturgy of the Word." General Audience. Zenit. January 31, 2018. https://zenit.org/articles/general-audience-on-the-liturgy-of-the-word/.

François, Wim. "The Catholic Church and Vernacular Bible Reading, Before and After Trent." *Biblicum Jassyense* 4 (2013) 5–37.

Frank, David B. "Do We Translate the Original Author's Intended Meaning?" *De Gruyter Open Theology* 2 (2016) 653–67.

Frei, Hans W. *The Eclipse of Biblical Narrative: A Study in Eighteenth and Nineteenth Century Hermeneutics*. New Haven, CT: Yale University Press, 1974.

Friedman, Marilyn. *Autonomy, Gender, Politics*. Oxford: Oxford University Press, 2003.

Frost, Anthony. "Tracing the Emergence of a Canon of Holy Scripture in Churches." *Anglican Historical Society Journal* 57 (2014) 26–39.

Fuller, Daniel P. "The Holy Spirit's Role in Biblical Interpretation." *International Journal of Frontier Missions* 14 (1997) 91–95.

Fulton, John. *Index Canonum: The Greek Text, an English Translation, and a Complete Digest of the Entire Code of Canon Law of the Undivided Primitive Church*. 3rd ed. New York: Thomas Whittaker, 1892.

Funk, Robert. *Language, Hermeneutic, and Word of God: The Problem of Language in the New Testament and Contemporary Theology*. New York: Harper and Row, 1966.

Furnham, Adrian. "Remembering Stories as a Function of the Medium of Presentation." *Psychological Reports* 89 (2001) 483–86.

Furnham, Adrian, and Barrie Gunter. "The Primacy of Print: Immediate Cued Recall of News as a Function of the Channel of Communication." *The Journal of General Psychology* 116 (1989) 305–10.

Gaarden, Marianne. "The Emerging Sermon: The Encounter between the Words of the Preacher and the Listeners 'Experience." *Academia* (2014) 1–10. https://www.academia.edu/23631542/the_emerging_sermon_the_encounter_between_the_words_of_the_preacher_and_the_listeners_experience.

———. "The Living Voice of the Gospel Needs a Preacher." Paper presented at the Pastoral Institute Aarhus, Denmark, 2013, 1–8. https://pure.au.dk/ws/files/56621840/The_Living_Voice_of_the_Gospel_needs_a_Preacher.pdf.

———. *The Third Room of Preaching: A New Empirical Approach*. Eugene, OR: Pickwick, 2021.

Gaarden, Marianne, and Marlene Ringgaard Lorensen. "Listeners as Authors in Preaching—Empirical and Theoretical Perspectives." *Homiletic* 38 (2013) 28–45.

Gadamer, Hans-Georg. "Aesthetics and Hermeneutics." In *The Gadamer Reader: A Bouquet of the Later Writings*, translated by David E. Linge and edited by Richard E. Palmer, 123–31. Evanston, IL: Northwestern University Press, 2007.

———. "The Continuity of History and the Existential Moment." *Philosophy Today* 16 (1972) 230–40.

———. *Gadamer in Conversation: Reflections and Commentary*. Translated and edited by Richard E. Palmer. New Haven, CT: Yale University Press, 2001.

———. "Hermeneutics as Practical Philosophy." In *The Gadamer Reader: A Bouquet of the Later Writings*, translated by Frederick G. Lawrence and edited by Richard E. Palmer, 227–45. Evanston, IL: Northwestern University Press, 2007.

———. "Language and Understanding." In *The Gadamer Reader: A Bouquet of the Later Writings*, translated by Richard E. Palmer and edited by Richard E. Palmer, 89–107. Evanston, IL: Northwestern University Press, 2007.

———. "On the Scope and Function of Hermeneutical Reflection (1967)." In *Hans-Georg Gadamer: Philosophical Hermeneutics*, edited by D. E. Linge, 18–43. Berkley, MA: University of California Press, 1976.

———. "The Power of Reason." *Man and World* 3 (1970) 5–15.
———. *Reason in the Age of Science*. Translated by Frederick G. Lawrence. Cambridge: MIT Press, 1984.
———. "Reflections on My Philosophical Journey." Translated by R. E. Palmer. In *The Philosophy of Hans-Georg Gadamer, The Library of Living Philosophers*, edited by L. E. Hahn, 24:3–64. Illinois: Open Court, 1997.
———. "The Relevance of the Beautiful." In *The Relevance of the Beautiful and Other Essays*, translated by Nicholas Walker and edited by Robert Bernasconi, 3–53. Cambridge: Cambridge University Press, 1986.
———. "Religious and Poetical Speaking." In *Myth, Symbol, and Reality*, edited by Alan Olson, 86–98. Notre Dame, IN: University of Notre Dame Press, 1980.
———. "Text and Interpretation." In *The Gadamer Reader: A Bouquet of the Later Writings*, translated by Richard E. Palmer and edited by Richard E. Palmer, 156–91. Evanston, IL: Northwestern University Press, 2007.
———. *Truth and Method*. Translated by Joel Weinsheimer and Donald G. Marshall. 2nd rev. ed. London: Bloomsbury, 1989.
Gamble, Harry Y. *Books and Readers in the Early Church: A History of Early Christian Texts*. New Haven, CT: Yale University Press, 1995.
Gargano, Innocenzo. "Scriptura Cum Legente Crescit: Dal Testo Scritto al Momento Celebrativo." In *Dall'Esegi all'Ermeneutica Attraverso La Celebrazione*, edited by R. Cecolin, 153–82. Padua: Edizioni Messagero Padova, 1991.
Garrett, Jan. "Hans-Georg Gadamer on 'Fusion of Horizons.'" *Man and World* 11 (1978) 392–400.
Garrison, Mary. "Alcuin's World through His Letters and Verse." PhD diss., University of Cambridge, 1996.
Geldhof, Joris. *Liturgical Studies as a Research Program*. Leiden: Brill, 2020.
Gelston, Anthony. "The Psalms in Christian Worship: Patristic Precedent and Anglican Practice." *Joint Liturgical Studies* 66 (2008) 1–40.
Gener, Timoteo. "Transformational Correlation: A Reformational Perspective on Cultural Theological Method in Conversation with David Tracy's and Paul Tillich's Correlational Approaches." In *That the World May Believe: Essays on Mission and Unity in Honour of George Vandervelde*, edited by M. Goheen and M. O'Gara, 29–43. Lanham, MD: University Press of America, 2006.
Gilles, Anne-Véronique. "La Ponctuation dans les Manuscrits Liturgiques au Moyen Age." In *Grafia E Interpunzione Del Latino Nel Medioevo*, edited by Alfonso Maierù, 113–33. Rome: Ateneo, 1987.
Gilliard, Frank D. "More Silent Reading in Antiquity: Non Omne Verbum Sonabat." *Journal of Biblical Literature* 112 (1993) 689–94.
Godin, Andre. *Psicologia delle Esperienze Religiose: Il Desiderio e la Realta*. Brescia: Queriniana, 1983.
Goldsworthy, Jeffrey. "Moderate Versus Strong Intentionalism: Knapp and Michaels Revisited." *San Diego Law Review* 42 (2005) 669–83.
Gothoni, Rene. *Words Matter: Hermeneutics in the Study of Religions*. Religions and Discourse 52. Bern: Peter Lang, 2011.
Graham, Elaine. "On Becoming a Practical Theologian: Past, Present and Future Tenses." *HTS Teologiese Studies/Theological Studies* 73 (2017) 1–9.
Graham, Elaine, et al. *Theological Reflection: Methods*. 2nd ed. London: SCM, 2018.

Graham, William A. *Beyond the Written Word: Oral Aspects of Scripture in the History of Religion*. Cambridge: Cambridge University Press, 1987.

———. "Scripture." In *The Encyclopedia of Religion*, edited by Mircea Eliade, 13:133–45. New York: Macmillan, 1987.

Graves, Michael. "The Public Reading of Scripture in Early Judaism." *Journal of the Evangelical Theological Society* 50 (2007) 467–87.

Gray, Donald, ed. *The Word in Season: Essays by Members of the Joint Liturgical Group on the Use of the Bible in Liturgy*. London: Canterbury, 1988.

Grayland, J. P. "Liturgy is an Act of the People of God and They Must Be Really Present." *La Croix International*. April 17, 2020. https://international.la-croix.com/news/religion/liturgy-is-an-act-of-the-people-of-god-and-they-must-be-really-present/12200.

Gregory the Great. *Homiliae in Hiezechielem Prophetam (Homilies on the Prophet Ezekiel)*. Edited by M. Adriaen. Corpus Christianorum Series Latina 142. Turnhout: Brepols, 1971.

Green, Laurie. *Let's Do Theology*. London: Continuum, 1990.

Greenblatt, Stephen. *Renaissance Self-Fashioning: From More to Shakespeare*. Chicago: University of Chicago Press, 1980.

———. *Shakespearean Negotiations: The Circulation of Social Energy in Renaissance England*. Oxford: Clarendon, 1988.

———. "Towards a Poetics of Culture." In *The New Historicism*, edited by H. Aram Veeser, 1–14. New York: Routledge, 1989.

Greenspoon, Leonard J. "Jewish Bible Translation." In *The Biblical World*, edited by John Barton, 397–412. New York: Routledge, 2012.

Griffiths, Alan. *Ordo Romanus Primus—Latin Text and Translation with Introduction and Notes*. Joint Liturgical Studies 73. London: Canterbury, 2012.

Grimes, Ronald L. *Beginnings in Ritual Studies*. 3rd ed. Columbia, SC: University of South Carolina Press, 1995.

———. "Liturgical Renewal and Ritual Criticism." In *The Awakening Church: 25 Years of Liturgical Renewal*, edited by Lawrence J. Madden SJ, 11–25. Collegeville, MN: Liturgical, 1992.

Grondin, Jean. "Hans-Georg Gadamer." In *The Blackwell Companion to Hermeneutics*, edited by Niall Keane, 397–403. Chichester: Wiley-Blackwell, 2016.

———. "The Hermeneutical Circle." In *The Blackwell Companion to Hermeneutics*, edited by Niall Keane, 299–305. Chichester: Wiley-Blackwell, 2016.

———. "Play, Festival, and Ritual in Gadamer: On the Theme of the Immemorial in His Later Works." In *Language and Linguisticality in Gadamer's Hermeneutics*, edited by Lawrence K. Schmidt, 43–50. Lanham, MD: Lexington, 2001.

Guardini, Romano. *The Church and the Catholic, and the Spirit of the Liturgy*. New York: Sheed and Ward, 1935.

Gunstone, John. "Contemporary Problems of Liturgical Time: Calendar and Lectionary." *Studia Liturgica* 14 (1982) 74–75.

Gy, Pierre-Marie. "Typologie et Ecclesiologie des Livres Liturgiques." *La Maison-Dieu* 121 (1975) 7–21.

Habermas, Jürgen. *Communication and the Evolution of Society*. Toronto: Beacon, 1979.

Hahn, Scott. "Worship in the Word: Toward a Liturgical Hermeneutic." *Letter and Spirit* 1 (2005) 101–36.

Hahneman, Geoffrey Mark. *The Muratorian Fragment and the Development of the Canon*. Oxford: Oxford University Press, 1992.

Haight, Roger. "Liturgy as Community Consciousness of Grace." In *The Awakening Church: 25 Years of Liturgical Renewal*, edited by Lawrence J. Madden SJ, 26–45. Collegeville, MN: Liturgical, 1992.

Halbwachs, Maurice. *On Collective Memory*. Chicago: University of Chicago Press, 1992.

Hameline, Jean-Yves. *La Poétique Du Rituel*. Paris: Les éditions du Cerf, 1997.

Hammond, C. E., and F. E. Brightman. *Liturgies, Eastern and Western: Being the Texts, Original or Translated, of the Principal Liturgies of the Church*. Oxford: Clarendon, 1896.

Hammond, Guyton B. "An Examination of Tillich's Method of Correlation." *Journal of Bible and Religion* 32 (1964) 248–51.

Harrington, Daniel. "Introduction to the Canon." In *The New Interpreter's Bible: A Commentary in Twelve Volumes*, edited by L. E. Keck, 7–21. Nashville: Abingdon, 2003.

Harrison, Peter. "Correlation and Theology: Barth and Tillich Re-Examined." *Studies in Religion/Sciences Religieuses* 15 (1986) 65–76.

Hassabis, Demis, and Eleanor A. Maguire. "Deconstructing Episodic Memory with Construction." *Trends in Cognitive Sciences* 11 (2007) 299–306.

Heidegger, Martin. *On Time and Being*. Translated by Joan Stambaugh. New York: Harper and Row, 1972.

Heinemann, Joseph. "The Triennial Lectionary Cycle." *Journal of Jewish Studies* 19 (1968) 41–48.

Heinz, Hanspeter. "The Celebration of the Sacraments and the Teaching of the Commandments in the Age of Religious Consumerism." In *Memory and History in Christianity and Judaism*, edited by Michael Signer, 145–69. Notre Dame: University of Notre Dame Press, 2001.

Hellwig, Monika K. "Twenty-Five Years of a Wakening Church: Liturgy and Ecclesiology." In *The Awakening Church: 25 Years of Liturgical Renewal*, edited by Lawrence J. Madden SJ, 55–68. Collegeville, MN: Liturgical, 1992.

Henderson, J. Frank. *Remembering the Women: Women's Stories from Scripture for Sundays and Festivals*. Chicago: Liturgy Training, 1999.

Herder, Johann Gottfried. *Ideen Zur Philosophie der Geshichte der Menschheit*. Volume 6. Edited by Martin Bollacher. Frankfurt: Deutscher Klassiker Verlag, 1989.

Herdt, Jennifer A. *Forming Humanity: Redeeming the German Bildung Tradition*. Chicago: University of Chicago Press, 2019.

Hervieu-Léger, Danièle. *Religion as a Chain of Memory*. New Jersey: Rutgers University Press, 2000.

Hildyard, Angela, and David R. Olson. "On the Comprehension and Memory of Oral vs. Written Discourse." In *Spoken and Written Language: Exploring Orality and Literature*, edited by Deborah Tannen, 19–33. Norwood: Ablex, 1982.

Hiltner, Seward. *Preface to Pastoral Theology*. New York: Abingdon, 1958.

Hoffman, Lawrence A. *Beyond the Text: A Holistic Approach to Liturgy*. Bloomington: Indiana University Press, 1989.

Hogan, John P. "Hermeneutics and the Logic of Question and Answer: Collingwood and Gadamer." *Heythorp Journal* 28 (1987) 263–84.

Holcomb, Justin S., and David A. Johnson. "Introduction: Mapping Theologies of Sacraments." In *Christian Theologies of the Sacraments: A Comparative Introduction*, edited by Justin S. Holcomb and David A. Johnson, 1–11. New York: New York University Press, 2017.

Holzherr, Georg, et al. *The Rule of Benedict: An Invitation to the Christian Life*. Collegeville, MN: Liturgical, 2016.

Hopkins, Dwight N. *Being Human: Race, Culture, and Religion*. Minneapolis: Fortress, 2005.

Hornsey, Matthew J., and Jolanda Jetten. "The Individual Within the Group: Balancing the Need to Belong with the Need to Be Different." *Personality and Social Psychology Review* 8 (2004) 248–64.

Hoy, David Couzen. *The Critical Circle: Criticism and History in Contemporary Hermeneutics*. Berkeley: University of California Press, 1978.

Hughes, Graham. *Worship as Meaning: A Liturgical Theology for Late Modernity*. Cambridge: Cambridge University Press, 2003.

Hughes, Kathleen. "Speaking in the Future Tense." In *The Awakening Church: 25 Years of Liturgical Renewal*, edited by Lawrence J. Madden SJ, 125–40. Collegeville, MN: Liturgical, 1992.

Hughes, Margaret I. "The Ease of Beauty: Liturgy, Evangelization, and Catechesis." In *Liturgy in the Twenty-First Century: Contemporary Issues and Perspectives*, edited by Alcuin Reid, 91–104. London: T. & T. Clark, 2016.

Huizinga, Johan. *Homo Ludens: A Study of the Play Element in Culture*. London: Maurice Temple Smith, 1970.

Hurtado, Larry W. "Manuscripts and the Sociology of Early Christian Reading." In *Texts and Artefacts: Selected Essays on Textual Criticism and Early Christian Manuscripts*, 99–114. London: T. & T. Clark, 2018.

Hutton, Patrick H. "The Halbwachs-Aries Connection." *Historical Reflections/Réflexions Historiques* 15 (1988) 311–22.

Immink, F. Gerrit. "Homiletics: The Current Debate." *International Journal of Practical Theology* 8 (2004) 89–121.

International Commission on English in the Liturgy. *Documents on the Liturgy, 1963–1979. Conciliar, Papal, and Curial Texts*, edited by Thomas C. O'Brien. Collegeville, MN: Liturgical, 1982.

Irwin, Kevin W. *Context and Text: A Method for Liturgical Theology*. Rev. ed. Collegeville, MN: Liturgical, 2018.

———. *Models of the Eucharist*. Mahwah, NJ: Paulist, 2005.

———. *What We Have Done, What We Have Failed to Do: Assessing the Liturgical Reforms of Vatican II*. Mahwah, NJ: Paulist, 2013.

Janowiak, Paul. *The Holy Preaching: The Sacramentality of the Word in the Liturgical Assembly*. Collegeville, MN: Liturgical, 2000.

Jauss, Hans Robert. *Aesthetic Experience and Literary Hermeneutics*. Translated by Michael Shaw. Minneapolis: University of Minnesota Press, 1982.

———. "Literary History as a Challenge to Literary Theory." *New Literary History* 2 (1970) 7–37.

———. *Question and Answer: Forms of Dialogic Understanding*. Translated by Michael Hays and edited by Wlad Godzich and Jochen Schulte-Sasse. Theory and History of Literature 68. Minneapolis: University of Minnesota Press, 1989.

———. *Towards an Aesthetic of Reception*. Translated by Timothy Bahti and edited by Wlad Godzich and Jochen Schulte-Sasse. Theory and History of Literature 2. Minneapolis: University of Minnesota Press, 1982.

Jerome and Gennadius, *Lives of Illustrious Men*. Translated by Ernest Cushing Richardson, United Kingdom: Aeterna, 2016.

Jewish Virtual Library. "Tractate Megillah—Babylonian Talmud." Meg. 3:5. American-Israeli Cooperative Enterprise, 1998–2022. https://www.jewishvirtuallibrary.org/tractate-megillah-chapter-3.

Johnson, William A. *Readers and Reading Culture in the High Roman Empire: A Study of Elite Communities, Classical Culture and Society*. New York: Oxford University Press, 2010.

———. "Toward a Sociology of Reading in Classical Antiquity." *American Journal of Philology* 121 (2000) 593–627.

Johnson, W. Walter. "The Ethics of Preaching." *Interpretation* 20 (1966) 412–31.

Jordahn, Ottfried. "What Makes the Liturgy Biblical?—Actions." *Studia Liturgica* 22 (1992) 134–45.

Jörns, Klaus-Peter. "Liturgy: Cradle of Scripture?" *Studia Liturgica* 22 (1992) 17–34.

Josephus. *The Life. Against Apion*. Translated by H. St. J. Thackeray. Loeb Classical Library 186. Cambridge, MA: Harvard University Press, 1926.

Jungmann, J. A. *The Mass of the Roman Rite: Its Origins and Development*. Translated by F. A. Brunner. Notre Dame, IN: Ave Maria, 2012.

Just, Felix. "Lectionary Statistics." The Catholic Lectionary. https://catholic-resources.org/Lectionary/Statistics.htm.

———. "Missale Romanum." The Catholic Lectionary. https://catholic-resources.org/Lectionary/Roman_Missal.htm.

———. "Real Presence and Virtual Liturgies." *La Croix International*. April 28, 2020. https://international.la-croix.com/news/religion/real-presence-and-virtual-liturgies-part-i/12261.

Kaufman, Gordon D. "Theology as Imaginative Construction." *Journal of the American Academy of Religion* 50 (1982) 73–79.

Kavanagh, Aidan. *On Liturgical Theology*. Collegeville, MN: Liturgical, 2017.

Kee, Howard Clark. "Defining the First-Century CE Synagogue: Problems and Progress." *New Testament Studies* 41 (1995) 481–500.

Keith, Chris. *The Gospel as Manuscript: An Early History of the Jesus Tradition as Material Artifact*. New York: Oxford University Press, 2020.

Kelber, Werner H. "The History of the Closure of Biblical Texts." *Oral Tradition* 25 (2010) 115–40.

———. "Oral Tradition in Bible and New Testament Studies." *Oral Tradition* 18 (2003) 40–42.

Kenneson, Philip. "Gathering: Worship, Imagination, and Formation." In *The Blackwell Companion to Christian Ethics*, edited by Stanley Hauerwas and Samuel Wells, 55–69. Oxford: Blackwell, 2004.

Kiefer, Thomas. "Hermeneutical Understanding as the Disclosure of Truth: Hans-Georg Gadamer's Distinctive Understanding of Truth." *Philosophy Today* 57 (2013) 42–60.

Kinast, R. L. *What Are They Saying About Theological Reflection?* Mahwah, NJ: Paulist, 2000.

Klaasen, John. "Practical Theology: A Critically Engaged Practical Reason Approach of Practice, Theory, Practice and Theory." *HTS Teologiese Studies/Theological Studies* 70 (2014) 1–6.

Klauser, Theodor. *Das Römische Capitulare Evangeliorum: Texte und Untersuchungen zu Seiner Ältesten Geschichte*. Liturgiegeschichtliche Quellen und Forschungen. Vol. 28. Münster: Aschendorffschen, 1935.

Klein, M. L. "Four Notes on the Triennial Lectionary Cycle." *Journal of Jewish Studies* 32 (1981) 65–73.

Klooster, Fred H. "The Role of the Holy Spirit in the Hermeneutic Process: The Relationship of the Spirit's Illumination to Biblical Interpretation." In *Hermeneutics, Inerrancy, and the Bible*, edited by Earl D. Radmacher and Robert D. Preuss, 451–72. Grand Rapids: Zondervan, 1984.

Knotts, Matthew W. "Readers, Texts, and the Fusion of Horizons: Theology and Gadamer's Hermeneutics." *Acta Universitatis Carolinae Theologica* 4 (2014) 233–46.

Knowles, Robert. *Anthony C Thiselton and the Grammar of Hermeneutics: The Search for a Unified Theory*. Milton Keynes: Authentic Media, 2012.

Konigsburg, Joyce Ann. "Worship as Compatible with Both Proper Human Autonomy and Relational Autonomy." In *In Spirit and in Truth: Philosophical Reflections on Liturgy and Worship*, edited by Wm Curtis Holtzen and Matthew Nelson Hill, 129–46. Claremont: Claremont School of Theology Press, 2016.

Kuhn, Thomas S. *The Structure of Scientific Revolutions*. 3rd ed. Chicago: University of Chicago Press, 2012.

Kunzler, Michael. *The Church's Liturgy*. New York: Continuum, 2002.

Kwasniewski, Peter. "The Reform of the Lectionary." In *Liturgy in the Twenty-First Century: Contemporary Issues and Perspectives*, edited by Alcuin Reid, 287–320. London: Bloomsbury T. & T. Clark, 2016.

Laney, Cara, and Elizabeth F. Loftus. "Truth in Emotional Memories." In *Emotion and the Law: Psychological Perspectives*, edited by B. H. Bornstein and R. L. Wiener, 157–83. New York: Springer, 2009.

Lang, Uwe Michael. "The Liturgy and Sacred Language." In *T&T Clark Companion to Liturgy*, edited by Alcuin Reid, 365–82. London: Bloomsbury, 2015.

Larson-Miller, Lizette. "Reality of Presence in Virtually Mediated Sacramentality: Has Sacramental Theology Sustained Us?" *Anglican Theological Review* 104 (2022) 37–53.

Lathrop, Gordon W. *Holy Things. A Liturgical Theology*. Minneapolis: Fortress, 1993.

———. *Saving Images: The Presence of the Bible in Christian Liturgy*. Minneapolis: Augsburg Fortress, 2017.

Lawrence, Fred. "Gadamer, the Hermeneutic Revolution, and Theology." In *The Cambridge Companion to Gadamer*, edited by Robert J. Dostal, 167–200. Cambridge: Cambridge University Press, 2002.

Leachman, James. "A New Liturgical Hermeneutic: Christian Maturation by Developmental Steps." *New Blackfriars* 90 (2009) 219–31.

Lenker, Ursula. "The 'West Saxon Gospels' and the Gospellectionary in Anglo-Saxon England: Manuscript Evidence and Liturgical Practice." *Anglo-Saxon England* 28 (1999) 141–78.

Lindbeck, George A. *The Nature of Doctrine: Religion and Theology in a Postliberal Age*. Philadelphia: Westminster, 1984.

Lonergan, Bernard. "Merging Horizons: System, Common Sense, Scholarship." *Cultural Hermeneutics* 1 (1973) 87–99.
Long, Thomas. *The Witness of Preaching*. Louisville, KY: Westminster John Knox, 1989.
Lowry, Eugene. *Living with the Lectionary: Preaching Through the Revised Common Lectionary*. Nashville: Abingdon, 1992.
Lynch, Gordon. *Understanding Theology and Popular Culture*. Oxford: Blackwell, 2005.
Mackenzie, Catriona, and Natalie Stoljar. *Relational Autonomy: Feminist Perspectives on Autonomy, Agency, and the Social Self*. New York: Oxford University Press, 2000.
Maggioni, Corrado. "Encountering Jesus Christ in the Liturgy." *Tertium Millennium* no. 1, 1997. http://www.vatican.va/jubilee_2000/magazine/documents/ju_mag_01031997_p-32_en.html.
Marini, P., et al. *A Challenging Reform: Realizing the Vision of the Liturgical Renewal, 1963–1975*. Collegeville, MN: Liturgical, 2007.
Martimort, Aimé Georges, ed. *The Church at Prayer*. Principles of the Liturgy. New York: Desclée Co, 1968.
———. *Les Lectures Liturgiques et Leurs Livres*. Turnhout: Brepols, 1992.
Martyr, Justin. *The First Apology, The Second Apology, Dialogue with Trypho, Exhortation to the Greeks, Discourse to the Greeks, The Monarchy or The Rule of God—The Fathers of the Church*. Volume 6. Translated by Thomas B. Falls. Washington, DC: Catholic University of America Press, 2010.
———. *Justin, Philosopher and Martyr: Apologies*. Edited by D. Minns and P. Parvis. New York: Oxford University Press, 2009.
Maurus, Hrabanus. "Homilia 39. PL 110, 73–74." In *The Craft of Thought: Meditation, Rhetoric, and the Making of Images 400–1200*, by Mary Carruthers, 275–76. Cambridge: Cambridge University Press, 2000.
Mayer, Richard E., and Laura J. Massa. "Three Facets of Visual and Verbal Learners: Cognitive Ability, Cognitive Style, and Learning Preference." *Journal of Educational Psychology* 95 (2003) 833–46.
McCarron, Richard. "Context for Preaching Resources in the Roman Catholic Church." *Journal of Religious and Theological Information* 4 (2001) 43–57.
McDonald, Lee Martin. *The Formation of the Christian Biblical Canon*. Peabody, MA: Hendrickson, 1995.
McFarland, Jason J. "The Why and How of Liturgical Theology: Dissecting a Method." *Studia Liturgica* 53 (2023) 265–90.
McGowan, Anne. "Living Lent and Engaging Easter: Scripture's Potential and Liturgy's Limits." In *Lively Oracles of God: Perspectives on the Bible and Liturgy*, edited by G. Jeanes et al., 55–74. Collegeville, MN: Liturgical, 2022.
McKinnon, J. W. *The Advent Project: The Later Seventh-Century Creation of the Roman Mass Proper*. Los Angeles: University of California Press, 2000.
McKnight, Edgar V. *The Bible and the Reader*. Philadelphia: Fortress, 1985.
Meeter, Daniel. "The Church Tells Time: The Observance of the Liturgical Year with the Lectionary." *Liturgy* 21 (2006) 35–41.
Mencher, Melvin. *Basic Media Writing*. Dubuque: Brown and Benchmark, 1998.
Mendelson, Jack. "The Habermas-Gadamer Debate." *New German Critique* no. 18 (1979) 44–73.
Mercer, J. A. "Interdisciplinarity as a Practical Theological Conundrum." In *Conundrums in Practical Theology*, edited by J. A. Mercer and B. J. Miller-McLemore, 163–89. Leuven: Brill, 2016.

Meschonnic, Henri, et al. "Poetics and Politics: A Round Table." *New Literary History* 19 (1988) 453–66.
Meyers, Ruth. "Missional Church, Missional Liturgy." *Theology Today* 67 (2010) 36–50.
Michalson, Gordon E. "The Response to Lindbeck." *Modern Theology* 4 (1988) 107–20.
Milbank, John. *Theology and Social Theory Beyond Secular Reason*. 2nd ed. Oxford: Blackwell, 2006.

———. *The Word Made Strange: Theology, Language, Culture*. Chichester: Wiley-Blackwell, 1997.

Miller, Marvin Lloyd. *Performances of Ancient Jewish Letters: From Elephantine to MMT*. Göttingen: Vandenhoeck and Ruprecht, 2015.
Miller-McLemore, Bonnie J. "Introduction: The Contributions of Practical Theology." In *Wiley Blackwell Companion to Practical Theology*, edited by Bonnie J. Miller-McLemore, 1–20. Oxford: Wiley-Blackwell, 2012.
Min, Eungjun. "Bakhtinian Perspectives for the Study of Intercultural Communication." *Journal of Intercultural Studies* 22 (2001) 5–18.
Mitchell, Henry. *The Recovery of Preaching*. San Francisco: Harper and Row, 1977.
Mitchell, Nathan. "Ritual as Reading." In *Source and Summit: Commemorating Josef A. Jungmann, SJ*, edited by Joanne M. Pierce and Michael Downey, 161–82. Collegeville, MN: Liturgical, 1999.

———. "The Spirituality of Christian Worship." *Spirituality Today* 34 (1982) 5–17.

Mitscherling, Jeff. "Resuming the Dialogue." In *Anti-Foundationalism and Practical Reasoning: Conversations between Hermeneutics and Analysis*, edited by Evan Simpson, 121–34. Edmonton: Academic Printing, 1987.
Moloney, Francis J. "Sacred Scripture at Vatican II." *Toronto Journal of Theology* 32 (2016) 183–200.
Moore, Allen J. "Practical Theology: The Emerging Field in Theology, Church, and World. Don S. Browning." *The Journal of Religion* 85 (1985) 428–30.
Moorhead, John. *Gregory the Great*. Early Church Fathers. Abingdon: Routledge, 2005.
Morrill, Bruce. "The Connection between Word and Rite in the Liturgy." *Pastoral Liturgy* 40 (2009) 9–12.

———. "Liturgical Music: Bodies Proclaiming and Responding to the Word of God." *Worship* 74 (2000) 20–36.

———. "Models of Liturgical Memory: Mystical-Political Dimensions, Mythic-Historic Tensions." *Studia Liturgica* 50 (2020) 40–54.

Mournet, Terence C. "The Jesus Tradition as Oral Tradition." In *Jesus in Memory: Traditions in Oral and Scribal Perspectives*, edited by Werner H. and Samuel Byrskog Kelber, 39–61. Waco, TX: Baylor University Press, 2009.
Moussa, N. "The Importance of Learning Styles in Education." *Institute for Learning Styles Journal* 1 (2014) 19–27.
Muller, Julian C. "Postfoundational Practical Theology for a Time of Transition." *HTS Teologiese Studies/Theological Studies* 67 (2011) 1–5.
Nardello, Massimo. "Method of Correlation and Ecclesiological Understanding: Developments from Paul Tillich's Theological Method." *Memorie Teologiche—Facoltà Teologica dell'Emilia Romagna* 7 (2014) 21–37.
Nedelsky, Jennifer. "Reconceiving Autonomy." *Yale Journal of Law and Feminism* 1 (1989) 7–36.
Nichols, Bridget. "Liturgical Hermeneutics: Interpreting Liturgical Rites in Performance." PhD diss., University of Durham, 1996.

Nielsen, Cynthia R. "Hearing the Other's Voice: How Gadamer's Fusion of Horizons and Openended Understanding Respects the Other and Puts Oneself in Question." *Otherness: Essays and Studies* 4 (2013) 1–25.
Nocent, A., and P. Turner. *The Liturgical Year: Advent, Christmas, Epiphany*. Volume 1. Collegeville, MN: Liturgical, 2013.
———. *The Liturgical Year: Lent, the Sacred Paschal Triduum, Easter Time*. Volume 2. Collegeville, MN: Liturgical, 2014.
O'Brien, Thomas C., ed. *Documents on the Liturgy, 1963–1979: Conciliar, Papal, and Curial Texts*. Collegeville, MN: Liturgical, 1982.
O'Collins, Gerald. "Dei Verbum and Biblical Scholarship." Lecture given at Catholic Biblical Association of Great Britain, St. Mary's College Twickenham, November 17, 1990. https://vatican2voice.org/5depth/ocollins.htm.
O'Collins, Gerald, and David Braithwaite. "Tradition as Collective Memory: A Theological Task to Be Tackled." *Theological Studies* 76 (2015) 29–42.
O'Collins, Gerald, and Edward G. Farrugia. *A Concise Dictionary of Theology*. 3rd ed. Mahwah, NJ: Paulist, 2013.
O'Connor, Tony. "Play." In *The Blackwell Companion to Hermeneutics*, edited by Niall Keane, 265–69. Chichester: Wiley-Blackwell, 2016.
Odenstedt, Anders. *Gadamer on Tradition—Historical Context and the Limits of Reflection*. Edited by Nicolas de Warren and Dermot Moran. Contributions to Phenomenology 90. Cham, Switzerland: Springer International, 2017.
O'Donoghue, Neil Xavier. "Effectively Communicating the Divine: A Proposed Rehabilitation of the 1998 Sacramentary." *The Irish Theological Quarterly* 82 (2017) 284–302.
O'Donohue, John. "The Inner Landscape of Beauty." Interview by Krista Tippett. *On Being*. February 28, 2008. https://onbeing.org/programs/john-odonohue-the-inner-landscape-of-beauty-aug2017/#transcript.
Office for the Liturgical Celebrations of the Supreme Pontiff. "The Liturgy, Work of the Trinity: God the Holy Spirit." https://www.vatican.va/news_services/liturgy/details/ns_lit_doc_20120307_dio-spirito_en.html.
———. "When to Celebrate." http://www.vatican.va/news_services/liturgy/details/ns_lit_doc_20120502_quando-celebrare1_en.html.
Okey, Stephen. *A Theology of Conversation: An Introduction to David Tracy*. Collegeville, MN: Liturgical, 2018.
Olick, J. K. "Collective Memory: The Two Cultures." *Sociological Theory* 17 (1999) 333–48.
O'Loughlin, Thomas. "The Bible in the Context of the Eucharist." In *Lively Oracles of God: Perspectives on the Bible and Liturgy*, edited by G. Jeanes et al., 33–54. Collegeville, MN: Liturgical, 2022.
———. "How Many Lectionaries Do We Need?" *Doctrine and Life* 69 (2019) 2–11.
———. "New Books, Old Assumptions: Identifying the Larger Dimensions of the Debate About 'Which Translation of the Lectionary Should We Use?'" *Australian Journal of Liturgy* 17 (2021) 198–207.
———. "A New Lectionary: Is It a Matter of Picking a Version?" *Pastoral Liturgy* 51 (2021) 1–5.
———. "New Lectionary Translations: What Is the Problem?" *La Croix International*. August 7, 2020. https://international.la-croix.com/news/religion/new-lectionary-translations-what-is-the-problem/12866.

———. "Sharing the Living Word: Looking at the Lectionary as it Approaches its Golden Jubilee." *Music and Liturgy* 43 (2017) 8–13.

———. "'Would You Read?': The Task of the Lector." *Anaphora* 1 (2007) 19–36.

Olson, Alan M. *Myth, Symbol, and Reality*. Notre Dame, IN: University of Notre Dame Press, 1980.

Olson, David R. "From Utterance to Text: The Bias of Language in Speech and Writing." *Harvard Educational Review* 47 (1977) 257–81.

O'Malley, John W. *Trent: What Happened at the Council*. Cambridge, MA: Harvard University Press, 2013.

O'Malley, Timothy P. "Liturgical Memory and Liquid Modernity." *Antiphon: A Journal for Liturgical Renewal* 22 (2018) 121–37.

Ong, Walter J. *Orality and Literacy: The Technologizing of the Word*. New York: Methuen, 1982.

Osmer, Richard R. "Practical Theology: A Current International Perspective." *HTS Teologiese Studies/Theological Studies* 67 (2011) 1–7.

———. "Toward a New Story of Practical Theology." *International Journal of Practical Theology* 16 (2012) 66–78.

Pacini, David S. "Professionalism, Breakdown, and Revelation." In *Building Effective Ministry: Theory and Practice in the Local Church*, edited by Carl S. Dudley, 133–52. San Francisco: Harper & Row, 1983.

Palazzo, Eric. "Art and Liturgy in the Middle Ages: Survey of Research (1980–2003) and Some Reflections on Method." *The Journal of English and Germanic Philology* 105 (2006) 170–84. http://www.jstor.org/stable/27712573.

———. "Art, Liturgy, and the Five Senses in the Early Middle Ages." *Viator* 41 (2010) 25–56.

Palazzo, Eric, and Madeleine Beaumont. *A History of Liturgical Books from the Beginning to the Thirteenth Century*. Collegeville, MN: Liturgical, 1998.

Palmer, Richard E. *Hermeneutics: Interpretation Theory in Schleiermacher, Dilthey, Heidegger, and Gadamer*. Evanston, IL: Northwestern University Press, 1969.

———. "Ritual, Rightness, and Truth in Two Later Works of Hans-Georg Gadamer." In *The Philosophy of Hans-Georg Gadamer*, edited by Lewis Edwin Hahn, 529–47. London: Open Court, 1997.

Parish, Helen. "The Absence of Presence and the Presence of Absence: Social Distancing, Sacraments, and the Virtual Religious Community During the Covid-19 Pandemic." *Religions* 11 (2020) 276–88.

Parris, David P. *Reading the Bible with Giants: How 2000 Years of Biblical Interpretation Can Shed New Light on Old Texts*. 2nd ed. Cambridge: Lutterworth, 2015.

———. "Reception Theory: Philosophical Hermeneutics, Literary Theory, and Biblical Interpretation." PhD diss., University of Nottingham, 1999.

Parvey, Constance F. "The Liturgy as Holy Play." *Liturgy* 6 (1986) 48–53.

Paul VI. *Missale Romanum—On New Roman Missal*. Apostolic Constitution. April 3, 1969. http://www.vatican.va/content/paul-vi/en/apost_constitutions/documents/hf_p-vi_apc_19690403_missale-romanum.html.

———. *Mysterii Paschalis—On Liturgical Year and New Universal Roman Calendar*. Motu Proprio. February 14, 1969. http://www.vatican.va/content/paul-vi/en/motu_proprio/documents/hf_p-vi_motu-proprio_19690214_mysterii-paschalis.html.

———. *Nostra Aetate: The Relationship of the Church to Non-Christian Religions*. Declaration. October 28, 1965. https://www.vatican.va/archive/hist_councils/ii_vatican_council/documents/vat-ii_decl_19651028_nostra-aetate_en.html.

Pembroke, Neil. *Pastoral Care in Worship: Liturgy and Psychology in Dialogue*. London: T. & T. Clark, 2009.

———. "A Spirit-Word-Community Hermeneutic for the 'Preaching as Reimagination' Approach." *HTS Teologiese Studies/Theological Studies* 77 (2021) 1–8.

———. "Theocentric Therapeutic Preaching: An Analogical Approach." *International Journal of Practical Theology* 17 (2013) 314–35.

Philo. *Every Good Man is Free. On the Contemplative Life. On the Eternity of the World. Against Flaccus. Apology for the Jews. On Providence.* Translated by F. H. Colson. Loeb Classical Library 363. Cambridge, MA: Harvard University Press, 1941.

———. *On Abraham. On Joseph. On Moses.* Volume 6. Translated by F. H. Colson. Loeb Classical Library. Cambridge, MA: Harvard University Press, 1989.

Pieper, Josef. *Only the Lover Sings: Art and Contemplation*. San Francisco: Ignatius, 1990.

Pinnock, Clark H. *Biblical Revelation: The Foundation of Christian Theology*. Eugene, OR: Wipf & Stock, 1998.

———. "The Role of the Spirit in Interpretation." *The Evangelical Theological Society* 36 (1993) 491–97.

———. *The Scripture Principle*. Vancouver: Regent College, 2000.

———. "The Work of the Holy Spirit in Hermeneutics." *Journal of Pentecostal Theology* 1 (1993) 3–23.

———. "The Work of the Spirit in the Interpretation of Holy Scripture from the Perspective of a Charismatic Biblical Theologian." *Journal of Pentecostal Theology* 18 (2009) 157–71.

Poe, Harry L. *The Gospel and Its Meaning: A Theology for Evangelism and Church Growth*. Grand Rapids: Zondervan, 1996.

Pontificia Commissio Biblica (Pontifical Biblical Commission). *The Interpretation of the Bible in the Church: Address of His Holiness Pope John Paul II and Document of the Pontifical Biblical Commission*. Rome: Libreria Editrice Vaticana, 1993.

Pontifical Council for Social Communications. "The Church and Internet." February 22, 2002. https://www.vatican.va/roman_curia/pontifical_councils/pccs/documents/rc_pc_pccs_doc_20020228_church-internet_en.html.

Power, David N. *The Word of the Lord: Liturgy's Use of Scripture*. Maryknoll, NY: Orbis, 2001.

Procter-Smith, Marjorie. "Lectionaries—Principles and Problems: Alternative Perspectives." *Studia Liturgica* 22 (1992) 84–99.

Rahner, Hugo. *Man at Play*. New York: Herder and Herder, 1967.

Rahner, Karl. *Theological Investigations*. Volume 4. Translated by Kevin Smyth. New York: Crossroad, 1960.

Ralph, M. N. *Breaking Open the Lectionary: Cycle A Lectionary Readings in Their Biblical Context for RCIA, Faith Sharing Groups, and Lectors*. New York: Paulist, 2007.

Ratzinger, Joseph Cardinal. *The Feast of Faith: Approaches to a Theology of the Liturgy*. Translated by Graham Harrison. San Francisco: Ignatius, 1986.

———. *The Spirit of the Liturgy*. San Francisco: Ignatius, 2014.

Rebenich, Stefan. *Jerome*. London: Routledge, 2002.

Reese, Thomas. "Reforming Catholic Liturgy Should Be Like Updating Software." Religion News Service, National Catholic Reporter, 2017. https://www.ncronline.org/opinion/signs-times/reforming-catholic-liturgy-should-be-updating-software.

Renoux, Athanase. *Le Codex Arménien Jérusalem 121*. Patrologia Orientalis. Turnhout: Brepols, 1969.

Reumann, John. "A History of Lectionaries: From the Synagogue at Nazareth to Post-Vatican II." *Interpretation* 31 (1977) 116–30.

Reynolds, Thomas E. "Practising Theology and Theologizing Practice." *Toronto Journal of Theology* 29 (2013) 169–74.

Ricoeur, Paul. *Interpretation Theory: Discourse and the Surplus of Meaning*. Fort Worth: Texas Christian University Press, 1976.

———. *Memory, History, Forgetting*. Chicago: University of Chicago Press, 2009.

———. *The Symbolism of Evil*. Translated by Emerson Buchanan. New York: Harper and Row, 1967.

Ringma, Charles. *Gadamer's Dialogical Hermeneutic: The Hermeneutics of Bultmann, of the New Testament Sociologists and of the Social Theologians in Dialogue with Gadamer's Hermeneutic*. Heidelberg: Universitätsverlag C. Winter, 1999.

Rise, Svein, and Staale Johannes Kristiansen. *Key Theological Thinkers: From Modern to Postmodern*. Farnham, UK: Ashgate, 2013.

Risser, James. *The Life of Understanding: A Contemporary Hermeneutics*. Bloomington: Indiana University Press, 2012.

Ritivoi, Andreea Deciu. "Hermeneutics as Project of Liberation: The Concept of Tradition in Paul Ricoeur and Hans-Georg Gadamer." In *Gadamer and Ricoeur: Critical Horizons for Contemporary Hermeneutics*, edited by F. J. Mootz and G. H. Taylor, 63–82. London: Continuum, 2011.

Robertson, Jon. "Hermeneutical Horizons: A Challenge to Moderns from Athanasius and Gadamer." *Cultural Encounters* 6 (2010) 35–42.

Robinson, J. M. C., and J. B. Cobb, eds. *The New Hermeneutic*. New York: Harper Row, 1964.

Rosier, Veronica. "The Spirit and Power of the Liturgy: Understanding Liturgical Catechesis." *The Australasian Catholic Record* 83 (2006) 387–405.

Rouwhorst, Gerard. "The Bible in Liturgy." In *New Cambridge History of the Bible*, edited by James Carleton Paget and Joachim Schaper, 822–42. Cambridge: Cambridge University Press, 2011.

Rue, Charles. "Dreaming of a Revised Catholic Lectionary: Proposing a Way Forward." *Australasian Catholic Record* 99 (2022) 321–32.

Ruin, Hans. "Memory." In *The Blackwell Companion to Hermeneutics*, edited by Niall Keane, 114–21. Chichester: Wiley-Blackwell, 2016.

Rumscheidt, Martin, ed. *The Way of Theology in Karl Barth: Essays and Comments*. Eugene, OR: Pickwick, 1986.

Rush, Ormond. *The Eyes of Faith: The Sense of the Faithful and the Church's Reception of Revelation*. Washington, DC: Catholic University of America Press, 2011.

Saenger, Paul. "Silent Reading: Its Impact on Late Medieval Script and Society." *Viator (Berkeley)* no. 13 (1982) 367–414.

———. *Space between Words: The Origins of Silent Reading*. Stanford, CA: Stanford University Press, 1997.

Saliers, Don E. "Symbol in Liturgy, Liturgy as Symbol: The Domestication of Liturgical Experience." In *The Awakening Church: 25 Years of Liturgical Renewal*, edited by Lawrence J. Madden SJ, 69–82. Collegeville, MN: Liturgical, 1992.

Sartori, Luigi. "Criteri Teologici per un Bilancio Prospettico." In *Scriptura Crescit Cum Orante*, Bibbia e Liturgia II, edited by A. N. Terrin, 255–75. Padua: Edizioni Messagero Padova, 1993.

Schattauer, Thomas. "Liturgical Studies: Disciplines, Perspectives, Teaching." *International Journal of Practical Theology* 11 (2007) 106–37.

Scheibler, Ingrid. "Art as Festival in Heidegger and Gadamer." *International Journal of Philosophical Studies* 9 (2001) 151–75.

Schellman, James M. "The Ministry of the Lector." *America—The National Catholic Review* 190 (2004) 21–24.

Schlimm, Matthew R. "Biblical Studies and Rhetorical Criticism: Bridging the Divide between the Hebrew Bible and Communication." *Review of Communication* 7 (2007) 244–75.

Schmemann, Alexander. *For the Life of the World: Sacraments and Orthodoxy*. Crestwood, New York: St. Vladimir's Seminary Press, 1973.

———. *Great Lent: Journey to Pascha*. New York: St Vladimir's Seminary Press, 1969.

Schnackenburg, Rudolf. *The Church in the New Testament*. New York: Burns & Oates, 1968.

Schniedewind, William M. *How the Bible Became a Book*. Cambridge: Cambridge University Press, 2004.

Schussler Fiorenza, Elisabeth. *Bread Not Stone: The Challenge of Feminist Biblical Interpretation*. Edinburgh: T. & T. Clark, 1990.

Schwartz, Barry. *Abraham Lincoln and the Forge of National Memory*. Chicago: University of Chicago, 2000.

Searle, Mark. *Called to Participate: Theological, Ritual, and Social Perspectives*, edited by Barbara Schmich Searle and Anne Y. Koester. Collegeville, MN: Liturgical, 2006.

———. "New Tasks, New Methods. The Emergence of Pastoral Liturgical Studies." In *Vision. The Scholarly Contributions of Mark Searle to Liturgical Renewal*, edited by Anne Y. Koester and Barbara Searle, 105–21. Collegeville, MN: Liturgical, 2004.

Seasoltz, Kevin R. "What Makes the Liturgy Biblical?—Setting." *Studia Liturgica* 22 (1992) 146–53.

Sefaria. "Mishnah Megillah." Talmudic Israel, c.190–c.230 CE. https://www.sefaria.org/Mishnah_Megillah.4?lang=bi.

———. "Talmud Berakhot." Talmudic Babylon, c.450–c.550 CE. https://www.sefaria.org/Berakhot.21a?lang=bi.

———. "Talmud Megillah." Talmudic Babylon, c.450–c.550 CE. https://www.sefaria.org/Megillah?lang=bi.

Sheerin, Daniel. "Interpreting Scripture in and through Liturgy: Exegesis of Mass Propers in the Middle Ages." In *Jewish Biblical Interpretation and Cultural Exchange: Comparative Exegesis in Context*, edited by Natalie B. Dohrmann and David Stern, 161–81. Philadelphia: University of Pennsylvania Press, 2013.

Skaggs, Michael A. "The Council as Shibboleth: The Rhetoric of Authenticity and Liturgical Space after Vatican II." *U.S. Catholic Historian* 33 (2015) 1–23.

Sloyan, Gerard S. "The Lectionary as a Context for Interpretation." *Liturgy* 2 (1982) 43–50.

———. "What Kind of Canon Do the Lectionaries Constitute?" *Biblical Theology Bulletin* 30 (2000) 27–35.

Smith, Christopher R. *After Chapters and Verses: Engaging the Bible in the Coming Generations*. Colorado Springs: InterVarsity, 2010.

Smith, James K. A. *Desiring the Kingdom: Worship, Worldview, and Cultural Formation*. Cultural Liturgies 1. Grand Rapids: Baker Academic, 2009.

Sodi, Manlio, and Achille Maria Triacca. *Missale Romanum: Editio Princeps 1570*. Vatican City: Libreria Editrice Vaticana, 1998.

Sovernigo, Giuseppe. "L'efficacia della Parola di Dio Celebrata. Aspetti Personali." In *Dall'Esegi all'Ermeneutica Attraverso la Celebrazione*, edited by R. Cecolin, 295–304. Padua: Edizioni Messagero Padova, 1991.

Spinks, D. Christopher. "Catching Up on a Conversation: Recent Voices on Theological Interpretation of Scripture." *Anglican Theological Review* 99 (2017) 769–86.

Stein, Robert H. "The Benefits of an Author-Oriented Approach to Hermeneutics." *Journal of the Evangelical Theological Society* 44 (2001) 451–66.

Steiner, George. *Real Presences*. Chicago: University of Chicago Press, 1989.

Stendahl, Krister. "Biblical Theology: Contemporary." In *The Interpreter's Dictionary of the Bible*, edited by G. A. Buttrick, 418–32. New York: Abingdon, 1962.

Stökl Ben Ezra, Daniel. "Seasoning the Bible and Biblifying Time through Fixed Liturgical Reading Systems (Lectionaries)." In *The Construction of Time in Antiquity: Ritual, Art, and Identity*, edited by Jonathan Ben-Dov and Lutz Doering, 227–47. Cambridge: Cambridge University Press, 2017.

Stovell, Beth M., and Stanley E. Porter. "Introduction: Trajectories in Biblical Hermeneutics." In *Biblical Hermeneutics: Five Views*, edited by Beth M. Stovell and Stanley E. Porter, 9–26. Illinois: InterVarsity, 2012.

Strawn, Brad D., and Warren S. Brown. "Liturgical Animals: What Psychology and Neuroscience Tell Us About Formation and Worship." *Liturgy (Washington)* 28 (2013) 3–14.

Stringer, Martin. "Gadamer and Hermeneutics." *Anaphora—The Journal of the Society for Liturgical Study* 1 (2007) 1–18.

———. "Text, Context and Performance: Hermeneutics and the Study of Worship." *Scottish Journal of Theology* 53 (2000) 365–79.

Stubbs, Michael. *Language and Literacy: The Sociolinguistics of Reading and Writing*. London: Routledge, 2015.

Suleiman, Susan Rubin, and Inge Crosman. *The Reader in the Text: Essays on Audience and Interpretation*. Princeton: Princeton University Press, 2014.

Sundberg, Walter. "Limitations of the Lectionary." *Word and World* 10 (1990) 14–20.

Sutcliffe, Peter Anthony. "Is There an Author in This Text? A Re-Evaluation of Authorial Intent Pursued as Ontological Disclosing the Being of the Entity of the Composition in Understanding an Author's Communication." PhD diss., University of Wales, 2012.

Swinton, John, and Harriet Mowatt. *Practical Theology and Qualitative Research*. London: SCM, 2006.

Synod of Bishops XII Ordinary General Assembly. "The Word of God in the Life and Mission of the Church—Instrumentum Laboris." Vatican City: Libreria Editrice Vaticana, 2008.

Szpunar, Karl K., and Kathleen B. McDermott. "Episodic Future Thought and Its Relation to Remembering: Evidence from Ratings of Subjective Experience." *Consciousness and Cognition* 17 (2008) 330–34.

Taft, Robert. *Beyond East and West: Problems in Liturgical Understanding*. Rome: Editione Orientalia Christiana, 1997.

———. "What Is a Christian Feast? A Reflection." *Worship* 83 (2009) 2–18.

Tatar, Burhanettin. *Interpretation and the Problem of the Intention of the Author: H.-G. Gadamer vs E.D. Hirsch*. Cultural Heritage and Contemporary Change. Series II A 5. Washington, DC: Council for Research in Values and Philosophy, 1998.

Tate, W. R. *Biblical Interpretation: An Integrated Approach*. Grand Rapids: Baker, 2008.

Taylor, George H. "Understanding as Metaphoric, Not a Fusion of Horizons." In *Gadamer and Ricoeur: Critical Horizons for Contemporary Hermeneutics*, edited by F. J. Mootz and G. H. Taylor, 104–18. London: Continuum, 2011.

Terrin, Aldo Natale. "Dialogo e Vero Perlocutorio in Liturgia." In *Dall'Esegi all'Ermeneutica Attraverso la Celebrazione*, edited by R. Cecolin, 121–52. Padua: Edizioni Messagero Padova, 1991.

Tertullian. "De Praescriptione Haereticorum (On the Prescription of Heretics)." In *The Complete Works of Tertullian (Illustrated)*, translated by Peter Holmes, 287–369. Delphi Ancient Classics Book 89. East Sussex: Delphi, 2018.

———. *Quinti Septimi Florentis Tertulliani De Anima*. Edited by J. H. Waszink. Boston: Brill, 2010.

The Benedictine Monks of Conception Abbey. *The Revised Grail Psalms—A Liturgical Psalter*. Collegeville, MN: Liturgical, 2012.

The British Library. *Cistercian Missal*. Digital Collections. Harley MS 1229. http://www.bl.uk/manuscripts/Viewer.aspx?ref=harley_ms_1229_fs001r.

———. *Epistolary of the Sainte-Chappelle*. Catalogue of Illuminated Manuscripts. Yates Thompson 34. https://www.bl.uk/catalogues/illuminatedmanuscripts/record.asp?MSID=8110&CollID=58&NStart=34.

———. *Odalricus Peccator Gospel Lectionary*. Digital Collections. Harley MS 2970. http://www.bl.uk/manuscripts/Viewer.aspx?ref=harley_ms_2970_fs001ar.

Thiselton, Anthony C. "Knowledge, Myth and Corporate Memory." In *Believing in the Church: Essays by Members of the Church of England Doctrine Commission*, 45–78. London: SPCK, 1981.

———. *The Two Horizons: New Testament Hermeneutics and Philosophical Description*. Grand Rapids: Eerdmans, 1980.

Thomas, Kenneth J., and Margaret Orr Thomas. *Structure and Orality in 1 Peter: A Guide for Translators*. New York: United Bible Societies, 2006.

Thomassen, Einar. "Some Notes on the Development of Christian Ideas About a Canon." In *Canon and Canonicity: The Formation and Use of Scripture*, edited by Einar Thomassen, 9–28. Copenhagen: Museum Tusculanum, 2010.

Thurneysen, Eduard. "Die Aufgabe Der Predigt." In *Die Aufgabe Der Predigt*, edited by G. Hummel, 105–18. Darmstadt: Wissenschaftliche Buchgesellschaft, 1971.

Tillard, J. M. R. *Church of Churches: The Ecclesiology of Communion*. Translated by R. C. De Peaux. Collegeville, MN: Liturgical, 1987.

Tilley, Terrence W. "Practicing the Faith: Tradition in a Practical Theology." In *Invitation to Practical Theology: Catholic Voices and Visions*, edited by Claire E. Wolfteich, 89–106. New York: Paulist, 2014.

Tillich, Paul. *Systematic Theology*. Chicago: University of Chicago Press, 1973.

Tracy, David. *The Analogical Imagination: Christian Theology and the Culture of Pluralism*. London: SCM, 1981.
———. *Blessed Rage for Order: The New Pluralism in Theology*. New York: Seabury, 1975.
———. "A Correlational Model of Practical Theology Revisited." In *Invitation to Practical Theology: Catholic Voices and Visions*, edited by Claire E. Wolfteich, 70–88. New York: Paulist, 2014.
———. "Creativity in the Interpretation of Religion: The Question of Radical Pluralism." *New Literary History* 15 (1984) 289–309.
———. *Filaments—Theological Profiles: Selected Essays*. Volume 2. Chicago: University of Chicago Press, 2020.
———. "The Foundations of Practical Theology." In *Practical Theology: The Emerging Field in Theology, Church, and World*, edited by Don Browning, 61–82. San Francisco: Harper and Row, 1983.
———. *Plurality and Ambiguity: Hermeneutics, Religion, Hope*. Chicago: University of Chicago Press, 1994.
Tracy, David, and John B. Cobb. *Talking About God: Doing Theology in the Context of Modern Pluralism*. Rochester, MI: Seabury, 1983.
Turner, Paul. *Words without Alloy: A Biography of the Lectionary for Mass*. Collegeville, MN: Liturgical Press Academic, 2022.
United States Conference of Catholic Bishops. *Fulfilled in Your Hearing: The Homily in the Sunday Assembly*. Bishops' Committee on Priestly Life and Ministry. Washington, DC: US Conference of Catholic Bishops Inc., 1982.
Upton, Julia. "Liturgy, Prayer, Pastoral Care and Pandemics." Paper presented at the Australian Catholic University Centre for Liturgy. Public Lecture Series. October 12, 2020.
Valenziano, Crispino. "Vedere la Parola—Liturgia e Ineffabilita." In *Dall'Esegi all'Ermeneutica Attraverso la Celebrazione*, edited by R. Cecolin, 53–74. Padua: Edizioni Messagero Padova, 1991.
Van De Geest, Hans. *Presence in the Pulpit: The Impact of Personality in Preaching*. Translated by Douglas W. Stott. Atlanta: John Knox, 1981.
Van Der Ven, Johannes A. *Discourse in Ritual Studies*. Empirical Studies in Theology 14. Leiden: Brill, 2007.
Van Ommen, Armand Léon. "Limping with the Living God: Reimagining Centre and Margins in the Liturgy." In *Lively Oracles of God: Perspectives on the Bible and Liturgy*, edited by G. Jeanes et al., 170–85. Collegeville, MN: Liturgical, 2022.
Vanhoozer, Kevin J. *Is There a Meaning in This Text? The Bible, the Reader, and the Morality of Literary Knowledge*. Grand Rapids: Zondervan Academic, 2009.
———. "The Reader in New Testament Interpretation." In *Hearing the New Testament*, edited by Joel B. Green, 301–28. Grand Rapids: Eerdmans, 1995.
Vatican Council II. "The Constitution on the Sacred Liturgy, *Sacrosanctum Concilium*, 4 December 1963." In *Vatican Council II: Constitutions, Decrees, Declarations*, edited by Austin Flannery, 117–61. Rev. trans. Collegeville, MN: Liturgical, 1996.
———. "Decree on the Apostolate of Lay People, *Apostolicam Actuositatem*, 18 November 1965." In *Vatican Council II: Constitutions, Decrees, Declarations*, edited by Austin Flannery, 403–42. Rev. trans. Collegeville, MN: Liturgical, 1996, 10.

———. "Dogmatic Constitution on Divine Revelation, *Dei Verbum*, 18 November 1965." In *Vatican Council II: Constitutions, Decrees, Declarations*, edited by Austin Flannery, 97–115. Rev. trans. Collegeville, MN: Liturgical, 1996.

———. "Dogmatic Constitution on the Church, *Lumen Gentium*, 21 November 1964." In *Vatican Council II: Constitutions, Decrees, Declarations*, edited by Austin Flannery, 1–95. Rev. trans. Collegeville, MN: Liturgical, 1996.

———. "Instruction on the Orderly Carrying Out of the Constitution on the Liturgy, *Inter Oecumenici*, 26 September 1964." In *Documents on the Liturgy, 1963– 1979: Conciliar, Papal, and Curial Texts*, edited by Thomas C. O'Brien, 88–110. Collegeville, MN: Liturgical, 1982.

Venturi, Gianfranco. "Criteri Interpretativi che la Chiesa Mette in Atto per una 'Lettura Liturgica' della Parola di Dio. Dall'analisi dei Testi." In *Scriptura Crescit Cum Orante*, edited by A. N. Terrin, 229–40. Padua: Edizioni Messagero Padova, 1993.

Vessey, David. "Dialogue, Goodwill, and Community." In *The Blackwell Companion to Hermeneutics*, edited by Niall Keane, 312–19. Chichester: Wiley-Blackwell, 2016.

Vezin, Jean. "Les Divisions du Texte dans les Evangiles Jusqu'à L'apparition de L'imprimerie." In *Grafia e Interpunzione del Latino Nel Medioevo*, edited by Alfonso Maieru, 53–68. Rome: Ateneo, 1987.

Vilhauer, Monica. "Beyond the 'Fusion of Horizons': Gadamer's Notion of Understanding as 'Play.'" *Philosophy Today* 53 (2009) 359–64.

Vincent, David. *The Rise of Mass Literacy: Reading and Writing in Modern Europe*. Cambridge: Polity, 2000.

Visentin, Pelagio. "Celebrazione Ecclesiale E Dinamismo Della Parola: Prospettive Teologiche." In *Dall'esegesi All'ermeneutica Attraverso La Celebrazione*, edited by Romano Cecolin, 183–91. Padua: Edizioni Messagero Padova, 1991.

———. "La Parola di Dio nel Contesto Celebrativo Secondo il Nuovo Lezionario della Messa." In *Scriptura Crescit Cum Orante*, edited by A. N. Terrin, 241–53. Padua: Edizioni Messagero Padova, 1993.

Visotsky, Burton. *Fathers of the World: Essays in Rabbinic and Patristic Literatures*. Tubingen: Mohr-Siebeck, 1995.

Vogel, Cyril. *Medieval Liturgy: An Introduction to the Sources*. Edited and translated by Niels Krogh Rasmussen et al. Washington, DC: Pastoral, 1986.

Vosko, Richard. *Art and Architecture for Congregational Worship: The Search for a Common Ground*. Collegeville, MN: Liturgical, 2019.

Wainwright, Geoffrey. "Bible et Liturgie: Danielou's Work Revisited." *Studia Liturgica* 22 (1992) 154–62.

Wakeling, Jennifer Maree. "Divine Resonance: Meaning-Generation via Instrumental Music Within Christian Worship." PhD diss., Australian Catholic University, 2019.

Warnke, Georgia. "Experiencing Tradition Versus Belonging to It: Gadamer's Dilemma." *The Review of Metaphysics* 68 (2014) 347–69.

———. *Gadamer: Hermeneutics, Tradition, and Reason*. Stanford, CA: Stanford University Press, 1987.

———. "Hermeneutics, Ethics, and Politics." In *The Cambridge Companion to Gadamer*, edited by Robert J. Dostal, 79–101. Cambridge: Cambridge University Press, 2002.

Waterford, William Bede. "Hearing and Reading Biblical Texts: A Study of Difference. Mark 6:30—8:27a." PhD diss., Griffith University, 2004.

Watson, Francis. "The Fourfold Gospel." In *The Cambridge Companion to the Gospels*, edited by Stephen C. Barton, 34–52. New York: Cambridge University Press, 2006.
Weinsheimer, Joel C. *Gadamer's Hermeneutics: A Reading of Truth and Method*. New Haven, CT: Yale University, 1985.
West, Fritz. *Scripture and Memory: The Ecumenical Hermeneutic of the Three-Year Lectionaries*. Collegeville, MN: Liturgical, 1997.
Wheelock, Wade T. "The Problem of Ritual Language: From Information to Situation." *Journal of the American Academy of Religion* 50 (1982) 49–71.
Whelan, Winifred. "English in the Roman Catholic Liturgy 1969-2002." *World Englishes* 32 (2013) 429–42.
White, Allan. "The Renewed Understanding of the Liturgy of the Word in the Reformed Liturgy." In *Liturgy in the Twenty-First Century: Contemporary Issues and Perspectives*, edited by Alcuin Reid, 174–88. London: T. & T. Clark, 2016.
White, James F. *Roman Catholic Worship: Trent to Today*. Collegeville, MN: Liturgical, 2003.
Whitehead, James D., and Evelyn Eaton Whitehead. *Method in Ministry: Theological Reflection and Christian Ministry*. Oxford: Sheed & Ward, 1995.
Wiener, Claude. "The Roman Catholic Eucharistic Lectionary." *Studia Liturgica* 21 (1991) 2–13.
Wikström, Owe. "Liturgy as Experience—The Psychology of Worship. A Theoretical and Empirical Lacuna." *Scripta Instituti Donneriani Aboensis* 15 (1993) 83–100.
Wilder, A. N. *Early Christian Rhetoric: The Language of the Gospel*. Cambridge, MA: Harvard University Press, 1964.
Wilkinson, Andrew, et al. *The Quality of Listening*. London: Macmillan Education, 1974.
Willander, Johan, and Maria Larsson. "Olfaction and Emotion: The Case of Autobiographical Memory." *Memory and Cognition* 35 (2007) 1659–63.
Willhauck, Susan. "The Urban Dictionary, Street Wisdom and God: An Intersection of Linguistics and Theology." *International Journal of Practical Theology* 17 (2013) 88–99.
Williams, Jack. "Playing Church: Understanding Ritual and Religious Experience Resourced by Gadamer's Concept of Play." *International Journal of Philosophy and Theology* 79 (2018) 323–36.
Williams, Rowan. "The Literal Sense of Scripture." *Modern Theology* 7 (1991) 121–34.
Williamson, Peter S. "Catholic Principles for Interpreting Scripture." *The Catholic Biblical Quarterly* 65 (2003) 327–49.
Willimon, William. "The Lectionary: Assessing the Gains and Losses in a Homiletical Revolution." *Theology Today* 58 (2001) 333–41.
Wils, Jean-Pierre. "From Ritual to Hermeneutics—An Exploration with Ethical Intent." In *Discourse in Ritual Studies*, edited by H. Schilderman, 257–75. Netherlands: Brill, 2007.
Wilson, Tim. "Chant: The Healing Powers of Voice and Ear." In *Music Physician for Times to Come: An Anthology*, edited by Don Campbell, 11–29. Wheaton, IL: Theosophical, 1991.
Wimsatt, W. K., and M. C. Beardsley. "The Intentional Fallacy." *The Sewanee Review* 54 (1946) 468–88.
Wink, Walter. *The Bible in Human Transformation: Toward a New Paradigm for Biblical Study*. 2nd ed. Minneapolis: Fortress, 2010.

Wolfteich, Claire E. "Catholic Voices and Visions in Practical Theology." In *Invitation to Practical Theology: Catholic Voices and Visions*, edited by Claire E. Wolfteich, 329–44. New York: Paulist, 2014.

———. "Reframing Practical Theology: Catholic Contributions and Conundrums." In *Conundrums in Practical Theology*, edited by Joyce Ann Mercer and Bonnie Miller-McLemore, 276–304. Boston: Brill, 2016.

Wolterstorff, Nicholas. *Acting Liturgically: Philosophical Reflections on Religious Practice*. Oxford: Oxford University Press, 2018.

Wright, Brian J. *Communal Reading in the Time of Jesus: A Window into Early Christian Reading Practices*. Minneapolis: Fortress, 2017.

Wright, Claire Louise. "The Fourth Dimension: Why Time is of the Essence in Sacramental Theology." *Australasian Catholic Record* 94 (2017) 35–44.

Wright, N. T. "How Can the Bible Be Authoritative?" *Vox Evangelica* 21 (1991) 7–32.

Wyckoff, John W. *Pneuma and Logos: The Role of the Spirit in Biblical Hermeneutics*. Eugene, OR: Wipf & Stock, 2010.

Yilpet, Yoilah K. "Knowing the Biblical Author's Intention: The Problem of Distanciation." *Africa Journal of Evangelical Theology* 19 (2000) 165–85.

Yong, Amos. *Spirit-Word-Community: Theological Hermeneutics in Trinitarian Perspective*. Burlington, VT: Ashgate, 2002.

Zimmerman, Jens. "Biblical Hermeneutics." In *The Blackwell Companion to Hermeneutics*, edited by Niall Keane, 212–25. Chichester: Wiley-Blackwell, 2016.

Zimmerman, Joyce Ann. "The Liturgy of the Word." *Liturgy* 16 (2000) 19–33.

Zumthor, Paul. *La Lettre et la Voix: De la 'Littérature' Médiévale*. Paris: Seuil, 1987.